Victorine du Pont

Cultural Studies of Delaware and the Eastern Shore

Victorine du Pont

The Force behind the Family

L E O N A R D   C .   S P I T A L E

NEWARK

Library of Congress Cataloging-in-Publication Data

Names: Spitale, Leonard C., author.
Title: Victorine Du Pont : the force behind the family / Leonard C. Spitale.
Description: Newark : University of Delaware Press, [2023] | Series:
   Cultural studies of Delaware and the Eastern Shore | Includes
   bibliographical references and index.
Identifiers: LCCN 2022009865 | ISBN 9781644532768 (paperback) |
   ISBN 9781644532775 (hardback) | ISBN 9781644532782 (epub) |
   ISBN 9781644532799 (pdf)
Subjects: LCSH: Bauduy, Victorine du Pont, 1792–1861. | Du Pont family. |
   Du Pont de Nemours, Pierre Samuel, 1739–1817—Family. | Brandywine Creek
   Valley (Pa. and Del.)—Social life and customs—19th century. | Christian
   women—Delaware—Wilmington—Biography. | School superintendents—
   Delaware—Wilmington—Biography. | Wilmington (Del.)—Biography.
Classification: LCC F174.W753 B388 2023 | DDC 975.1/2092
   [B]—dc23/eng/20220323
LC record available at https://lccn.loc.gov/2022009865

A British Cataloging-in-Publication record for this book is available from the British Library.

References to internet websites (URLs) were accurate at the time of writing. Neither the author
nor Rutgers University Press is responsible for URLs that may have expired or changed since
the manuscript was prepared.

⊖ The paper used in this publication meets the requirements of the American National Standard for Information Sciences—Permanence of Paper for Printed Library Materials, ANSI
Z39.48-1992.

udpress.udel.edu

Distributed worldwide by Rutgers University Press

Manufactured in the United States of America

Victorine Elizabeth du Pont

Contents

Illustrations

Genealogies

The du Ponts

Samuel du Pont's Family

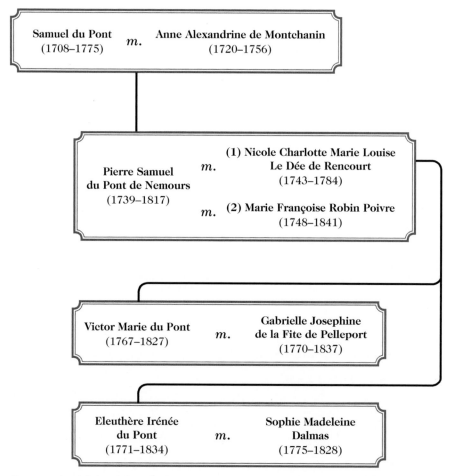

Samuel du Pont (1708–1775) m. Anne Alexandrine de Montchanin (1720–1756)

Pierre Samuel du Pont de Nemours (1739–1817) m. (1) Nicole Charlotte Marie Louise Le Dée de Rencourt (1743–1784)

m. (2) Marie Françoise Robin Poivre (1748–1841)

Victor Marie du Pont (1767–1827) m. Gabrielle Josephine de la Fite de Pelleport (1770–1837)

Eleuthère Irénée du Pont (1771–1834) m. Sophie Madeleine Dalmas (1775–1828)

Figure 1. Genealogical chart for Pierre Samuel du Pont de Nemours. Artwork by Jim Gemmell Creative.

The du Ponts

Victor Marie du Pont's Family

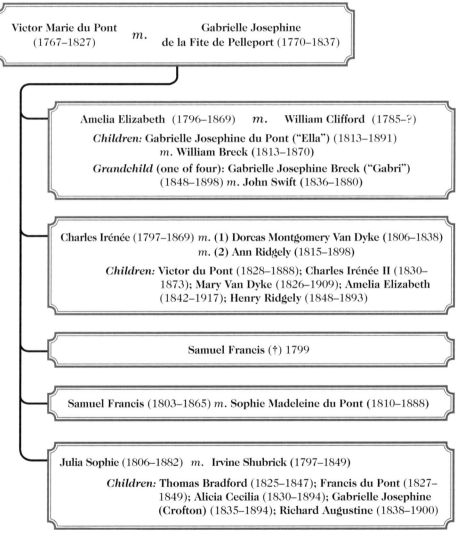

Victor Marie du Pont (1767–1827) *m.* Gabrielle Josephine de la Fite de Pelleport (1770–1837)

Amelia Elizabeth (1796–1869) *m.* William Clifford (1785–?)
Children: Gabrielle Josephine du Pont ("Ella") (1813–1891) *m.* William Breck (1813–1870)
Grandchild (one of four): Gabrielle Josephine Breck ("Gabri") (1848–1898) *m.* John Swift (1836–1880)

Charles Irénée (1797–1869) *m.* (1) Dorcas Montgomery Van Dyke (1806–1838) *m.* (2) Ann Ridgely (1815–1898)
Children: Victor du Pont (1828–1888); Charles Irénée II (1830–1873); Mary Van Dyke (1826–1909); Amelia Elizabeth (1842–1917); Henry Ridgely (1848–1893)

Samuel Francis (†) 1799

Samuel Francis (1803–1865) *m.* Sophie Madeleine du Pont (1810–1888)

Julia Sophie (1806–1882) *m.* Irvine Shubrick (1797–1849)
Children: Thomas Bradford (1825–1847); Francis du Pont (1827–1849); Alicia Cecilia (1830–1894); Gabrielle Josephine (Crofton) (1835–1894); Richard Augustine (1838–1900)

Figure 2. Genealogical chart for Victor Marie du Pont. Artwork by Jim Gemmell Creative. (†) Died in infancy.

The du Ponts

Eleuthère Irénée du Pont's Family

Eleuthère Irénée du Pont (1771–1834) *m.* Sophie Madeleine Dalmas (1775–1828)

Victorine Elizabeth (1792–1861) *m.* Ferdinand Bauduy (1791–1814)

Lucille (†) 1795

Evelina Gabrielle (1796–1863) *m.* James Antoine Bidermann (1790–1865)
Children: James Antoine Bidermann (1817–1890)

Alfred Victor (1798–1856) *m.* Margaretta Elizabeth Lammot (1807–1898)
Children: Victorine Elizabeth (Kemble) (1825–1887); Emma Paulina (1827–1914); Eleuthère Irénée (1829–1877); Lammot (1831–1884); Alfred Victor (1833–1893); Mary Sophie (du Pont) (1834–1869); Antoine Bidermann (1837–1923)

Eleuthera (1806–1876) *m.* Thomas Mackie Smith (1809–1852)

Sophie Madeleine (1810–1888) *m.* Samuel Francis Du Pont (1803–1865)

Henry (1812–1889) *m.* Louisa Gerhard (1816–1900)
Children: Henry Algernon (1838–1926); Evelina (1840–1938); Ellen Eugenia (Irving) (1843–1907); Louisa Gerhard (1845–1863); Sara (Duer) (1847-1876); Victorine Elizabeth (Foster) (1849–1934); Sophie Madeleine (Chandler) (1851–1931); Mary Constance (†) (1854); William (1855–1928)

Alexis Irénée (1816–1857) *m.* Joanna Smith (1815–1876)
Children: Frances Elizabeth (Coleman) (1838–1902); Eugene (1840–1902); Alexis Irénée (1843–1904); Irene Sophie (Dimmick) (1845–1877); Eleuthera Paulina (Bradford) (1848–1906); Francis Gurney (1850–1904); Thomas Mackie (†) (1852–1853); Joanna Maria (Dimmick) (1854–1901)

Figure 3. Genealogical chart for Eleuthère Irénée du Pont. Artwork by Jim Gemmell Creative. (†) Died in infancy.

du Pont Family Portraits

Figure 4. *Victor Marie du Pont, 1767–1827.*
François Jules Bourgoin, 1806.

Figure 5. *Gabrielle Josephine de la Fite de Pelleport, 1770–1837.* Louis Boilly, oil on canvas, 1794.

Figure 6. *Eleuthère Irénée du Pont, 1771–1834.* Rembrandt Peale, oil on canvas, 1831.

Figure 7. *Sophie Madeleine Dalmas du Pont (Mrs. E. I. du Pont), 1775–1828.* Unknown artist, watercolor on ivory, 1791.

Figure 8. *Evelina Gabrielle du Pont (Mrs. James Antoine Bidermann), 1796–1863.* Rembrandt Peale, oil on canvas, 1813.

Figure 9. *Alfred Victor du Pont, 1798–1856.* Clawson Hammitt, oil on canvas, 1919.

Figure 10. *Eleuthera du Pont Smith (Mrs. Thomas Mackie Smith), 1806–1876.* Rembrandt Peale, oil on canvas, 1831.

Figure 11. *Sophie Madeleine du Pont (Mrs. Samuel Francis Du Pont), 1810–1888.* Rembrandt Peale, oil on canvas, 1831.

Figure 12. *Henry du Pont, 1812–1889.* J. E.
Torbert, photographer, 1892.

Figure 13. *Alexis
Irénée du Pont,
1816–1857.* John
Sartain, engraver,
undated.

Foreword

Pontiana. The name connotes utopian visions—of places that exist nowhere, save in the imagination, and are as unattainable as they are perfect. Such a place was the product of the fertile mind of Pierre Samuel du Pont de Nemours. A child of eighteenth-century France, he parlayed his considerable intellectual gifts and talents with the pen into a political career that brought him to the heights of power and influence during the ancien régime, the French Revolution, and the Napoleonic era. He was witness to, and author of, numerous theories and initiatives aimed at perfecting government and the governed. An early proponent of physiocracy, a doctrine that figured land as the ultimate source of prosperity and well-being, he dreamed and wrote about the best ways to cultivate places, and the minds of the people who dwelt in them, as a path to the realization of ideal polities.

As his dissatisfaction with France's social and political experiments mounted, Pierre Samuel cast his eyes across the Atlantic and began to see the young, still "unspoiled" American nation as the place upon which he might project his ambitious societal vision. In letters and treatises written for his frequent correspondent Thomas Jefferson, he outlined the economic and educational features of a model community—one in which the inhabitants would thrive economically, spiritually, and civically. The success of such a community would be predicated on providing citizens with a liberal education, notable for its breadth of subjects but grounded not so much in rote mastery of classical learning as in mastery of oneself. His aim, he confided to Jefferson, was to buy land in the new world and create a place called "Pontiana"—a manifest utopia, sustained by people inspired to work and learn in equal measure.

What followed, of course, has been oft chronicled: as Pierre Samuel's vision matured, it assumed the form of an entrepreneurial venture, complete with business plans, stock issuance, and land purchases, initially in New Jersey and then, by 1802, on the banks of the Brandywine Creek in Delaware. From that point, the story of the family du Pont and its namesake company traces a familiar arc—a more than two-hundred-year epic of innovation, industrial growth, and service to community and country. This story has been animated by well-limned, familiar characters such as the company's founder, Eleuthère Irénée du Pont, and Pierre Samuel du Pont, the twentieth-century steward of a global empire. These men, like the patriarch before them, have come to embody this tale of fortunes built and dreams realized.

But . . . what of Pontiana? What became of the utopian vision that filled the pages of Pierre Samuel's letters and philosophical treatises? The name, and the concept, drop out of the historical record after the Jefferson correspondence. We could be excused for believing that Pontiana was more fable than fact—an idea whose time never came. To adopt this viewpoint, however, is to ignore the life and contributions of a character in the du Pont drama who has received relatively little notice to date: Victorine Elizabeth du Pont. The eldest child of E. I. and Sophie du Pont, Victorine passed most of her years on the land that housed her family, their company, and its workers. Within this world created by her forebears and identified primarily with the men who ran the black-powder enterprise, she carved out a unique role and a purpose for herself; she became instrumental to the success of the community that grew within and around this family precinct. Drawing upon a brilliant mind honed by a sparkling academic career during her youth, Victorine became "first tutor" to her siblings and nieces and nephews, designing and supervising the learning of the young people in her family who would mature into leaders in business, politics, and the cultural sphere.

This pedagogical impulse, however, was not channeled solely in service to her kin. Over several decades, and until the time of her death, she created and superintended a school on the family compound that provided the children of local workers with an educational experience that, in rigor and accessibility, was the exception to the rule in antebellum America. Generations of these children in the Brandywine Valley, beneficiaries of her inspired teaching and stewardship, succeeded in becoming literate and numerate and in cultivating habits of mind that would enrich the life and work of their community.

Viewed through the lens of her achievements as a pioneering and innovative educator, Victorine can be rightly judged the true philosophical heir of her grandfather, the man who conjured an inspiring pedagogical and civic vision for his family's place in the new world. It was left to Victorine to realize this vision, not in its abstract, utopian form but as a tangible, indispensable cultural facet of the community in which she lived. In Victorine's hands, a terrestrial version of Pontiana, created to meet the challenges of *her* world, in *her* day, took root and prospered.

And in author Lennie Spitale's hands, we have a vivid, nuanced account of this remarkable figure who navigated and surmounted the strictures faced by women in her era to improve her corner of the world. This compelling volume encourages us to take another look at a story that we thought we knew well—and to encounter within it a character, and perspectives, that have been awaiting illumination. In words Victorine admired from the poet Bernard Barton, she may now "be remember'd as a light that flung/Its first fresh lustre on the unwrinkled brow."

Dr. David Cole
Former Executive Director of the Hagley Museum and Library

Preface

In the first half of the nineteenth century, there were two sources of power in the rustic mill community north of Wilmington, Delaware. One was a river; the other was a woman. The Brandywine River was a force that powered the wheels of industry for the manufacturers along its banks. The woman, Victorine du Pont, served and taught those who lived in the community and left a legacy whose influence upon her family lingers to the present day.

For over 220 years (until its recent merger with Dow Chemical and subsequent restructuring), DuPont, the company established by Eleuthère Irénée du Pont in 1802, was primarily a family business. E. I. du Pont de Nemours and Company was birthed at the dawn of a century that produced some of America's greatest industrial giants, adding the name of du Pont to the likes of Morgan, Astor, Vanderbilt, and Rockefeller. By the 1870s, publishers realized that interest was high, not only in the company, but in the people behind it. The du Pont story, both fascinating and complex, wove like a persistent thread throughout America's industrial fabric. Individual family members have been the subjects of numerous biographies, and fresh accounts continue to appear. Few, however, have contained biographies of the family's women. Although several of them have made significant contributions to the family's legacy, their notable accomplishments have received far less publicity. The life of one daughter, in particular, has arguably made the greatest impact upon the entire du Pont family than any other; and yet a complete account of her life has never been published.

Victorine Elizabeth du Pont was the eldest child of the company's founder, Eleuthère Irénée (E. I.) du Pont, and his wife, Sophie Madeleine Dalmas. Born in Paris in the middle of the French Revolution, and seven years old when the family emigrated to America, Victorine was the only member of the next generation old enough to retain clear memories of their native country. Two years after arriving in America, the family settled on the rustic banks of the Brandywine River in Northern Delaware, where her father established a black-powder company. After watching the family home rise to completion in 1803, Victorine would grow to adulthood in that house, marry in its parlor, administrate its operations, and spend the next half-century living in it. Through a lifetime of correspondence with friends and relatives, she would unwittingly chronicle the first sixty years of the du Pont saga in America and provide the most intimate view into the lives and events of that pioneer generation.

In modern times, Irénée du Pont Jr., the great-great-grandson of E. I., remarked that Victorine's story "has been overlooked by the writers of popular histories of Du Pont, both company and family."[1] His nearby cousin, Francis Irénée du Pont, adds that she was "without doubt," the educational and spiritual "force" behind the family.[2] Intellectually curious and well read, she was educated in Philadelphia from ages thirteen to seventeen at a prominent boarding school for young women, where she achieved the school's highest academic award for best overall student. Excelling in several disciplines, including literature, science, history, medicine, and botany, she was fluent in both French and English, studied Italian and German, and knew Latin well enough to teach it. An insatiable reader, she consumed an eclectic range of classic and contemporary literature throughout her lifetime, all the while staying abreast of the latest authors in America and Europe.

Growing up in an age when women were permitted few opportunities to oversee institutional projects, Victorine's efforts in education, medicine, and religion would transform an entire community. Responsible for providing the primary education of her youngest siblings, and that of her cousins, nieces, and nephews, she also had a profound moral and educational influence upon the first two generations of American-born du Ponts, some of whom would go on to become leaders of the company. The late John Beverley Riggs, who compiled the Hagley Museum and Library's *Guide to Manuscripts*, described her as "a woman of great perception and force," and affirmed that through the French traditional role of the eldest sibling, she "exerted great influence in all matters concerning their affairs."[3]

Recovering from the fires of a personal tragedy, which dramatically altered the course of her life, Victorine chose to engage some of the harsher social realities of her community. Many of her neighbors struggled to survive the economic uncertainties of life in a rural manufacturing village, while the absence of schools and churches all but eliminated their educational and religious opportunities. Regarding the latter, she achieved societal breakthroughs for her community and, with them, brought occasional pain and conflict upon herself. Growing up on the grounds of what quickly became America's leading producer of black powder, she would personally experience the devastating effects of over eighty explosions during her lifetime. In addition to those threats, the fires, floods, and diseases of the day brought her frequently to the gravesides of friends and family.

Victorine du Pont died on the eve of the Civil War, but not before leaving a sixty-year record of the family's early history to the generations that followed. While a remarkably intact hoard of her correspondence has survived, the majority has yet to be transcribed into print. Between the ages of eight and sixty-eight, she filled several hundreds of pages with observations of her times, her family and friends, academic and literary interests, Christian faith, and the unique accomplishments of a selfless life. Like a wind upon the parlor curtains, she left an unseen (and largely unrecognized) influence upon the du Pont family and the millworkers' community in which she lived. Reconstructed primarily through her unpublished letters, this poignant but little-known journey has been carefully reassembled.

Acknowledgments

To my wife, Gwen, a constant encourager and a clear-eyed critic. She graciously read several versions of the manuscript, provided numerous suggestions and critiques that improved the storyline, and has shared her home for over a decade with the ghost of Victorine du Pont. All I can say is thank you, Hun. I love you very much.

This twelve-year journey of research and writing began in the fall of 2009, when Gwen and I first visited the Hagley Museum and Library's historic 235 acres in Greenville, Delaware. Since then, I have met several other travelers along the way, each appearing at timely intervals to offer their assistance and encouragement. The first of these was Marge McNinch, author of several works of Delaware history, and the cheerful archivist at Hagley who greeted me with helpful leads. The late Lynn Ann Catanese was chief curator of Library Collections and the author and compiler of *Women's History: A Guide to Sources at Hagley Museum and Library*. Lynn was a wealth of information to me in terms of what was in the stacks regarding the du Pont women.

Lucas Clawson, reference archivist and Hagley historian, provided me with many helpful resources. Whenever I thanked him, he always grinned and responded with his trademark "That's what we're here for!" Over at the museum's library, Max Moeller, the gracious curator of Imprints and Published Collections, was the go-to person. Max provided me with many answers, materials, and direction. Other library staff, such as Judy Stevenson, Lynsey Sczechowicz, Jennifer Johns, and Angela Schad, cheerfully worked with me on selecting the illustrations. Other members of the Hagley family included Angela Williamson, former director of volunteers, who read an early draft and asked if I would be willing to share what I had learned with their guides and volunteers. Their enthusiastic response encouraged me to continue. Sara Wells, at Visitor Services, has been a consistent cheerleader for the project, as have numerous other Hagley staff and volunteers with whom I have worked "on the hill." I wish I could name you all. Dr. David Allen Cole, former executive director of the Hagley Museum and Library, kindly agreed to write the foreword, and his earnest support for bringing Victorine's story to light went a long way toward that end.

Susan Newton and Lynn McCarthy at the Winterthur Museum, Garden and Library in Wilmington, Delaware, graciously shared their expertise in providing photos of some of the impressive portraits from the museum's collection. Alison K. Matsen, Winterthur volunteer and teacher of French, German, and Spanish, was an invaluable assistance in translating many of Victorine du Pont's French letters. Joining her on the translation team was Jacques Cattiaux, a former Parisian and longtime family friend. *Merci beaucoup* to you both.

Interviews with present-day descendants of the Bauduy, Des Chapelles, and Garesché families provided important background information, materials, and testimonies. I am especially grateful for the cheerful assistance of Betty Torno, Joanna Dhody, and Kathleen Brandt, whose dedicated research on their families was essential to the story. On the du Pont side, I will always be indebted to two men, especially. Francis Irénée du Pont, the great-great-grandson of Alexis du Pont (Victorine's youngest brother); and Irénée du Pont Jr., the great-great-grandson of Eleuthère Irénée du Pont (Victorine's father and the founder of the company). Both men spent numerous hours introducing me to their family's history, showing me records, artwork, and historical memorabilia in their own possession, while relating many fascinating personal anecdotes. Their input and personal enthusiasm for the project was often the steam that kept me going.

Other supportive travelers have been: Chaplain Jack Crans, of County Corrections Gospel Mission, and Rev. Dr. Peter Lillback, the president of Westminster Theological Seminary in Glenside, Pennsylvania. The author of the national best seller *George Washington's Sacred Fire*, Dr. Lillback read the manuscript and took it upon himself to forward two copies to friends, one of whom was Francis Irénée du Pont, mentioned above. Rev. Marty Machowski, author of numerous children's books, read the manuscript and made encouraging suggestions. My California sister, Fran Spitale, also made several insightful observations for which I was grateful.

Dr. Julia Oestreich, director of the University of Delaware Press, who said Victorine's story "intrigued" her from the beginning, and whose exceptional editorial skills were greatly appreciated, deserves a special thank you. She has made this a better book. That she instinctively knew there was a story worth telling here was a huge encouragement.

A heartfelt thanks to all of you.

Note to the Reader

In transcribing Victorine du Pont's correspondence, maintaining the integrity of the original text was a personal goal. However, in the case of archaic word forms or the peculiarities common to informal correspondence, editorial intervention was sometimes required.

A small number of grammatical devices common to nineteenth-century writers also created challenges. For example, Victorine and her correspondents were liberal in their use of "the dash," employing it frequently—and interchangeably—as a paragraph break, period, comma, or semicolon. When used for those punctuations, I have replaced it with its modern counterpart; but when used for emphasis or impact, such as the "em dash" may be used today, it was retained.

Words that have evolved into different spellings (such as "staid" for "stayed") were conformed to today's renderings, except when communicating a more vivid sense of the times. In the latter case, these are identified with the use of [*sic*]. Other antebellum practices, such as the abbreviation of words or the capitalization of common nouns ("We had a small school on acct of the Freshet") were corrected to avoid distraction or confusion. Words that had been underlined for emphasis were italicized; and sentences that failed to begin with a capital letter (or proper nouns that lacked them) were supplied with one.

In the case of abbreviations, such as those that occur frequently in the diary of Rev. Samuel Crawford Brincklé, the words have been fully spelled out. These include such entries as: "would" for "wd"; "morning" for "m'g"; "which" for "wh," etc.

The Du Pont Name

When referring to the company, the capital "D" for Du Pont was used. When referring to the name of an individual, or to the family as a whole, the smaller case has been employed ("Eleuthère Irénée du Pont, esteemed by generations of du Ponts, was the founder of the Du Pont Company").

The only exception to the rule of a small *d* for individuals is for Samuel Francis Du Pont ("the Admiral"), who signed his last name with the capital *D*. His wife, Sophie, adopted the same practice after their wedding.

Eleuthère Irénée du Pont is occasionally referenced by the abbreviation of his first and middle names, E. I.

CHAPTER 1

France, 1792–1795

August of 1792 left little hope that the French monarchy would survive. Earlier in the month, an armed force of angry revolutionaries had stormed the Palace of the Tuileries, decimated the Swiss Guard in a fierce battle, and taken the king and queen into custody. The menacing winds of *La Terreur* would soon be unleashed against the nobility, the clergy, and many of those in the professional classes who were perceived (rightly or wrongly) to be loyal to the king. Thousands of citizens would flee the country in fear for their lives.

Yet, in a small apartment at 146 Rue de l'Oratoire, a teenage mother was giving birth to her first child—a daughter. Eleuthère Irénée du Pont and Sophie Madeleine Dalmas, very much in love, found themselves staring with humbled amazement into the cherub-like face of the one they called their "little angel."[1] Married less than a year, Sophie had just turned seventeen and Eleuthère Irénée twenty-one. The plump little girl who was captivating their mutual attention had arrived in time to greet her first dawn. Victorine Elizabeth du Pont was born at 5:00 a.m. on August 30, 1792, in the heart of the City of Light, in the middle of the French Revolution.

In late eighteenth-century Paris, it was customary to require baptism in a Roman Catholic church in order to become officially registered in the city's rolls. But the young father, Eleuthère Irénée du Pont, was not a member of that religion. Although his family's genealogy, stretching back to the 1500s, had included a number of Roman Catholics (including his mother), the du Ponts had been predominantly French Protestant. In his autobiography, the young man's father, Pierre Samuel du Pont de Nemours, had declared that, historically, they were Huguenots;[2] but in actual practice, neither the father nor his two sons were strict adherents of either faith. In order to establish legal recognition for their newly arrived angel, however, the couple agreed to have her baptized in the Roman Catholic parish of Fort-Louis-en-l'Isle, the city's oldest district.

Yet Irénée (as he preferred to be called) knew that securing Victorine's registration was a far smaller hurdle than the one he and Sophie had already faced. In

Figure 14. *Pierre Samuel du Pont de Nemours, 1739–1817.* Ernest Moore, oil on canvas, 1907.

1790s France, parental consent for marriage was still required, and Irénée's own father, Pierre Samuel, had been vehemently opposed to their union. Pierre Samuel du Pont de Nemours was a short man (a bit over five feet, three inches), but enraptured by grandiose ambitions and noble concepts—be they philosophical, political, pedagogical, or economical. By 1792, the fifty-three-year-old had gained significant influence in the court of King Louis XVI, and in Parisian society in general. The French philosopher Voltaire, with whom he corresponded, noted that du Pont seemed to encompass "two species, one a little different from the other: finance and poetry."[3] From the 1760s throughout the 1780s, du Pont de Nemours had been a member of a small group of influential economists dedicated to the concepts of physiocracy.[4] At age twenty-eight, he had caught the attention of his fellow economists after publishing his book *Physiocracy* in 1767. In 1774, King Louis XVI appointed him as his Inspector General of Commerce. He was later to become a member of the National Constituent Assembly in 1789–1790, during which he would serve a brief term as its president.[5] When this group dissolved in September 1790, he boldly decided to launch a new business venture—a publishing company in the heart of Paris.

The then-unmarried Irénée had obtained an apprenticeship at the gunpowder factory at Essonne, which at that time was producing one hundred tons of powder a year for France.[6] Irénée had been taken under the personal tutelage of the famous French scientist Antoine Lavoisier, a friend of the family and the overseeing chemist in charge of the powder works.[7] By early 1791, however, Irénée had developed an interest beyond that of the refinement of French gunpowder. He and his cousin Lamotte[8] were known to be making long trips to the town of Metz during their days off, and it was rumored that both boys were "smitten with two little sisters."[9]

The gossip turned out to be true. Irénée had fallen in love with a fifteen-year-old girl named Sophie Madeleine Dalmas, the daughter of a prominent villager.

He approached his father with his desire to make Sophie his wife but was met with a resounding "no." Harsh words were exchanged, and the discussions did not go well. Desperate and afraid, Irénée turned to the pen for his defense. "My dear Papa," he wrote on August 15, 1791, "The first thing that I must tell you . . . is that I love Mademoiselle Sophie Dalmas a thousand times more than I love myself and that I am willing if necessary to sacrifice my life and my happiness for her."[10] The lovesick lad went on to describe her qualities, her notable family background, and his absolute conviction that she was the one he wished to have as the mother of his children. "Do not," he pleaded, "condemn to a great sorrow the son whom you have always made so happy. . . . I finish, my dear Papa, imploring you to realize that you are to decide on more than my life."[11] The gallant flourish of words fell upon deaf ears. A week later, the moonstruck suitor was forced to write a second letter: "The only thing that could have increased my unhappiness, my dear papa, was that you, my Father, my friend and my judge, should refuse to listen to me. I cannot, however, believe that this severity is from indifference and I think it is because of your mistaken idea of my feelings. . . . Try to understand if you can how agonizing are all these uncertainties, when for me they mean either perfect happiness or eternal sorrow."[12]

Pierre Samuel finally responded with a lengthy letter on August 26, patiently explaining to his desperate son why getting married at the present time was unwise—on multiple levels. Most of his arguments had to do with Irénée's youth, his lack of professional and material preparedness, and the obvious immaturity he was displaying by his desire to marry immediately.

> The first loves of early youth are like straw. They burn, but you cannot hope that their heat will melt the inexhaustible and stubborn mine of the perplexities of life. . . . What do I ask of you then? First of all to be a man; to show intelligence and strength; not to be a child who two years ago seemed to promise much, but who has deteriorated in every kind of industry, ambition and accomplishment from exactly the time when you fell in love. . . . Do not torment me. You will waste your trouble and give me exceeding and bitter grief which will hurt us both.[13]

At this point, the father knew that any further debate with his son was useless, so he decided to launch a counter-offensive in another direction—he wrote to the girl's mother. Unfortunately for Pierre, the flanking maneuver to the Dalmas family did not produce the hoped-for alliance; the girl's parents were in favor of the marriage. Stymied, the elder du Pont decided to affix a four-year moratorium upon the young couple's marriage plans, but two months later, in November 1791, Irénée married Sophie—with the full consent of his father.

What could have happened within the space of two short months to bring about such a complete reversal by the elder du Pont? Although their letters do not provide

Figure 15. *Eleuthère Irénée du Pont,*
1771–1834. Unknown artist, sketch, c. 1791.

a direct explanation, ensuing events suggest at least two contributing factors. The first was the departure of Antoine Lavoisier from the powder works at Essonne. The brilliant chemist had been reassigned to a position at the treasury department, leaving Irénée without his mentor. Without Lavoisier's special interest in the trajectory of his career, his prospects for advancement were now greatly diminished. How would he support Sophie? The second factor was that Pierre Samuel was becoming overwhelmed with the multiple demands of his new publishing business. Never one to concern himself with what he considered minutia, his level of frustration with the many mundane—yet necessary—details of operation was rapidly increasing. Irénée, on the other hand, was a plodding workhorse who knew that scrupulous attention to every aspect of one's business was a necessary element of its success. In the end, it is likely that a deal was struck. If the son was willing to devote his energies to his father's fledgling business, then "Papa" would give his approval to the marriage.

Pierre's consent was not insincere. The authentic joy with which the elder du Pont received his new daughter-in-law is well documented in many of his subsequent letters. They contain frequent, effusive compliments about her beauty, industry, and faithfulness. As for Irénée and Sophie, the young couple could hardly believe their good fortune; anything, they felt, could be endured as long as they were together. After finding a small apartment at 146 Rue de l'Oratoire, the joyous lovers wasted no time in celebrating the triumph of their union. By the opening months of 1792, it was discovered that Sophie was pregnant.

Irénée's older brother, Victor Marie du Pont, after whom little Victorine was named, then married Gabrielle Josephine de la Fite de Pelleport in April of 1794.

Figure 16. *Victor Marie du Pont, 1767–1827.*
Unknown artist, pencil drawing, c. 1791.

Her family had come from nobility but had fallen on harder times. Through Victor's prior association with the French legation to America, he was appointed head consul for the French Ministry of Foreign Affairs over the two Carolinas and Georgia. He and Gabrielle spent four happy years (1794–1798) in a comfortable residence in Charleston, South Carolina, during which time two children were born to them, Amélie (Amelia) in January of 1796, and Charles Irénée in March of 1797.

In personality, the two sons of Pierre Samuel couldn't have been more different. Victor was the classic extrovert; Irénée was the quiet, reserved man, preferring the solitude of his studies and the company of a few familiar friends over the dances and fêtes of high society. Although his father would have disavowed it, Irénée had grown up with a sense that Victor was the favorite, and that paternal expectations of success had rested more upon the shoulders of the eldest son than upon those of the younger. However, by the end of 1788, indications that Pierre Samuel was beginning to change this perception can be observed in a letter he wrote to Irénée: "For the second time I am trusting to an untried youth my hope, the honor of my name, on which I cannot help setting some value, the peace, the happiness, the purpose of my life. . . . I am trying this time with a more hopeful feeling because . . . you have a gentler nature than your brother; because having lived with me more you love me better; and because though younger than he your mind is a little more developed."[14] Although heavily in debt, father and son poured their du Pont diligence into their publishing business and engaged those duties that suited each man best.

SHADOW OF THE GUILLOTINE

Pierre Samuel du Pont de Nemours was a man of letters, but he had taught his sons how to handle a sword. When King Louis XVI and his queen Marie Antoinette were fleeing the palace as it was being stormed on August 10, they met a familiar face. Family historian Bessie Gardner du Pont recorded:

> Du Pont de Nemours [had] assembled and drilled a little band of fifteen of his relatives and friends—his son Irénée among them. . . . As Louis XVI and the royal family left the palace to ask protection of the Legislative Assembly, he stopped to say, "Ah! Monsieur du Pont, one always finds you where one has need of you." When the defense collapsed and the Swiss guard was exterminated, Du Pont de Nemours and his son were among the eight survivors of their little company. With great presence of mind they marched fully armed out of the palace, across the Place Vendôme, and did not separate till they were well away from the mob, who took them for a detachment of the ordinary guard.[15]

Although corroboration of these events is sparse,[16] there can be little doubt as to the bravery of that small group of men—or of Irénée's loyalty to his father. Sophie was just three weeks away from delivering their first child, and the young husband's heart would surely have been torn between two struggles—one outwardly, with the king's enemies, and the other, a fierce inner desire to be with his wife. But Irénée could have never abandoned his father in such perilous circumstances. *Rectitudine Sto* (Upright I stand) was the family motto.[17]

Following his confrontation with the mob in the courtyard of the Tuileries, it now became necessary for the elder du Pont to go into hiding. Irénée was less well known and, as an active member of the national guard, drew little suspicion from the revolutionaries. But it was clear that the time for Pierre Samuel to disappear had come. Aided by friends, he hid in the dome of the Paris observatory for a few weeks, until he managed to slip out of the city. After posing as a doctor in a small town, he eventually arrived at his country home in Bois-des-Fossés, about sixty miles southeast of Paris.[18] Pierre's departure, however, greatly increased Irénée's workload at the same time his wife's due date was rapidly approaching. While her father-in-law was still in hiding, seventeen-year-old Sophie gave birth to her first child on August 30, 1792. Three days later, in what became known as the September Massacres, vigilante mobs stormed the prisons of Paris and slaughtered the inmates.

By the end of September, Irénée sent his wife and four-week-old daughter to Bois-des-Fossés for safety. Irénée now shouldered the sole responsibility for running what was quickly becoming a rather extensive printing establishment; his regular (sometimes nightly) tours of duty with the national guard only added to his workload. Four months passed before he was able to tear away long enough to spend a few precious days at Bois-des-Fossés in January of 1793. Upon his return to Paris, he learned that the king had been beheaded during his absence.[19]

Under the inflammatory rhetoric of Jacobin leaders, most notably men like Jean-Paul Marat and later Maximilien de Robespierre, the powder keg finally

Figure 17. *Sophie Madeleine Dalmas (Mrs. E. I. du Pont) and her daughter Victorine du Pont.* Unknown artist, oil on canvas, 1793–1795.

exploded during the frightening ten-month period known as the Reign of Terror, which began in September of 1793 and lasted until the end of July 1794.[20]

Sophie did her best to keep Irénée informed of Victorine's progress in a series of letters: "Our little angel embraces you with all her heart, she repeats your name constantly. I love so to hear her say Papa, that sweet word which makes my life's happiness, that whenever she says it I tremble with joy."[21] On the occasion of their daughter's first birthday, an oil painting of mother and daughter was most likely created by Irénée's first cousin, Philippe Gudin.[22] Kept in his room in Paris, it was the first and last thing the lonely husband looked at each day: "In spite of the pleasure it gives me, I feel that your face is much better reproduced in my heart than on that canvas."[23]

By February of 1794, the separations from Sophie and his daughter had become so intolerable that Irénée sent for them to join him in Paris. The brief but happy reunion almost certainly resulted in the conception of their second child; a daughter they would name Lucille. Tragically, in what became the first great loss of their lives, Lucille would die just two days after her birth.

On May 8, 1794, Irénée's mentor and friend Lavoisier was beheaded by guillotine. Due to Irénée's former apprenticeship at Essonne, he was appointed by the Committee of General Safety as a commissioner overseeing the manufacture of saltpeter, one of three essential components of black powder.[24] By July, the radical elements of the interim government finally decided to do something about the absence of "Citizen Du Pont de Nemours." The order went out for his arrest, and he was found at his country estate. He was apprehended by Jacobin soldiers on July 22, 1794, nearly two full years since he had fled Paris. Leaving her beloved daughter with family, Sophie followed the soldiers out into the night in order to help arrange for her father-in-law's needs at the prison—a feat of love and loyalty that the old man would never forget.

Having been arrested toward the end of the Reign of Terror, the elder du Pont's conditions at La Force prison were not wholly intolerable. In the shadow of the guillotine, the irrepressible patriarch began two writing projects, one which included a major work on national education, and the other, his autobiography. Although he had friends on the (oxymoronically named) "Safety Committee," they did not get around to determining his case until the end of August. As the weeks passed, he realized how closely he came to being terminally shaved by the "national razor." In a letter to Irénée on August 12, he wrote: "The tyrant [Robespierre] said that none of our heads should be saved. . . . Seven days later—even four days earlier, and you would have loved, but you would have mourned your poor old father who would have gone to swell the number of murdered patriots."[25]

The "poor old father" would have likely lost his head if Robespierre had not first lost his. The mercurial tide of politics turned once again, and "the tyrant" was shot in the jaw by a policeman during a Saturday night committee meeting. A victim of his own fomented practice of swift and arbitrary execution, he was guillotined the very next day, along with seventy-one members of his radical party. After nearly six weeks of imprisonment, du Pont de Nemours was released, returning once again to the tranquil surroundings of Bois-des-Fossés. Irénée's brother Victor, who had recently returned from America but was not above suspicion as a royalist (and whose wife, Gabrielle, was vehemently so), had also joined the rural conclave.

The Little Woman

During Pierre Samuel's seclusion, little Victorine had grown very attached to him—and he to her. As the patriarch's first grandchild, she would secure a position in his heart that would remain for life. The inquisitive pair spent many hours together investigating the local fields and forests, with *Bon Papa* pointing out various flora and fauna to the wide-eyed toddler. Pierre had been among the first to appreciate her unusual level of curiosity and quickness to learn. It was here at Bois-des-Fossés, under the early tutelage of her grandfather, that Victorine's young heart was first stirred by the joy of learning. The fields behind the farmhouse were her classroom; every plant and tree were the curricula of the moment, and every animal and bird a skittish classmate. She wanted to know everything—and there seemed nothing that *Bon Papa* could not explain. She had observed him writing for hours at his desk, but she was too young to know that her personal tutor had once been hired to tutor a prince, served as a consultant on national education for a king, and assisted in conducting France's economic policies.[26]

Grandfather was also the first to use Victorine's given name in correspondence. For the first two years of their daughter's life, Sophie and Irénée referred to her exclusively as, "our little one," "little angel," or "our little love."[27] It was only after Pierre's arrival at Bois-des-Fossés that Sophie began to employ "our dear little Victorine."[28] The doting mother had recently noted the development of a contemplative side to her toddler as well, an ability to preoccupy herself with her own thoughts. Writing to Irénée from the lawn behind the farmhouse one afternoon, she observed, "Your little one is very good. She spends half the day playing quietly like a little woman, sitting on a rug on the lawn beside her mother."[29]

For Sophie, too, Victorine's education had begun to take center stage, and with it, her fear that she was ill equipped to match the child's potential: "Ah! my Irénée, if you knew how I regret that I did not have a brilliant education. I could teach our child so many things that I have never learned."[30] Her observations regarding Victorine's intellectual potential were reminiscent of those Pierre Samuel's mother, Anne Montchanin,[31] had made about *his* exceptional abilities two generations earlier. But there the similarity had ended. Opportunities for gifted women of the eighteenth century were negligible when compared to their male counterparts. While the prolific grandfather would go on to leave his mark upon French history in such varied fields as economics, politics, education, literature, and philosophy, these paths were usually closed to women. As a mother of her times, it was less the unfairness that Sophie bemoaned, than the misfortune of chance. "It is a great pity that she is not a boy," she said, "she has such a memory and learns so easily that she can be made a charming child."[32]

Fortified by her academic father-in-law's assessment of Victorine's intellectual promise, Sophie determined to do whatever she could to improve her three-year-old's educational opportunities.

CHAPTER 2

America's Turn

In October of 1798, Sophie sent the six-year-old Victorine to Paris for a two-month stay with Pierre and his new wife, the widowed Madame Françoise Poivre.[1] Sophie had sent Victorine to Paris so that she could be in a more intellectually stimulating environment. She assured Irénée that

> I am making a great sacrifice, but I know how necessary it is to her happiness and her education; for her intelligence which should be developing is necessarily losing when she lives entirely with children only two years old. I am sure, my dear, that she will give you some trouble, but you will be repaid by her loving caresses; remember above all, my Irénée, how much she values them from you and how grieved she would be if she thought you loved her any less. . . . If you could have seen her indecision about leaving me—the desire to be with you and yet not to leave me—ah! my Irénée, I am sure that you would love her even more.[2]

The transplanted girl wailed as loudly for Sophie as she had done for her father when he was away. In October, under the guidance of the new Madame du Pont de Nemours (*Bonne Maman*), Victorine had her first occasion to write a letter to her mother. "My dear Maman I will soon see you and it makes me very happy. I love you dearly and Lina and Alfred. Victorine Dupont."[3]

"Alfred" referred to Alfred Victor, the family's first son, who had just been born on April 11, 1798. "Lina" was two-year-old Evelina Gabrielle, to whom Sophie had given birth on May 31, 1796. The toddler was now talking incessantly, and referring to her big sister as "Torine," a term that Sophie mimicked for a time. The two played together constantly, with older sister, of course, directing the activities and making up the rules. Victorine was now reading and writing quite well and looked forward to receiving letters and packages from her father and grandparents. Like most children, she had developed a sweet tooth and had no timidity in requesting that such treats be sent to her. Displaying an early generosity of spirit, a trait that would mark the woman in adulthood, she rewarded the other occupants of the house for good behavior. Sophie noticed with amusement that "[Victorine] is very

proud that she can offer us some of her own candy, but I think that you would better bring some more when you come, for we are often 'very good.'"[4]

In January of 1799, Victorine was again sent to Paris, where she continued to
receive help with her English. Sophie's letters during this year indicate that she was
finding her daughter increasingly strong-willed. She hinted to Irénée that Victorine
would be quite charming "if only she were obedient."[5] It had been evident to
Sophie from the beginning that the girl was driven by a strong desire to please her
father, often displaying abject sorrow whenever she knew she had disappointed
him. Sophie recognized this attachment and urged her husband to employ it stra-
tegically. "She loves you very, very dearly and is eager to do all that you ask her to,"
she explained to Irénée. "If you have time to write to her it would please her
immensely; but do not let her know that I wrote about her, she would be in despair."[6]

THE FINAL STRAW

By this time, Pierre Samuel had wearied of farm life and could not resist the temptation to be back in the heart of French politics. Returning to Paris in the summer
of 1795, he returned to his duties at the printing company, writing and publishing
numerous political articles. By October, he was also serving in the legislature as a
member of the Council of Elders—one of two branches (along with the Council of
the Five Hundred) within the newly established government. A third group, made
up of five men who served as "directors," were tasked with executing the business
of the other two councils. Due to their more visible responsibilities, the new entity
became known as the "Government of the Directory."

Despite the Directory's early accomplishments,[7] the average citizen still saw
little change in their economic conditions. By the time the fledgling government
held its first elections in April of 1797, acts of violence erupted at many voting sites
throughout the country. Unnerved by this renewed threat of chaos, three of the
five members of the Directory usurped the others and ordered the arrest of several members from both chambers for suspected royalist motives. Du Pont de
Nemours was one of those swept up in the arrests, and this time Irénée was picked
up along with him. In their absence, their print shop was overrun by hooligans
who tore the place apart and succeeded in damaging several presses. When one of
the usurping directors, Jean François Reubell, realized that du Pont de Nemours
and his son were among those taken into custody, he moved swiftly to facilitate
their release the following day. But this event proved to be the final straw for the
elder du Pont. Citing bad health, he submitted his resignation to the Council of
Elders on September 13, 1797.

The indefatigable fifty-eight-year-old now turned his attention westward. *Bon
Papa* (as he was affectionately called by his children and grandchildren) gave
instructions for the dissolution of the printing company and made plans to leave for
America. He then set about creating a new company that would serve as the family's
base of operations in the new world, naming it Du Pont de Nemours Père et Fils et
Compagnie. In his *Philosophie de l'univers*, published shortly before the family's

departure, Pierre Samuel announced, "It is now America's turn. The temperate, moderate, judicious and republican government of the United States offers almost the only asylum where persecuted men can find safety, where fortunes can be rebuilt through work, [and] where the prudence of heads of families may invest their last savings."[8]

For the two years before departing to America, Irénée took a course in English whenever his work permitted. "I have already gained one thing by it," he informed Sophie. "I have found a new phrase in which to tell you how I love you. You know, my sweetheart, that a thousand would not suffice to tell you of the love with which you have filled my heart. '*I thee love with extreme fondness*; je t'aime avec idolatrie.'"[9]

New Century, New Country

The family's newly established enterprise, Du Pont de Nemours Père et Fils et Compagnie, solicited a small number of French investors who were given promising expectations of large dividends by the senior du Pont. When father and sons drafted a list of potential undertakings to pursue in America, seven projects had come quickly to their minds. For Pierre Samuel, land development based upon physiocratic principles had been his predominant dream; he viewed the land of America as the potential fulfillment of "Pontiana," the name he intended to call his utopian world. Irénée, for his part, was prepared to put his hand to whichever endeavor his father thought best, but his experience with gunpowder had never been far from his mind. Recalling his years with Antoine Lavoisier, he suggested another possibility—the production of black powder. Although his father thought the idea too risky, "project number eight" was added to the list.

By the spring of 1799, it was decided that an advance party would sail for America in order to secure a residence for the combined families, and to establish preliminary business arrangements. This group consisted of Pierre Samuel's wife Françoise, her son-in-law Bureaux de Pusy, and his daughter Sara.[10] They departed on May 10, and although their ship was captured by the British and held for six weeks, they eventually arrived in America in September of 1799, a month before the second party sailed.

For Sophie, this couldn't come soon enough. The girl from Metz was now twenty-four years old, with three children, and another child already buried. For the first eight years of her marriage, she had endured one long separation from her husband after another and had yet to experience their own "corner of the world," as she and Irénée referred to it.[11] Although a united life with Irénée was her greatest desire, Sophie had other reasons for anticipating the journey to America; she had grown more convinced that Victorine needed the stability of her father's presence. The observant mother knew better than anyone else that Irénée's absences had negatively affected their seven-year-old daughter and had contributed to an underlying anxiety in the child: "Victorine is still very grieved at your departure, especially in the evenings; she cries herself to sleep."[12] In adulthood, the girl would struggle with bouts of anxiety—a weakness she would commonly refer to as "fretting."

Irénée continued to work feverishly in order to conclude the family's remaining business before their departure date. "If I ever get out of the chaos in which I am living," he told Sophie, "my existence will be as happy as it is miserable today. I will be with you and our children and you will fill every moment of my life with happiness—how different from my life now!"[13] Ultimately, a greatly relieved Irénée completed his work in time to embark with his wife and three children. They were joined by Pierre Samuel, Victor, his wife Gabrielle, and their two children, as well as Charles Dalmas, Madame Bureaux de Pusy,[14] and her infant son Maurice.

The journey aboard the *American Eagle* was lengthier and more dangerous than anyone had expected; in fact, the entire du Pont saga could have terminated, en masse, at sea. Gabrielle's summation, as recorded in her "Notre Transplantation en Amérique," is perhaps still the best eyewitness description. "We finished the century at sea, fighting a terrible north-west wind that drove us far from our port. . . . Supplies began to fail,—the passengers to quarrel,—the sailors to rob our trunks. The Captain lost his bearings and if two English ships in succession had not given us food and told us where we were, we must have perished almost in sight of land. But after ninety-three days at sea we landed . . . at the little city of New Port [Rhode Island]."[15] In his recounting of the event, historian Ambrose Saricks added: "The American Marie out of Boston came upon the distressed Eagle, when rations were so low that the passengers were eating horse beans, after cleansing them of worms."[16]

Victorine was now seven years old and wary enough to sense the tensions felt by her family members. She knew that her sister Lina had been sick for most of the voyage and had overheard her mother express fears that they might lose her. The ship was boarded twice by armed sailors from English warships, and she had watched in puzzled fear as these "enemies of France" carried rations of food aboard for the starving passengers. In spite of the long, perilous journey, the American coastline finally came into view on the iconic date of January 1, 1800.[17] Such a symbolic convergence of timing was not lost on Victorine's idealistic grandfather. In a letter to Françoise Poivre, he told his wife that "We saw Block Island, on the 1st of January, the first day of the year and of the Century! And I saluted America, happy daughter, heiress of an unfortunate Europe."[18]

The beleaguered *American Eagle* docked at Newport, Rhode Island, on January 3, 1800.[19] The advance party led by Bureaux de Pusy had succeeded in purchasing a comfortable property overlooking the water at Bergen Point, New Jersey. The house, which Pierre Samuel romantically dubbed *Bon Séjour* (or "Goodstay," as the family referred to it in English) was a large, two-story home, but its accommodations were inadequate for a party that now consisted of twenty persons. Although Bureaux de Pusy had contracted carpenters to begin major expansions, Victor and his wife volunteered to cross the bay with their two children, Amélie and Charles, to secure lodgings in New York City. This departure served the dual purposes of alleviating the crowded accommodations at

Goodstay while enabling Victor to establish the New York office for Du Pont de Nemours and Sons.

Determined not to lose ground with Victorine's education, Irénée and Sophie decided that eight-year-old Victorine would join her aunt and uncle in lower Manhattan, at 91 Liberty Street, so that she could attend school; Evelina followed soon after, leaving only two-year-old Alfred with his mother at Goodstay. Examples of Victorine's earliest American letters, written in French, were sent from the Liberty Street address and were transported to Goodstay via ferry. On one small page she wrote, "My dear little mama you do not write as often as I would like. I would like you to come. Lina send you kisses. So do I. Goodbye my dear little mama, Victorine."[20]

Victorine's middle name, which appears as "Elisa" on her birth certificate, was anglicized to "Elizabeth" shortly after the family's arrival in America. She attended a school in the city that taught both English and French, and quickly advanced in both languages. Although the du Pont children would continue to write to the older generation in French and speak it while at home with them, English became the conversational tongue between the siblings and cousins.[21] By her teenage years, Victorine would be speaking English as well as any native-born American. Her command of the new language became so proficient that her grandfather labeled her the "chief grammarian of the family."[22] Although Pierre Samuel could speak passable English, he never mastered it. He had concluded that, at his age, it was not worth the effort to vigorously pursue it. In America, the grandfather was much more interested in pursuing Pontiana, the agricultural Eden of his physiocratic dreams.

BLACK POWDER

The name Louis de Tousard[23] is not prominently featured in most American history books, due in part to his having been eclipsed by the fellow soldier with whom he arrived in the new country—the Marquis de Lafayette. Tousard's area of expertise was artillery, and he had proved to be an asset to Washington's inexperienced army.[24] Irénée met Tousard in 1800, in the parlor of Victor's house on Liberty Street. Gabrielle recalled: "Colonel Tousard, who was our guest . . . spoke of a small establishment in Pennsylvania where cannon powder was made. Irénée . . . was curious to see the mills. He went and was much amused to find that the owners of them were quite contentedly making powder by the methods that were used in the time of Louis XIV—and making a very good profit."[25]

Accompanied by Tousard, Irénée visited other manufacturers in the New York and Pennsylvania areas and discovered that they were largely using techniques introduced by the Dutch some fifty years previously. As a result, the overall quality of American gunpowder during this period was greatly inferior to that of France and England. Irénée was increasingly convinced that by implementing the superior methods he had learned from Lavoisier, he could make a good profit producing black powder. He showed his financial projections to his father and, after considerable scrutiny, the venerable patriarch agreed.

This decision, however, made it imperative for Irénée to return immediately to France to purchase the necessary machinery and learn everything he could about the latest methods in powder manufacture. Irénée's stay in France proved to be more successful than he had dared to hope. The timing of his arrival proved fortuitous, for his own purposes and those of Napoleon Bonaparte as well.[26] The new leader of the French nation was bent on destroying England's sea-trading capabilities, and Irénée's proposal to establish a powder company could result in the establishment of an additional source of gunpowder for France and a competitor to England's dominance of the industry in America. He not only gave his consent, he ordered "the chiefs of the French Powder Department [to offer] all the technical assistance at their command. It was arranged that Government draftsmen should draw the plans for Irénée's machinery, that the machines should be built at cost in the Government's shops, and, if necessary, trained workmen should be released to form the nucleus of the American plant's crew."[27]

It was quite a birthday present for Irénée, who turned thirty while he was in Paris, an event that did not go unremembered by his nine-year-old daughter:

> I am really upset at not having been near you to wish you a happy birthday and to hug you with all my heart. I beg you to come back soon. . . . I am going at present, my dear good papa, to another school, . . . which I like a lot more than the other. One gives at this school some "ex"s, which mean "excellents." It's for when one is happy with you; and some "VB" for "very bad" when you don't know your lessons. And at the end of the month one gives a certificate to the girl who has the most "ex"s. On this card there is: "This certificate is given to Miss____ for her untiring attention to her lessons during a month." I hope, my dear good father, that I will soon have a certificate.[28]

This endearing avowal supports the notion that she was beginning to view academic achievement as a means of pleasing her parents—especially her father. As a child at Bois-des-Fossés, she had reacted to his absences with tears, resistance, and moodiness, but after only two years in America, she appears to have discovered a more constructive path.

After an absence of seven months, Irénée returned to America on July 14, 1801. Victor did not return with him, as his work in the old country was not yet finished; but the brother's extended presence in France helped to facilitate the ensuing details of Irénée's agreement with Bonaparte's government. Production of the new machinery began almost as soon as the younger brother had departed France, and the first shipments began to arrive in America as early as September. Now that Irénée had the freedom to exert his energies toward the establishment of his own business, he wasted no time in taking the next step—finding a suitable location for his powder works. Pierre Samuel had explored various sites along the Potomac River on a previous excursion, but when Irénée later examined them he found none suitable for his purposes. In September, he told his father: "There is absolutely no opportunity in Maryland or Virginia near Federal City [Washington, DC] . . . all worthless. . . . I will stay a day at Wilmington to see the Brandywine."[29] Unknown to Irénée, the decision to spend "a day at Wilmington" would set into motion a series of events that would establish the course of the du Pont family for the next two centuries.

CHAPTER 3

Wilmington, Delaware

The rustic settlement that eventually became the city of Wilmington, Delaware, is located near the juncture of two rivers, the sedate Christina and the rambunctious Brandywine, which tumbles in from the northwest. Like the union of the two rivers, Wilmington brings together a mixture of diverse cultures.

In the mid-Atlantic region, enclaves of French refugees from the Haitian Revolution were located in both Philadelphia and Wilmington, Delaware. By 1793, nearly forty families of French émigrés had found refuge in the Delawarean city. This included three close-knit families who had formerly lived within twenty miles of each other in Port-au-Prince—the des Chapelles, Gareschés, and de Bauduys. Of importance to these loyalist émigrés was that their children married well—and preferably into other French families. Two sons of Jean Garesché, for example, married two daughters of Pierre Bauduy. In the future, both daughters would become like sisters to Victorine du Pont.

Within ten years of his arrival from Santo Domingo, Peter Bauduy had established himself as one of Wilmington's most ubiquitous and prominent businessmen. Multitalented, he was both an artist and an architect,[1] and he pursued any enterprise that could potentially turn a profit. As a speculator in real estate properties in and around the greater Wilmington area, he held several strategic parcels. Bauduy's diversity of investments ranged from coach making to cotton mills. In 1804, he teamed up with eleven other men to establish the Spring Water Company, the first venture to successfully supply water to Wilmington residents.[2] With his hand in several of the city's earliest enterprises, and his numerous connections among the French community of émigrés, Bauduy was well positioned to provide assistance to any newcomer to the area, especially if one were a fellow Frenchman.

Figure 18. *Peter Bauduy, 1769–1833.* Possible
self-portrait, oil on wood, undated.

THE BANKS OF THE BRANDYWINE

In September 1801, Irénée and Bauduy met for the first time at Eden Park, Bauduy's
home in Wilmington. As Irénée outlined his plans for a black-powder manufactory, the idea intrigued the entrepreneurial Bauduy, who was impressed by the
scope and practicality of du Pont's vision. While it was clear to him that Irénée
had a superior grasp of the powder business, he also sensed an underlying determination in the man that boded well for the business's prospects.

Bauduy immediately suggested a few parcels of land that he thought might be
suitable for du Pont's purposes. Desirous to make the best use of his time, Irénée
took Bauduy up on his offer to visit them. When he and Irénée visited the ninety-
five-acre farm along the Brandywine River owned by a man named Jacob Broom,[3]
both men agreed that of all the places they had scouted, this one held the most
promise. The Brandywine descended rapidly in that stretch, and the waterpower
it produced was more than sufficient for Irénée's purposes. Even the steep hills that
cradled the creek on both of its sides matched his topographical preferences. The
only drawback was that the owner proved to be as obdurate as the unquarried granite embedded in his land. Broom's price was high and, as negotiations continued,
Bauduy referred to him "as a miser of the first class."[4]

An additional obstacle facing Irénée was that, as a noncitizen, he was barred
from purchasing land under Delaware law. Here again, Bauduy was able to provide a solution. William Hamon, a former marquis who had married Bauduy's
sister Minette, agreed to buy the property in his own name, thereby effecting a
proxy purchase for Irénée.[5] Bauduy then facilitated Irénée's application for citizen-
ship, prompting Irénée to reaffirm his appreciation for his new friend's assistance:

"It is not the city of Wilmington that I prefer to other places, but its inhabitants, and [should you be persuaded] to return to France or to San Domingo, the Brandywine would lose all its charm for me."[6]

On April 27, 1802, the tough negotiator Broom finally sold his property for $6,740. "It is to you, my dear friend," wrote Irénée to Bauduy on June 25, "that I owe the fact that I have done so, both because of the trouble you took in the matter and because without you and your family I would never have decided to locate my business in Wilmington."[7]

Four days later, Irénée suffered an unexpected disappointment as he watched his beloved father and stepmother ascend the gangplank of the *Virginia*, bound for France. Pierre Samuel's abrupt decision to leave America was a discouragement to both of his sons, neither of whom had been aware of his intentions to return to his native country. But the former statesman had been nursing a desire to be once again in the center of French politics. When Napoleon's offer of amnesty to those who had fled the country during the Revolution proved sincere, Pierre decided to relocate the company headquarters to Paris and promote its interests from there. Upon his return to the French capital, du Pont de Nemours received an enthusiastic welcome by his old associates. He also enjoyed a favorable interview with Napoleon, whose wife, Josephine, granted him a card of admission that enabled him to present himself at the palace whenever he wished. Victorine's grandfather was indeed back in his element.

Not quite ten when *Bon Papa* departed, Victorine would not see her grandfather again until she was twenty-three. The following year, she lamented:

> I am very sorry that the previous year has passed without us having had the plea-
> sure of embracing you, but I hope that this year will be happier. Your kind letter
> my dear *bon Papa* gives me the greatest pleasure. I thank you very much for the
> good advice that you were kind enough to give me. I will do my best to follow it
> and to one day be worthy of you my *bon Papa* and my [grandmother, father and
> mother]. . . . I kiss you with all my heart as well as *bonne Maman*.[8]

Considering the torchbearer role she would later fill among the next generation of du Ponts, this aspiration to "be worthy" of her grandfather and her parents, suggests that even at age eleven, she was beginning to sense that the older generation represented (or perhaps embodied) a higher responsibility.

On July 19, 1802, twelve weeks after the purchase of Broom's property, Irénée moved his family from the New Jersey shores of Goodstay to the sleepy banks of Delaware's Brandywine River. William Dutton described the transition: "It took them four days to drive the 130-odd miles from Bergen Point, New Jersey, over roads deep with ruts and dust. Their house on 'the Brandywine,' as the stream was to become affectionately known to them and succeeding generations, was the first of their own that Irénée and Sophie had possessed. It was a crude, two-story structure of native stone built in the hillside."[9]

Eleuthère Irénée du Pont wasted no time in launching his dream. He and Bauduy hired workmen, carpenters, stone masons, and scores of laborers to clear the land and begin construction for the various buildings along the river. Trees were felled, rocks cleared, foundations laid, and millraces dug for waterpower. As the orderly chaos along the riverbank progressed, construction on the family home began in early September 1802. Bauduy, exercising his architectural talents, drew up the original drafts and oversaw the construction. The foundation was laid atop a steep hill overlooking the river, which would enable Irénée to observe the mills when they were in operation. As the land was cleared, Sophie described the vista to her brother, Charles Dalmas, who was still at Goodstay: "You cannot imagine the view of the countryside we have now that some of the trees next to the site have been cut down—we overlook the entire Brandywine and the valley."[10]

With the frequent contact between Irénée and Peter, the social relationship between their two families grew proportionately. It was not long before Victorine met Mr. Bauduy's eldest son, the slender, fair-haired Ferdinand. Due to time spent together at family gatherings, their common French heritage, and age proximity, the two children soon found themselves enjoying an easy and unpretentious friendship. On the numerous occasions when their fathers were occupied with events at the mill, they could be seen exploring the hills, woods, and streams surrounding Jacob Broom's old property.

By the close of 1802, the Bauduys and du Ponts each had three children consisting of two girls and one boy. Ferdinand and Victorine had just turned eleven and ten respectively; Mimika Bauduy was nine; Cora Bauduy and Evelina du Pont were each six; and little Alfred du Pont was four. Peter's wife, Juliette, informed her daughter Mimika, who was boarding at the St. Mémin School in Burlington, New Jersey, that: "When you come home, you will find here a little companion whom I am sure you will like very much. It is Victorine du Pont, whose parents live in the country as you know. She is a charming little girl and [your sister] Cora is much better since she is here."[11]

Although many of her future acquaintances would prefer the gaiety of city life over her rustic river community, Victorine loved the Brandywine Creek and its lush sylvan setting.[12] The seclusion of the river and the steep, narrow valley gave her a sense of security. In one of her earliest jaunts through the woods, she had discovered a large gray boulder near a peak directly above the river, which she referred to simply as "my rock."[13] The limber ten-year-old would climb to its gently sloping top and sit contentedly for an hour or two at a time, lost in her own thoughts or in the pages of a book. The gurgle of the river below, the crackling sounds of small creatures in the shrubbery, and the cheerful twitter of songbirds in the branches above her head added to her sense of belonging. Unlike her experiences in France, here along the Brandywine River her family was safely ensconced about her. Although she was to see many changes to "the neighborhood," her daily appreciation for its emerald landscape never diminished. Like her father, she loved the natural, untamed beauty of the place. Even as Papa's business increasingly filled the air with plumes of billowing steam and smoke, acrid smells, and chronic noise, she never failed to appreciate her surroundings.

When the family home was completed in the early summer of 1803, it marked the fulfillment of a twelve-year-old dream for Irénée and Sophie—the attainment of their "little corner of the world." For their eldest daughter, who was able to still recall the painful separations from her father and the lonely tears of her mother while in France, she could share her parent's joy at a level her younger siblings could not. For the next fifty years, Eleutherian Mills (the name they would give to the house *and* the business) would become the nexus of Victorine's relational world.

Troubled Waters

In Delaware, the early summer of 1803 found Irénée and Sophie moving into their new home atop the steep rise overlooking the Brandywine. The family was excited, but the year spent in the dank air of a rustic cottage near the river had taken a toll on Sophie's health, and she developed a chronic backache. Meanwhile, construction of the mill buildings continued feverishly throughout 1803, requiring Irénée's full attention. Victorine had never known a time when her father had not been driven by the demands of his work, learning early that there was a painful correlation between his duties and his physical presence. This awareness had created an intense desire to ease his burdens. In young adulthood, she would confide to her mother that "I have always regretted not being a boy because I would have been useful to my family; but because that is not possible I at least wish to contribute to your happiness."[14] Victorine accepted the nineteenth-century reality that her opportunities were limited due to her gender, but this never quenched her desire to seek ways in which she might be useful.

In the spring of 1804, just two years after the purchase of Broom's land, the company's first kegs of gunpowder were packaged and sent off to Victor du Pont's office in New York City. Irénée's brother immediately went to work on advertising and seeking customers. "I am going to occupy myself with the sale of your powder," he wrote on May 2, "and I hope to dispose of more than you can make."[15] One fortuitous contract in particular would account for nearly half the company's total powder output for that first year. Twenty-two thousand pounds of it was soon "belching defiance to Barbary pirates"[16] off the coast of Algiers, helping to precipitate the conclusion to America's first foreign conflict.[17]

The gunpowder produced at the manufactory that came to be called Eleutherian Mills repeatedly proved in government tests to be superior to English powder, which at the time had been considered the world's finest. Given the poor quality of American powder, one would have anticipated the company's profit trajectory to have trended smoothly upward, but such was not to be the case. Payment was slow, competition stiff, and government agents were free to purchase from sources of their own choosing. Although test after test proved his powder superior to that of other manufacturers, Irénée found himself locked out of many government contracts. He couldn't help but conclude that much of this was tied to his nationality. He lamented to his father that: "In spite of the equality, the rights of liberty, and the excellent government of this country, we foreigners are always in a position inferior to that of other citizens."[18]

But Irénée's troubles were not entirely external; deep-seated problems were beginning to appear much closer to home. Peter Bauduy, the man who had initially done so much to aid Irénée's settlement in Wilmington, was slowly becoming the source of his greatest discontent. As the friendships between their children grew deeper, the divide between the fathers grew wider. At the root of the problem were the dual issues of incompatible personalities, and an early misunderstanding regarding Peter's role in the company. Bauduy chafed at the idea of being thought merely a "clerk of the manufacture" and asserted that "It has never seemed to me that a partnership between Mr. Irénée Dupont and Peter Bauduy is derogatory to either [of us]. . . . I have always understood that I was to conduct the outside affairs and you the interior discipline and management."[19] His perception regarding their individual roles makes it clear that his view of "partnership" exceeded that of a simple investor. Irénée came to believe that Bauduy's ultimate goal was nothing short of co-ownership of the company. One can understand his frustration, for example, when bills were arriving "addressed to Mr. Bauduy *owner of the powder mills*, or *at his powder mills on the Brandywine.*"[20]

The diplomatic Victor, perceived by both men as someone who could understand their individual viewpoints, was pressed into the role of mediator. Eventually, Victor succeeded in brokering a sort of "cease-fire." As expressions of good faith, Irénée agreed to give Bauduy more recognized status, and the latter backed off his demands to be viewed as an equal within the company. The cease-fire lasted from 1808 to the beginning of 1814. During these six years, production at the mills increased dramatically, a situation that favorably positioned the company to meet the demands of the upcoming War of 1812.

CHAPTER 4

Emergence

Madame Capron, an educator of aristocratic young women in France, had fled to America in 1791, rightly fearing that her former connections with the nobility were a threat to her life during the Revolution. While feelings of political animus against France were on the rise, schools for young ladies run by highly educated French women, many of whom had taught in circles of nobility, were all the rage among America's rapidly growing upper-middle class. After establishing a school in Elizabeth, New Jersey, and later in Philadelphia, Capron relocated to Wilmington, Delaware. Her enrollment records for the 1803–1804 term included an eleven-year-old scholar named Victorine du Pont.

While her school taught basic educational subjects, the primary thrust of Capron's curriculum emphasized French heritage and the enhancement of a young woman's "finishing" skills.[1] Although the school did not survive, it was unlikely that Victorine would have remained for another term. By year's end she had felt largely unchallenged, and lamented that she had learned "very little" while she was there.[2] The idea of receiving enough knowledge to adequately adorn a husband's arm in society, while excelling in the social graces of feminine charm, musical skills, and etiquette, did not greatly interest the granddaughter of du Pont de Nemours. Victorine believed that genteel society pressured young women into traditional roles by stressing those graces over fields of academic study. Regarding musical skills, for example, she loved to play the piano (the influence of her mother and aunt), but she thought it "a pity that what ought to be considered merely as an amusement should become the chief thing which people in general pay most attention. But let us not envy those brilliant accomplishments. Girls who are fit merely to shine in a crowd, are very seldom happy at home."[3] Victorine wanted something different, and she would pursue an educational path more suited to her own personal goals: "I often rejoice that I did not receive one of those superficial educations, which may perhaps suit fashionable ladies, but that would have rendered me unfit for the private life I am destined to lead."[4]

MADAME RIVARDI'S SEMINARY FOR YOUNG LADIES

Upon finishing her term at Madame Capron's, Victorine learned that Ferdinand Bauduy's sisters, Mimika and Cora, had been sent to a new boarding school in Philadelphia. The excited sisters told her that the "seminary" was run by a French couple named Rivardi, whose curriculum and methods of teaching were both interesting and avant-garde. Everything the girls told Victorine about the school raised hopes that here may exist the type of educational experience for which she had longed. The twelve-year-old immediately spoke to Papa, who subsequently visited the establishment on one of his business trips to Philadelphia. Impressed by what he saw and heard, Irénée felt that the Rivardi's school might just provide the type of challenging environment that could nurture his daughter's academic interests. He also believed it was time for his eldest daughter to experience life beyond the family enclave, and the provincial setting in which she had thus far existed. After talking it over with Sophie, they informed their daughter that she would be boarding at Madame Rivardi's Seminary for Young Ladies—starting next term. The excited girl was enrolled on July 17, 1805, six weeks shy of her thirteenth birthday.

When Victorine left the family home for Philadelphia in the summer of 1805, it was with a mixture of apprehension and anticipation. She would sorely miss her parents and siblings, but on the cusp of her teenage years, the desire to experience the friendship and intimacy of girls her own age had been growing more acute. Physically, she was of good health, slender, and tall for her age. Her hair had darkened into the deep chestnut color she would maintain for most of her life. Pierre Samuel had expressed that of all the women in the family, with the exception of her blue eyes, Victorine most resembled her grandmother, Marie Le Dée, whom he described as "a tall brunette, built like a nymph, and with soft although black eyes, deserved the praise for her beauty, for her noble and simple grace, for her modesty, and above all for her intelligence."[5] At Madame Rivardi's seminary, she would be introduced to young women with whom she could build not only a social connection, but an intellectual bond, as well. For many of the young women who attended the school, the Rivardi years were a rich foundational experience; but for Victorine du Pont, they proved especially formative. Her three years at the seminary, and the five years that followed, had a significant impact upon her academic, spiritual, and social development, and aided a sense of self-discovery.

Academically, she received from Madame Rivardi a comprehensive and specialized curriculum that included arithmetic, art and drawing, botany, drama and plays, embroidery, English, epistolary style, essays, geography, grammar, history, languages, music (instrumental and compositional), philosophy, poetry, prose, science, and writing skills. Field trips, such as their "botanical walks," were a regular part of the curriculum, as were trips to museums, art galleries, and theaters. Student-led performances of plays and concerts were also conducted for the benefit of visiting family members and community leaders.

Victorine's first letter home announced a determination "that Madame Rivardi will never be displeased with me."[6] Indeed, the celebrated matron was impressed with the latent potential she saw in this slender thirteen-year-old from the backwoods of Delaware; but her standards were high, and she quickly went to work setting the bar for her young protégé. By October of 1805, she sent the following report to Victorine's father:

> [Victorine] took the second mark in writing and answered correctly all the questions that were asked her in grammar, geography and history. I am very pleased with her except for her lack of industry and her sewing. We have frequent little discussions about it and (in order to persuade her to work) I have even threatened to ask her mother not to come until the work [is] finished. Of course the threat made her shed many tears—but as I am telling you this in confidence I must beg you not to know of it when you see our little penitent. I hope that I shall never again have to make this complaint.[7]

The wise headmistress had touched the young student in her most vulnerable spot—the threat of becoming a disappointment to her parents. Not only would the punishment deprive her of the much-hoped-for visit with her mother, but the cause would be due to a "lack of industry," a sure stab in the heart for the daughter of Irénée and Sophie du Pont. She, who secretly lamented that she had not been born a boy in order to have been more help to the family, was now in danger of having the charge of laziness brought against her name.

Mrs. Rivardi's "little penitent" would never again give the clever woman a reason to repeat the complaint. The motivation of pleasing Rivardi—with the ultimate goal of making her parents proud—was all the incentive Victorine needed. Her progress from that point on was so noticeable that by May of 1806, less than a year after her arrival, she had advanced to the highest grade. Victorine wrote to her father, "My dear papa, How happy I am to inform you that I was *promoted* [to] the first class. . . . Mrs Rivardi mentioned me in a book which was exposed in the school room, for my attention to my studies, & progress. I cannot tell you how gratified I am, to her, for all the encouragement that she has conferred on me. I *will* continue to do all in my power to deserve them."[8]

By the time another year had passed, the fourteen-year-old had attained the school's highest level of recognition—the remarkable distinction of becoming Madame Rivardi's "best overall student," a title she would hold until her graduation. With this newfound recognition, "Vic" (as she was often called by her classmates) gained a level of esteem she had not previously experienced. When one considers that many of her fellow scholars were the daughters of well-to-do merchants and dignitaries from the entire mid-Atlantic region, the Brandywine nymph had accomplished no small feat.

Irénée was bursting with pride as he wrote to his father: "Victorine wins everyone's affection; she is Madame Rivardi's best pupil; every month her name is at the head of her class in every subject, though there are pupils who are much older and have been in school longer than she; and I have no doubt that next month I shall have the pleasure of telling you that she has earned the school's first prize. The teachers are loud in their praises of her gentleness, her industry, her friendliness."[9]

A number of Victorine's classmates would leave a lasting impression upon her. Several remained acquaintances for many years after graduation: two became sisters-in-law and one would become her brother Alfred's mother-in-law. A partial list of her classmates at Madame Rivardi's included: Mimika and Cora Bauduy, Phoebe Pemberton Morris,[10] the gifted songstress Anne Halverson, the "very beautiful" Estelle Pageot (who later married Napoleon's ambassador to the United States),[11] and "our Wilmingtonian Miss Stokes."[12]

But of the numerous friends and acquaintances she had made during her stay at Madame Rivardi's, her closest were Rebecca Ralston, Antoinette Brevost, and Anna Potts Smith. Of the three, Ralston was clearly Victorine's "most intimate friend."[13] It would be through her friendship with "Becky" that Victorine's world-view would be entirely transformed. Before her arrival at the school, her understanding of spiritual things had been influenced by the deistical views of her grandfather and father. Here in Philadelphia she was exposed to a more orthodox view of Christianity. Although Victorine's conversion would be a slow, deliberative process of inquiry and investigation, the original spark was ignited by Becky and the Ralstons. For Victorine, the nascent Christian faith that began to be nurtured in the Ralston family home would eventually become the mainstay of her life.

A year older than Victorine, Becky was the daughter of the influential Ralstons of Philadelphia. Her mother, Sarah, was the pious daughter of Matthew Clarkson, a former mayor of the city, and her father was the prominent merchant, Robert Ralston, whose import–export firm had grown into one of the city's most successful enterprises.[14] In their room at Madame Rivardi's, Victorine learned that Rebecca's parents were known for their Christian faith and philanthropic efforts. Sarah Ralston shared her husband's religious convictions "and furthered his charitable purposes upon all occasions."[15] In 1808, for example, Robert Ralston conducted a meeting in their home that led to the establishment of the nation's first Bible society, which continues in Philadelphia to the present day.[16] In attendance were William White, first presiding bishop of the Episcopal Church in the United States, and Dr. Benjamin Rush—a signer of the Declaration of Independence and George Washington's surgeon general. Rush's daughter, Julia, was one of Victorine's classmates.[17] To the French girl from Delaware, it seemed that the school had more than a smattering of young ladies who openly identified themselves with the Christian religion.

The Ralston family home, Mount Peace, was situated close to the school, which meant that Victorine was a frequent guest for meals and overnight stays. The tall brunette quickly became a favorite of Becky's numerous siblings. Describing those visits to her sister Lina, Vic wrote: "I was received in the most cordial manner by all members of this truly amiable family. They seemed quite delighted to see me and showed me so much attention that I cannot but feel most grateful to have such kind friends."[18]

To this point, Victorine had not thought too deeply about religious matters. Although du Pont genealogical records reveal a sprinkling of Roman Catholics (including Irénée's mother),[19] the predominant faith of the du Pont family since the 1500s had been Huguenot, a form of Calvinistic Protestantism. Pierre Samuel du Pont de Nemours, like many of his philosophical peers, renounced both Protestantism and Roman Catholicism in favor of a more deistical system of religious thought. His decision influenced his two sons—as well as his first grandchild, Victorine du Pont.

The Ralstons' lifestyle challenged Victorine's perspective. As a frequent visitor to their home, she could see that their experience with the Divine was markedly different than her own. They read the Bible regularly and sought the society of others who held the same beliefs. They observed Sundays for worship and conducted daily prayer times in their home. Victorine noted that it wasn't just Becky's parents who were religious; the whole family—down to its youngest members—seemed to incorporate that same bigger-than-life view of religion. Although the emphasis seemed extreme to her, she found the peaceful environment of the Ralston home increasingly attractive, and the warmth in which she was received gave her a pleasant feeling of belonging. Moved by the unfeigned piety of this devout Presbyterian home, she slowly began to explore the tenets of their faith.

Commenting on Victorine's religious journey years later, her future sister, Sophie du Pont, would report that "Altho' brought up to live & reverence God, [she] had not belonged to any church, & her first deep religious impressions had been made by assisting [at the] family worship of the father of one of her schoolmates, Mr Robert Ralston of Phila[delphia]. Her religious convictions and feelings gradually increased by the study of God's Word under the teaching of the Holy Spirit, without the special influence of any church."[20] Becky was not the only classmate who professed to be a Christian, but it is clear that she and her family had the largest initial impact upon Victorine's conversion. The two friends maintained a close relationship throughout the decade following their graduation, staying frequently at each other's homes. When Becky visited the Brandywine, Victorine introduced her to local friends and activities: "We went in the boat . . . as far as the [Gilpin] paper mill & as you may easily fancy, I did not fail giving Rebecca a sample of my skill in the art of rowing."[21]

The second member of the Rivardi sisterhood was the loyal Antoinette Brevost. Her father, the educator John Brevost, had moved his wife and daughter to Philadelphia after a failed attempt to open a school near Wilkes-Barre.[22] He found employment with the newly arrived Rivardis as a teacher of mathematics, and moved his family into the school. Antoinette would become known for her unfeigned loyalty and devotion to parents and friends. Both of these were virtues that Victorine highly respected, in addition to her admiration for Antoinette's intellect and amiability.[23] Reciprocally, Antoinette found her greatest social happiness in the relationship she developed with the girl from rural Delaware, whose accepting friendship she grew to cherish. A glimpse of Antoinette's affection can be seen at the end of their first year, when she and several classmates had been simultaneously confirmed at their church. After supplying Victorine with a complete rundown of the names each girl had chosen for herself, she concluded with: "Thus my dear, in future I may as well be called Victorine, as . . . Antoinette . . . your devoted and loving, *A. Victorine Brevost*."[24]

The third member of the triad was Anna Potts Smith, the daughter of the devout Robert and Rebecca (Potts) Smith. The second of eight children, she was born on December 14, 1793, and baptized the following month in the Second Presbyterian Church of Philadelphia by the pious Rev. Ashbel Green. Among Madame Rivardi's students, it was generally conceded that Anna was the most gifted poet among them. Victorine admired her creativity, wit, and outspokenness; she knew that her friend held strong opinions about politics, literature, and current affairs—and was unafraid to express them. In Anna's later years, an admiring visitor described her as possessing a mind that was "of the order of genius rather than talent, with intuitive flashes of perception."[25]

On a summer day in 1818, Anna was visiting Victorine at Eleutherian Mills while another guest was also present—Irénée's good friend, Daniel Lammot.[26] The latter was a successful textile manufacturer, and a recent widower. Victorine introduced Anna to Daniel, who was eleven years her senior, and the guests soon took a more than passive interest in each other. Following a period of courtship that lasted for eighteen months, the couple were married on December 2, 1819. The carefree, independent-thinking poet became, in one happy moment, a first-time bride and an instant mother of Daniel's four children. Five years later, Daniel's seventeen-year-old daughter from his former marriage, the lovely Margaretta Elizabeth Lammot, would marry Victorine's brother Alfred—effectively turning Anna into Alfred's mother-in-law. The outspoken girl that Victorine had admired at Madame Rivardi's for her wit, sophistication, and poetic ability, would now become an integral part of her own family.

Although the two Rivardi chums did not always agree (Anna tended to be more progressive than Victorine in her views), Vic always described her as "the kindest of friends."[27] For Anna's part, her feelings were reflected in her own unique fashion in 1813: "For yourself dear Victorine, I have always more thoughts than my paper can hold. . . . Till I have a window in my heart you will never read them all."[28] Perhaps the most concrete example of Anna's affection for her old classmate was revealed when she named her first daughter Eugenia Victorine.[29]

Socially, Victorine's emergence from her Brandywine cocoon upon the advent of her impressionable teenage years dramatically expanded her view of the world. The intimate environment of the boarding school had her rubbing shoulders with people who represented a broader spectrum of American culture and ideas than she had hitherto experienced. At Madame Rivardi's, Victorine discovered social acceptance, camaraderie, and an unexpected measure of popularity. The ebullient banter bouncing off the walls of the girls' bedrooms had included not only in-depth literary discussions, but also the predictable topics of boys, fashion, gossip, and the latest fads.

Irénée's eldest child also discovered more about her own uniqueness, in particular finding that a certain level of esteem followed her academic accomplishments. The level of success she attained through her studies—especially in the fields of literature, botany, embroidery, science, and history—contributed to an ever-increasing sense of self-confidence. Already fluent in French and English, she possessed a knack for languages in general. She could read Latin, had taught herself Italian (teaming up with Aunt Gabrielle), and had moderate familiarity with Spanish. At Anna Smith's urging, Victorine had also begun to study German. Her letters reveal that by her mid-teens she showed an impetus to be more creative and playful, frequently spicing her paragraphs with examples of literary wit or tongue-in-cheek humor. Victorine was experiencing a sense of "fitting in" and, for the first time, a healthy dose of acceptance and affection—even popularity—beyond the family home. By the time of her graduation in 1808, the sixteen-year-old daughter of Eleuthère Irénée du Pont had every reason to feel confident and optimistic about her future.

CHAPTER 5

Post-Rivardi Years

[Victorine] is well informed, gentle and attractive; the devil of it is that others are beginning to find her so.

—Eleuthère Irénée du Pont to Pierre Samuel du Pont de Nemours, November 22, 1809

The year after Victorine had begun her studies in Philadelphia, her mother gave birth to her first American-born child. Eleuthera du Pont arrived in December of 1806, bringing with her an unexpected Christmas gift. The backaches that had plagued Sophie for the past three years mysteriously disappeared after she delivered her new daughter. "She has brought back Sophie's good health," wrote Irénée to his father, "[and] since she has been nursing the baby she has regained all the plumpness and vigor that she had when Victorine was a baby."[1] Eleuthera's arrival marked the beginning of a transcendent bond between the two sisters. Although fourteen years separated them, Victorine experienced an immediate attachment to the newborn. Writing to her cousin Amelia, she confided that it was she who had been responsible for naming the new addition: "No one knows it yet, [but] it is I who chose that name. I found it very pretty but I am afraid that not everyone has my taste."[2] Although French families often named a daughter after the mother, Victorine had bestowed the child with the feminine version of her *father's* name.

During 1809, Victorine had been helping her eleven-year-old brother Alfred with his preparatory studies for boarding school and she offered to do the same for her cousin, Charles Irénée, who was now twelve. "Victorine," noted Aunt Gabrielle with appreciation, "had the kindness to allow him to share the lessons which she was giving Alfred before they went to Mount Airy School."[3] Mount Airy Seminary in Germantown, Pennsylvania, had just been established as a boarding school for boys,[4] and Alfred and Charles enrolled in 1809. Victorine's academic assistance to her brother and cousin foreshadowed her position of "first tutor," a role that fell quite naturally upon the shoulders of the granddaughter of Pierre Samuel Du Pont de Nemours. With very few exceptions, Victorine went on to provide the preliminary education of not only her own siblings, but of nearly every du Pont descendant along the Brandywine for the next two generations. A partial list of the preliminary subjects she taught included French, English, spelling, reading, writing, history, geography, and mathematics—all before her pupils were sent to their respective schools. For the girls, she also provided supplemental activities like dancing, drawing, sewing, and piano lessons.

Irénée too availed himself of her academic skills. Due to her bilingual fluency in French and English, and his paternal trust in her handling of sensitive documents, he frequently asked his daughter to transcribe or compose important business letters for him.[5] Her role as a sort of impromptu "private secretary" to her father began when she returned from Madame Rivardi's in 1808. Among her other tasks, she copied his incoming and outgoing letters and opened his correspondence when he was away.[6] Although Victorine was not involved in the operations of the company, or in day-to-day decision-making, this informal role of *secrétaire* exposed her to many of its internal affairs.[7] Through these critical communications, she became familiar with many of the people and institutions with whom the company interacted—the agents, suppliers, customers, salesmen, lenders, and investors that were necessary to its operations. She also knew many of them personally, since several came to visit, dine, or spend the night at Eleutherian Mills.

While Victorine was happy to be useful to her father, his unscheduled requests often interrupted an active social life. Responding to Evelina, who was still at Madame Rivardi's in 1811, she acknowledged that she would have answered sooner, "had I not been constantly occupied [for] two days in transcribing some papers for papa. . . . I snatched a few minutes yesterday to write to Mrs Rivardi and I was scarcely done before papa brought me a great long paper to copy. You may [tell] our friends that I will surely answer their letters as soon as this *indigestion* of writing will be over."[8] Ten years later, a note she sent to Eleuthera reveals that the "indigestion" had not abated: "Last night I sat up till 12 writing for Papa."[9]

The first five years following her graduation were gratifying ones for Victorine. During that time, she welcomed two new siblings. On September 20, 1810, Victorine reported to Evelina the arrival of yet another little girl.[10] This time, the name Sophie Madeleine would grace the newborn; a decision that greatly pleased Irénée. The tiny babe proved to be Irénée's final girl, and the opportunity to memorialize the name of the woman he loved would never repeat itself. On August 8, 1812, Henry du Pont, the first of a pair of boys to be born in America, made his debut. When Irénée announced the news to his father, he engaged in a bit of speculative prophecy: "This little one may live to be the head of our American family."[11] Nearly forty years later, Henry would indeed take over the company's leadership and run it in the black from that point on. The dual nicknames of "Boss" and "General" would become appropriate epithets of his reign. The other American-born boy, Irénée and Sophie's last child, would be born on Valentine's Day, 1816. Victorine reported that the miniature Cupid, Alexis Irénée, was "a thin little blue-eyed fellow, whom everybody mistakes for a little girl, from his delicate appearance. To prevent mistakes, Mama has just put him in a rifle dress, but [it does not] make him look more manly."[12]

The numerous letters to Evelina at Madame Rivardi's abound with humor, local news, and big-sisterly advice. Her tone is upbeat (even when scolding) and reflects a certain joie de vivre. "Tini," as she was sometimes called during this period, wanted to be kept abreast of friends she still had at the school and prodded her sister for information: "Send me all you pick up good or bad, true or false. It will always afford a moment's amusement and prevent you from sending me any *blanks*, which are the things I hate in a letter as much as in conversation."[13] Although Lina was only four years younger, she had been homesick. Vic encouraged her through those early months and sent her motherly advice on such diverse topics as clothing and hairstyles, use of time, study habits, and feminine hygiene. On one occasion, while she was describing her sister's rosy academic setting, she unwittingly painted her own happy state as well: "You are just in that bright season of life when every object dances gaily before your fancy, decked with all the charms of novelty."[14]

A RENEWED INTEREST

A significant reason for her happiness at the time was her renewed connection with Ferdinand Bauduy. Ferdinand and his best friend Jerome Keating,[15] both newly graduated from St. Mary's in Baltimore, had paid visits to Madame Rivardi's throughout Victorine's last year there, since both of Ferdinand's sisters (Mimika and Cora) were attending the school. The childhood friends had seen little of each other during the previous four years, and the time apart had brought significant, but pleasant, changes. To Ferdinand, the pretty but gangly friend of youth had matured into a "tall and lovely"[16] young woman whose slender, attractive form was not lost on the young man's admiring eyes. Quickly renewing their friendship, the two found themselves anticipating new opportunities to be together, which, their friends noted, were becoming more frequent. Ferdinand's father, Peter Bauduy, also noticed their renewed interest, and mentioned it to Irénée: "My son has told me that ever since he left college, he has seen and thought of no one but V."[17]

Epistolary evidence for the deeper feelings "V" may have had for any young man during this period is scant, but the topic of prospective beaus was, nonetheless, a hot one among the Rivardi group of friends. Du Pont historian Mary Johnson observed that Victorine and her classmates were "fully absorbed with the venerate notion of marriage, they believed that they had to find *the one man* most compatible with their individual characters."[18] Antoinette Brevost would later tell her friend that apart from Ferdinand's "amiable qualities," he had "one *great claim* to your affection—I mean that of having *appreciated* your worth from his *earliest youth*."[19] And if Victorine's father was late in recognizing the special attraction between the two friends, her Uncle Victor had not been. In a letter to his father, he described Ferdinand as the one "with whom [Victorine] had been in love since they were children."[20]

Victorine turned seventeen at the end of August 1809, and although Irénée chose to ignore the implications of her relationship with Ferdinand for as long as he could, by autumn he could no longer remain in denial. Not only was he aware of Ferdinand's growing interest, but his thirty-three-year-old company accountant, Raphael

Duplanty, had surprised him by mentioning *his* intentions for Victorine. Preoccupied with the constant demands of his powder mills, Irénée had been taken aback by the romantic notions of the two men. Summarizing his alarm to his father, he expressed:

> The business difficulties are diminishing—the family ones are beginning. The picture you have made for yourself of Victorine is not exaggerated; she is well informed, gentle and attractive; the devil of it is that others are beginning to find her so. . . . Among her suitors the principal ones are Duplanty and Ferdinand—Mr. Bauduy's son. I think the first is too old for her and the second too young. Duplanty is a very worthy man, full of energy and ability; his character is good and I am really fond of him. If the question were for myself, I would marry [her to] him with pleasure. Ferdinand is a nice boy; he has no vice that I know of; the match would be perfectly suitable; but his father has behaved to me in a way that it is hard to forget, though I have nothing to find fault with now. . . . However, Victorine is so perfectly sensible that I have no uneasiness in leaving it to her to decide and that is a great relief to me.[21]

His father's response wasn't the most reassuring; the older man floated the suggestion that Victorine should marry her mother's brother, Uncle Charles. "Isolated as you are," Pierre had written to his son, "I had fancied that [Charles] Dalmas would be the first to think of marrying Victorine . . . [but] I do not know whether marriage between uncle and niece is permitted in your country. If your boys were not younger than your girls, the marriages that I should prefer for our colony would be between the cousins. In that way we should be sure of honesty of soul and purity of blood."[22]

In fairness, neither Victorine nor Ferdinand had been thinking seriously of marriage to this point; both were enjoying their post-graduate season of life. Although both Bauduy and du Pont were given to indulging their children, neither would have agreed to a marriage in which the groom could not adequately provide for his bride. Peter knew Ferdinand had a bent toward laziness: "I admit, my dear boy, that I myself—when I remember how indolent you have been ever since you were a child—am uneasy for you."[23] But a new opportunity for his son's viability as a suitor was about to take shape.

Irénée, who had always wanted the family reunited, convinced his brother Victor, who was failing at trying to establish a general store in Upstate New York, to join him along the Brandywine, where he promised Victor assistance in establishing a business.[24] Irénée owned a fine herd of Merino sheep and suggested that his brother could start a textile mill with him as a silent partner. Peter Bauduy then offered to become a partner in the operation so that he could establish his son Ferdinand in business. He supplied most of the capital, including the land "as part of his investment."[25] Duplanty became a fourth partner and, by the spring of 1810, the textile mill of Du Pont, Bauduy & Company was officially launched on the opposite side of the creek from the powder mill. Charles returned to the Brandywine from Mount Airy Seminary to join his father at the newly formed textile mill and became a partner in the company,[26] while Alfred was eventually sent to Dickinson College in 1816 to study under Thomas Cooper, the renowned chemist and educator.[27] Irénée contracted to build a home for his brother's family on the hillside adjacent to the textile mill. The house was completed in the summer of 1811 and Gabrielle named it Louviers, for her hometown in France. The name would eventually make its way into local usage as a designation for the general locale of Victor's house and mill.

The partners of the new textile company planned to send Ferdinand to Europe for two years to learn the trade, with a particular focus on the dyeing process. But Duplanty's competition had injected a sense of urgency into the senior Bauduy's heart. What if Victorine were to show a renewed interest in the older man while his son was away? Although she had previously turned Duplanty down, Peter knew that marriages were made for financial stability as well as love, and that age disparity was not a major obstacle among his French merchant class. Had not he— just five days previously—hosted the marriage of his own daughter Mimika to the successful businessman Vital Garesché? The groom had been twenty-seven and she but sixteen.[28] With this fresh example in mind, Peter suddenly viewed his son's two-year absence as a threat to the union for which he had been hoping, and decided to act upon a rash, paternal impulse by alerting Ferdinand to Duplanty's intentions. He urged Ferdinand to immediately submit his own marriage proposal. "Before you is the possibility of a wonderful future," the father had persuaded his son, "united to one who with every physical charm has much sweetness and amiability . . . and for all that you have only to give two years of serious application. . . . I have persuaded [Irénée] to agree that before you leave for France . . . you will be allowed to pay your addresses to V. so that you may know before you sail whether she shares your hope for the future and whether she is willing to give you her promise."[29]

To Peter Bauduy, the all-important goal was "to know before you sail." He was convinced that a formal engagement would lock the girl into a commitment and preclude the possibility of marriage to anyone else while his son was away. He succeeded in conveying this sense of urgency to his son, who immediately sat down to pen his own proposal. Peter then took it to Eleutherian Mills. "[Ferdinand] has given me a sealed letter that he wanted to beg you to deliver," he explained to Irénée, "but he had not courage to ask you himself. . . . He has assured me that it contains nothing that is not absolutely respectful, and he promises that if you will be good enough to do this for him, when he next sees you he will show you how well he has used his time and how eager he is to deserve Victorine."[30]

Irénée had no intention of interfering with his daughter's choice of a husband, but he did have an intractable position as to *when* such a union should occur. Writing to his father, Pierre Samuel, he vented:

> You know of [Peter Bauduy's] propositions concerning Victorine. They were finally resolved into a request that she should become engaged to his son before his journey to Europe. I did not consent to this American arrangement which

seems to me the height of absurdity between two young people who have seen very little of each other and between whom the subject has never been mentioned. To promise Victorine to a young man who is about to spend two years in France would be to bind her to one who would be bound in no way whatever. I therefore refused my consent to any such engagement. I did it as politely as possible but the way in which my decision was received makes me believe that the one idea of this strange family is to prevent V. from marrying before the son returns; that it is the factory he wants to marry, and the chief idea is to be sure that V. shall not marry anyone else who might be helpful to me. I am much dissatisfied with both father and son in this affair.[31]

Although Irénée was a bit naive about how deeply involved the childhood friends had become, Victorine nevertheless turned the young suitor down. She had, essentially, two primary reasons for the refusal—one which she could verbalize, and one she could not. The first was that the proposal had caught her truly by surprise and was wildly out of keeping with her perception of the relationship's pace. Unaware of the urgency now driving father and son, the request had seemed "audacious" to her.[32] She tried to convince the disheartened lover that it was in both their interests to wait until he returned from Europe to discuss the matter of marriage; but until then, she could make him no promises one way or the other. Second, and perhaps more importantly, she knew that her father's outward objections to a prolonged engagement were rooted in deeper, more unspoken fears. Her ears had not been deaf to the many outbursts she had overheard in the family home related to her father's turbulent relationship with Peter Bauduy. She was convinced that formally binding herself to a union with the Bauduy family—at least for the present—would only increase Papa's anxiety and unnecessarily add to his burdens.

Ferdinand was disappointed by the refusal but knew that Victorine had no immediate plans to marry anyone else, especially since she had already given his current rival, Duplanty, a gracious but very emphatic "No." But while the refusal dejected Ferdinand, it stabbed his father in the heart of his pride. Victorine's rejection had made it look to Peter that his son had been played for a fool. He was convinced that Irénée had put her up to it and was not appeased by explanations of timing. He sent a rash note to Irénée demanding the return of Ferdinand's letter, "as nothing in the world is more foolish than the letter of a lover—especially to a person who does not return the sentiment. . . . It can only be an unpleasant souvenir to Victorine, since she considers it *very audacious* and its contents must seem ridiculous to her."[33] Unfortunately, the refusal diminished Victorine's currency in the eyes of Ferdinand's injured father. He told Irénée, "You will admit, my friend, that one must have a wonderful imagination and be devoid of common sense to believe that if a man has been in love with a lady for two years and has done his utmost to please her, without her even noticing his devotion, it is improbable that he will succeed better in two years of absence."[34]

Ferdinand sailed for Europe on May 18, 1810. His mission was scheduled to take him first to Sweden, and then on to Holland and Paris. Since the assignment was to include specializing in the art of dyeing (a process the inexperienced Americans were finding difficult to master), Irénée asked his father to use his contacts to direct the lad when he arrived in Paris. As far as Irénée was concerned, the young man's departure now freed him up to refocus on business matters. His mills were producing at capacity, and the coming war with England would force him to erect more buildings to keep up with the demand.

Patriotism and the War of 1812

The U.S. Congress approved President Madison's declaration of war with England on June 18, 1812. The timing was propitious for E. I. du Pont, who had already made plans to leave the following day for Washington, DC, on business. Building in some leisurely time to enjoy the sights, he thrilled his nineteen-year-old daughter when he invited her to join him. The journey took three weeks to complete and was a rare example of Irénée at leisure. For Victorine, it was surely one of the most memorable and happy events of her life. As they traveled, the days were devoted to sightseeing, reading, and examining the numerous flowers and plants they encountered. Employing their favorite term for this activity to Evelina, she gushed, "We often have stopped on the road to *Botanize* [sic] and really we have found some beautiful flowers."[35] Two weeks later, the city of Washington held its annual Fourth of July celebrations. Victorine and her father were among the enthusiastic crowd that met first at the Capitol building, and then later at the President's house, which Victorine referred to as "the palace."

> The most *brilliant* day of our stay in W[ashington] was certainly the 4th of July.... Mrs. Madison, the president, all the great Ladies of the court & their husbands, sat in the middle of the Congress hall, in the best place to *hear* and *see*. We were so fortunate as to procure a seat near them, so that we did not lose a word of Mr. Rush's fine address.[36]
>   ... [On leaving the Capitol] the President was escorted by the cavalry as far as the palace. As he passed, the whole band struck up Madison's March.[37] Then the Secretarys [sic] & their Ladies went off in the same style.... We were introduced into the drawing room [of the president's house], where stood the greatest crowd I ever beheld in my life. We could scarcely find out the President & his Lady to make our *bows*.[38]

As war progressed, British warships maintained a tight blockade of the Eastern Seaboard. By the spring of 1813, rumors were spreading of a likely attack on the Brandywine mills, especially upon the gunpowder-producing enterprise of Eleuthère Irénée du Pont. Irénée and Victor, along with other mill owners, received permission from Delaware Governor Joseph Haslet on May 18, 1813, to organize a militia to protect these highly strategic targets and the citizens living there. The "Brandywine Rangers," consisting of two hundred men, were formed into two companies, one of which was overseen by Irénée and the other by Victor.[39] The Rangers created a temporary, supplemental force to the regular state militias, which often performed their military drills at "Camp DuPont," a wide, sloping hillside near the Brandywine River two miles south of Irénée's mills.

Writing to Lina from home, Victorine announced: "We are *immersed* in war preparations and of course we talk of nothing else. Papa is going to give all the officers a *huge horn*, that each may sound the alarm in case of danger. . . . The uniforms [of the Brandywine Rangers] are to be blue and gold . . . and the hats will be after the Spanish fashion tacked up on one side with a feather. I think it will look very handsome indeed."[40] Victorine admired and supported the patriotism of the young men who placed themselves in harm's way for the sake of the war effort. Wanting to help where she could, she frequently made the ten-mile trip to Kennett Square, Pennsylvania, where she volunteered with other women to help feed and nurse militia men who had been wounded in the conflict.[41] Victorine's patriotic sentiments were unfeigned. When Philadelphia's state militia, the Washington Guards, sent hundreds of men to defend the Brandywine upon Irénée's request, Victorine proudly extolled the hospitality of Mr. Warner, a neighbor who had freely given them food and refuge on his property. At the same time, she vehemently renounced the reception given by another farmer in Chester, Pennsylvania, who had charged the men for their room and board and "stowed 15 of them in one room! Was there ever anything more abominable? If I had been the Captain," she vented to Evelina, "I would not have paid a cent and given him a beating with the bargain. However my dear, you may tell the Philadelphians that they may send us more troops for we take good care of those we have."[42]

While the war presented a direct threat to du Pont homes and businesses, it also created an unprecedented opportunity for the expansion of the powder mills. Having wisely encouraged then-President Thomas Jefferson to stockpile saltpeter, a necessary ingredient of black powder, Irénée took a calculated risk. In 1813, the visionary entrepreneur purchased an additional thirty-two-acre lot attached to, and just below, his own yards. The parcel, known as "Hagley," had been recently acquired by the wise speculator Thomas Lea, who in turn sold it to E. I. for the exorbitant price of $47,000.

CHAPTER 6

Ferdinand

While Ferdinand was in Europe pursuing his apprenticeship in textiles and the art of dyeing, Victorine was engaged in the multihued activities of her postgraduation social life. She and her chums engaged in boating, hiking, and horseback riding while in the country and visited museums, theaters, and art studios while in Philadelphia. They attended soirees in various homes or meandered through the shops on Chestnut Street. Gossip about potential beaus or upcoming marriages were frequent topics of conversation. On one occasion, Cousin Amelia (known to Victorine and her sisters as either "Emily" or "Melie")[1] approached her with a "dream list"—following the popular fancy that if the names of available bachelors were placed under one's pillow in the evening, the heart's hidden choice from among that list would be revealed in a dream that night. Vic confided to sister Lina that: "I forgot to put it under my pillow until last night, & [as usual] I did not dream of anyone at all. . . . One of the poets [says], 'In sleep when fancy is let loose to play, our dreams repeat the wishes of the day.' But I am not quite of this opinion & I think *chance* has a great share in those mighty visions."[2]

Cousin Amelia became the first of the next du Pont generation to marry. In September of 1812, the sixteen-year-old exchanged vows with William Clifford, the manager of Victor's woolen mill. Although the man was twenty-seven and only recently arrived from England, Amelia had fallen head over heels in love with him. Tragically, one of her father's workers, also a recent immigrant from England, recognized the foreman as a man named Nathaniel Clifford Perkins—who still had a wife and children back in Gloucester. Victor sent him packing and had the marriage legally dissolved, but six months later, on June 8, 1813, little Gabrielle Josephine became the first grandchild presented to the du Pont brothers.

Whether or not Ferdinand appeared in Victorine's dreams as a result of Amelia's list is unknown, but his name seldom appears in letters to her friends during this exuberant period; in fairness, however, neither does the name of *any* particular young man. Victorine's refusal of her childhood friend was never intended to convey that she'd had no feelings for him, only that his timing had been premature. Privately, she felt that Ferdinand was not ready, and that in some ways, he was still very much a youth. Also, his father's intervention—viewed as a rash attempt at manipulating her future—had somewhat galled her.

Although not ready for marriage, she and her friends did read romantic novels, especially those by Sir Walter Scott, the Scottish writer she referred to as "our favorite author."[3] She had read *Marmion* "over and over," as well as *The Lay of the Last Minstrel*, and was rereading the epic poem *The Lady of the Lake*.[4] Poetry in general remained a faithful companion to Victorine, as it was for many of the well-read women of her times. Were it not for the survival of her substantial collection of poetry, a clearer appreciation for her inner feelings would have surely been lost. The eldest daughter had a strong aversion to what she described as "making a parade" of her feelings,[5] but in the secret world of poetry, the bards often gave voice to that which her own tongue could not. Although many of her selections were chosen simply because she thought the lines "pretty" or "fine," other samplings jolt the reader with their stark, emotional intensity. These latter poems, several of which she penned herself, unearth a complex and passionate level of feeling that Victorine usually kept veiled.

Although visits to her city friends were frequent, she was happiest when at home: "I am really anxious to see [Becky], but I seem to have taken root here, and habit, which always does a great deal for me, has nailed me to this spot so fast that even the expected prospect of seeing my Philadelphia friends is hardly strong enough to set me in motion."[6] The friendly woods, rivers, and runs of her ancient green valley were the backdrops that cradled her sense of identity. Peter Bauduy had badly misread her when he thought she preferred the bustle of city life to "a dreary life on the Brandywine."[7]

As for Mr. and Mrs. Bauduy, Victorine's refusal of their son had renewed a notion they had entertained ever since Juliette's younger sister, Fortunée, had married the titled Bernard de Sassenay. Although the de Sassenays had returned to France, the wish of the two families had always been that their children, Clara and Ferdinand, would someday marry. Since the two young people would be often in each other's company while Ferdinand was in France, their parents hoped their relationship would grow. Ferdinand, meanwhile, had "wasted nine months" as his father put it, before he was able to secure an apprenticeship in Paris.[8] Much to the lad's chagrin, the delay forced him to extend his stay for a third year. To date, he had shown little interest in Clara. Although their parents desired such an interest, Ferdinand protested that he would do nothing that could jeopardize his chances with Victorine. The elder Bauduy relayed his son's excuse to Clara's father, Bernard de Sassenay, but could not contain his resentment toward the "contaminated" du Pont family: "[Victorine's] parents will never be my friends. To tell the truth, I am trying hard to be Christian and wish my enemy well. I have never had such antipathy toward anyone like the father, and no doubt he feels the same toward me. Father, mother, daughters, are all false and dishonest and nothing could be worse than to become related to such people. What a difference, my friend, if you and Fortunée became a second family to my Ferdinand. This happy event would bring us closer and fulfill our wishes."[9]

As the busy year of 1812 was drawing to a close, Irénée grew increasingly aware that Ferdinand was due to return the following spring. His curiosity was piqued to know what might be the young man's current intentions toward Victorine. Irénée dared not raise the subject to Victorine for fear of upsetting the status quo, so he turned to his father for a bit of detective work: "Try to find out Ferdinand's ideas concerning Victorine. His father tells me that he is very eager to marry her."[10] It would appear, however, that Peter's assurances to Irénée were merely an attempt to keep his son's options open. Judging by the letters he was simultaneously writing to his brother-in-law de Sassenay, Peter was still advocating for a union with the latter's daughter. In the end, it seems that his relentless persuasions may have paid off. In April of 1813, Ferdinand was preparing for his return to America—apparently engaged to Clara de Sassenay.

This stunning turn of events was reiterated to Ferdinand's sister Mimika, by Clara's mother: "Your brother . . . is sorry to leave us and to be separated from his 'wife' for two or three years. You will be surprised to know that little Clara is now the favorite . . . He said he is in love with her and they have exchanged promises to each other. We have approved. He will come back in two or three years for his cousin and make her his wife. This union which brings us closer will please you, I hope, my dearest."[11] If more than a mother's wish, what could have been the reason for Ferdinand's sudden change of heart? For nearly three years, the young man had clung to the hope that he may yet win Victorine's hand. What incentive could have induced him to change his mind on the eve of returning to Wilmington? Perhaps his father's pressure, combined with Victorine's silence on the subject, had finally convinced him that there was no hope. Or perhaps it was that the "pretty, kind and sweet" Clara, now fourteen, had finally caught his eye.[12]

Ferdinand arrived in Wilmington on June 18, 1813, after an absence of exactly three years and one month. The war with England was marking its first anniversary, and orders for gunpowder were flooding into Irénée's young company. Sales for 1812 had totaled $148,597, and 1813 would add $107,291 more.[13] While Irénée was consumed with the pressure to keep up with wartime demand and the construction of his new mills at Hagley, a new development was brewing within the family. If the news of Ferdinand's engagement to Clara de Sassenay had seemed a surprising turnaround, Victorine's renewed interest in Ferdinand also turned heads. She, who three years previously had expressed little interest in marrying anyone, was now saying "yes" to the man who was engaged to his cousin in France.

The topic of Victorine's original refusal had quickly resurfaced between the old friends. She was no longer the gleaming seventeen-year-old he had left behind, but a charming woman of nearly twenty-one, who seemed much more certain of what she wanted. For his part, the years abroad had erased much of the boyish naivety he had clumsily brought to his marriage proposal. Although his stride now bore the confident air of one who had seen a bit more of the civilized world than had the average Wilmingtonian of his age, Victorine was pleased to note that the basic gentleness of his character, which had attracted her in the beginning, had not diminished.

The embers of love did not take long to rekindle. Sparked by the pleasure of his return (and perhaps fanned by the awareness of a rival), Victorine knew, perhaps as she had not known before, that she wanted to marry him. She confessed her feelings first to her mother, who, recalling all that she and Irénée had sacrificed to be together, was sympathetic to the rekindled romance. Aware of her husband's anxieties regarding such a match, however, Sophie waited for the right moment to break the news. Hoping to explain why the embers had so quickly reignited, she hinted to Irénée that Victorine's earlier refusal of Ferdinand had been partially motivated out of deference to him.

Uncle Victor reaffirmed this to his father in France: "I have a great secret to tell you. Irénée is at last convinced that it was entirely because of her respect for him that Victorine refused Ferdinand, with whom she had been in love since they were children; she sacrificed her own happiness to the dislike she believed her father felt for the whole Bauduy family. Irénée now says that he never refused Ferdinand, though he and all his people—who are very proud, very irritable, and very sensitive—took it for refusal, and he will do what he can to bring about a reconciliation."[14] Irénée's response makes it clear that his daughter's happiness superseded any antipathy he felt for the groom's father. He would always, as he had affirmed, allow Victorine to make up her own mind.

In spite of all the work pressing for his attention, Irénée did take the time to "bring about a reconciliation," and by August, he and Peter had approved the public announcement of marriage between their eldest children. The summer bustled forth with wedding plans and trips to Philadelphia. Amidst shopping excursions and visits with friends, both Victorine and Evelina had been sitting for portraits by the rising artist Rembrandt Peale.[15]

On the joyous Tuesday evening of November 9, 1813, in the parlor of Eleutherian Mills, Victorine du Pont became Mrs. Victorine Elizabeth (du Pont) Bauduy. The ceremony was officiated by Father Patrick Kenny, the family priest of both the Bauduys and Aunt Gabrielle, Victor's wife. As was the custom among the merchant class, the lovebirds spent the next ten days being hosted at grand dinners in various homes. Following these local events, the newlyweds went to Philadelphia to stay for a time with Cora (Bauduy) and John Garesché, to facilitate similar fetes with their urban friends. "My dear Evelina," wrote Vic, "I do not know how in the world I shall contrive to return all the visits and accept or refuse *politely* all the invitations that pour upon me every day. Everyone wants to give us a party."[16]

After three bustling weeks, it was finally time for Ferdinand to earn his living. He was scheduled to leave for New York on his first business trip for Du Pont, Bauduy & Company. On Tuesday morning, November 30, the reluctant youth left for New York. They had estimated that his trip would require a separation of two to three weeks. So it was with alarm that only six days later, the young bride awoke to find the shadowy figure of a man in her room: "I heard someone open my door at

6 o'clock & soon beheld a man bearing a candle. Just as I was going to scream out with fear, I [recognized Ferdinand]. You may depend it was a most joyful meeting."[17]

Ice on the rivers had prevented the steamboats from sailing, and Ferdinand (not unhappily) had been forced to return. Within a few days, the lovers were back at Eleutherian Mills enjoying the sanctuary of their own room, which had been set up in the library on the first floor. Upon their return, Victorine experienced two disappointments: the first was that she had narrowly missed Evelina, who had just returned to Madame Rivardi's; and the second was that Ferdinand was immediately resent to Albany. The weather had warmed considerably, and the business partners thought his assignment sufficiently important to make a second attempt at traveling there. Mingling her tears with the sniffles of a lingering cold, Victorine said her second goodbye in as many weeks to her disconsolate husband.

Ferdinand dreaded the trip—far less for the wintry conditions than for his separation from the girl he had so recently won. To his credit, he dutifully accepted his responsibilities, but the young man had just turned twenty-three, was newly married, and very much in love. Upon arrival in New York City for the journey to Albany, he poured out his heart to his forlorn bride:

> I found out when I arrived that the steamboat will not leave for Albany until tomorrow and I could have stayed with you for one more day. This makes it worse for I miss you so much already. There is no happiness for me without you; everything is sad and dismal. More than ever you are my life and I need you. Far from you I am not pleased, no matter where. Nothing can amuse me and I think always of you. My mind is far away with the one I love. My consolation is to think of you; I am always with you in thought. I ask myself constantly, "What is she doing? Where is she?" Oh, dearest Victorine, what would I give to be near you! But I still have two weeks of misery. . . . I beg you to take care of your cold and keep in good health, and think sometimes of the one who adores you.[18]

The following lines, written in her own hand, may well have been her response.

> Oh heavy is my heart my love, & thoughtful is my brow
> And cares scarce felt when thou art near, how busy are they now!
> And irksome are the tedious hours, and lonely is the day
> And heavy, heavy is my heart when thou art far away.[19]

Ferdinand did return two weeks later, but not with his customary cheerfulness. His countenance was pale, and he seemed unusually weak and tired. By January 7, he had taken to his bed with recurring bouts of chills, pain, and high fever. Doctor Pierre Didier, the beloved physician for both families, was called in to examine him. The diagnosis was serious: Ferdinand had contracted a virulent case of "inflammatory rheumatism," a nineteenth-century term often associated with rheumatic fever. For ten straight days, the young man battled with fever and weeping sores that broke out over his entire body. Victorine never left his bedside. Day and night she attended to his various needs, and cooled his feverish, aching body with wet cloths. When the doctor was absent, she faithfully applied whatever measures he had prescribed. On Monday, January 20, he appeared to be showing some improvement, and family members on both sides began to give rise to their hopes. But no sooner had he improved than his condition worsened. On Tuesday the young husband, who had so recently attained his highest joy by marrying the girl he had loved since childhood, died at Eleutherian Mills, seventy-three days after his wedding.

Pierre Provenchère, the close family friend of the Bauduys, recorded the event in some detail to his daughter, Amelia:

> The illness he succumbed to was an inflammatory rheumatism. This sickness, very common just now, makes itself felt by a chill in different parts of the body, with great pain which soon spreads to the arms, legs, shoulders and chest. The parts so attacked swell up with great aches, fever breaks out with shuddering and headache with delirium. . . . After 24 hours of thinking him out of danger, the illness took on symptoms of putrefaction which were evidenced by red pimples all over the body with small white and viscous pustules on them. All this happened in three days.[20]

Victorine, inconsolable, fell into a state of disbelief and shock; her mother Sophie could do nothing but hold her.

At Eden Park, Juliette Bauduy was devastated, having now lost both her youngest and oldest child within the span of four months. Her and Peter's infant daughter, Louise, had died in September of whooping cough.[21] Peter, who had been at the bedside when his son had died, could not bear to break the news to his wife. In a letter to Irénée just two days after Ferdinand's death, he described his grief in the most heartrending terms.

> I left your house, my good friend, stricken with horror and not knowing what to do in my great sorrow. I could not decide how to meet my wife, to whom such a shock in her present condition might be disastrous, especially if I were not with her. I could not bear to see my poor son, and I could not help my dear daughter [Victorine], whose only comfort then was with her dear and worthy mother. . . . We told [Juliette] of our loss by degrees.
>
> . . . I cannot speak to you of my grief, my friend. It is very great. How terrible it must have been for you, my friend, when you returned to your home. May this sorrow unite us; be my friend, I have lost the best one I had. I shall never recover from it. My most sincere devotion is consecrated forever to my good Victorine; she was the dearest thing on earth to my poor Ferdinand. . . . Let us throw a veil over the past, my friend. Send me word how Victorine is each day. . . . My heart aches—I cannot write one word of Victorine; her grief adds to mine. As long as my heart beats she will have her place there as my daughter—her whom my son loved most dearly.[22]

Ferdinand was laid to rest in the graveyard of Old Swedes Church in Wilmington, which in 1814, was one of the few places in the largely Quaker city where Roman

Catholics could be interred. The congregation of Old Swedes, in an act of Christian charity, had voted to set aside a portion of their cemetery where Catholics could bury their dead. When they met at the funeral, Peter and Irénée wept together and reaffirmed their love and friendship. And while the brief season of peace between the two men would not last, the shared grief of the moment had been sincere.[23]

CHAPTER 7

Mourning on the Brandywine

Victorine's youthful exuberance, so characteristic of the previous nine years, evaporated on the chilly afternoon of January 21, 1814. An oral tradition has lingered that Victorine never again slept in the room that she and Ferdinand shared so briefly as husband and wife.[1] Retreating to her chamber on the second floor, where she and Evelina had formerly shared a bed, the shocked twenty-one-year-old buried herself in a blanket of grief.

For Peter and Juliette Bauduy, Victorine now became a living memorial to the one thing their son had so cherished in life. "You were his darling," wrote a grieving Juliette, "his heart's choice; with this title you will always be a dear daughter to me. . . . I press you to my heart."[2] Her husband reiterated the same sentiments in a touching letter he wrote in May. Within its pages was enclosed a lock of Ferdinand's golden-brown hair: "I attach for you, here enclosed, my dear and good daughter, an object which belonged to him whom we cry over so bitterly, and which belongs to you. I press you against my heart and I will keep you there as long as I exist."[3] Ferdinand's grieving sisters, Mimika and Cora Garesché, wrote regularly to Victorine in the days and weeks that followed, each urging her to find consolation in her faith.

Two weeks after his son's death, Peter sent his carriage to Eleutherian Mills so that Victorine could spend a few days with them at Eden Park. The grieving daughter-in-law was able to endure only a few days before she had to return to the seclusion of her family home; she found that sharing the grief with her in-laws only exacerbated her own. But however difficult the visit had been for Victorine, it had proved a comfort to the Bauduys. In a follow-up note, Peter expressed, "To weep with you, my dearest, was a great consolation and a relief to my grief."[4]

As the weeks passed at Eleutherian Mills, Victorine remained inconsolable. Irénée stood awkwardly by as Sophie cradled their daughter in her arms. The widowed bride ate little, wept much, and seldom left the confines of the house. Her weight loss was visible, and she developed a severe chest cold. There is some evidence that Victorine may have been pregnant at the time of Ferdinand's death and later miscarried, but her own correspondence does not confirm this.[5] If true, it would surely add a more tragic dimension to her grief, and perhaps explain why a growing number of family and friends began to fear for the young widow's life. A despondent Irénée confessed to his worried father: "I have not courage to write about that poor child—neither I nor those belonging to me were born for happiness."[6] Victorine's friend Anna Smith pleaded, "May I not hope dear Victorine that when the violence of grief is past, you will turn to the affection of your friends for comfort; that you will find in their fondness a power to soothe; [and that] for their sakes Victorine, you will have still a tender interest in prolonged existence."[7]

The longest chronological gap in Victorine's letters is the eight-month period from January to August of 1814. Secluded at home, correspondence with family members was unnecessary; but she had, nevertheless, been pouring out her heart to her closest friends—Rebecca Ralston, Anna Potts Smith, and Antoinette Brevost. Although her letters to them did not survive, Victorine saved several (if not all) of their responses. It is clear that her friends shared a mutual anxiety over her physical and emotional state. Underlying their frequent pleas for better care of her health was the angst that she had lost her will to live. Their greatest fear was not that she would raise her hand against herself, but that she would not lift it in her defense. They knew she was ill and growing physically weaker—and were alarmed at her level of indifference. Rebecca Ralston went to be with Victorine immediately after Ferdinand's death and stayed for a few days. Her letters are a blend of heartfelt compassion, spiritual encouragement, and a chum's friendly admonition toward better health.

> I always esteemed you as a dear friend, but now I feel as if I could make any sacrifice to relieve your anguish but, my love, you know as well as myself my insufficiency. I feel a consolation in finding by your letters you look to that power which alone is able to assist you. Be firm in your reliance there and you will, I trust, be comforted. . . . I feel uneasy at hearing your cough continues and that you are growing very thin. Do my dear girl take care of yourself and, when you can, use moderate exercise.[8]

The friends appealed to her fledgling Christian faith as the greatest source of solace. Although Victorine's theology was not well formed at this point, her friends displayed a familiarity with her level of understanding—and built their encouragements upon it. It is clear that they sought to steer her gently toward the spiritual harbor of resignation. Among Christians of Victorine's day, it was a commonly shared belief that a sort of "holy resignation" to the perfect will of a sovereign, infinitely wise, and loving God was the desired haven for storm-tossed sorrow.

The letters of Anna Potts Smith emphasize religion, but her assurances of loving concern spill forth with disarming transparency. Her vividly creative expressions make it easy to understand why she was named Madame Rivardi's poet laureate. Anna's theology was perhaps not as refined as Rebecca's, but her faith was no less certain. A week after Ferdinand's death, she expressed:

Alas! My dear friend, of *myself* I cannot attempt giving you any [consolation], but I would have you turn to *the God who can*. He can heal the heart which he has pierced. He can calm the mind which he has shaken. *He* can teach your heart to sacrifice even its cherished sorrows & to lean on *him* in peaceful resignation to *his* will. Oh my dear Victorine, *this* world indeed has now little to engage your affections & how sweet, how consoling is it to reflect that in that region of immortal bliss, for which your husband has departed before you, you will be again united. And oh, Victorine, will it throw a shade on the transporting prospect of never-ending happiness to look back on a comparative *moment* of suffering? Will it lessen the rapturous hope of a reunion with the object of your fondest affection to recollect that but few of the fleeting moments of sad mortality were spent together? No, my dear friend, you are not separated forever. . . . O may [your friends] have the satisfaction of seeing you resigned! I wish it were possible that I, like them, could join my prayers with yours & mingle my tears with those of my beloved friend.[9]

This tender letter was quickly followed by another, more colorful, appeal: "How soothing is the holy balm religion administers. Gently she withdraws the mind from its sufferings—with a tender hand she 'binds up the wounds of the broken heart.' She is the handmaid of a *great Physician* & on *him* she teaches the heart to rely. . . . Oh my beloved Victorine this is your God—he is mine."[10]

Antoinette Brevost's gentle encouragements tended to elicit transparent disclosures from Victorine, such as her repeated attempts at self-consolation by immersing herself in thoughts of Ferdinand. Antoinette tried to affirm this practice but cautioned her against the excessive sorrow it produced: "Yes my love think of him forever—but try to do it with composure."[11] Antoinette, like Anna and Rebecca, was encouraged that Victorine had turned to her Bible for solace. "O my beloved friend, I rejoice at the idea of your consulting that Divine book. . . . I become daily more firm in the belief that the holy writings open the way to peace of mind in this world, and happiness in the next."[12]

Whatever the collective impact of her faithful friends may have been, Victorine broke free of her self-imposed seclusion by May, and felt well enough to leave the Brandywine. Her first visit was to Philadelphia for a stay with Rebecca and her family. When news spread to other urban acquaintants that Victorine had left her river fortress and was visiting with the Ralstons, she received numerous callers. The etiquette of the day usually required a reciprocal visit to those who had made the initial call, but the young widow was in no state of mind to accommodate the practice. In a letter to her mother, she confessed:

My dear Mama, I felt truly bad yesterday that I wasn't to be found here when Papa came to see us. We were spending the day at Anna Smith's. It was my first time out and even though I was in a carriage, I came back quite tired. I'm still very weak and I have taken the notion to stay constantly at home, without mentioning that I am quite sure that to walk in the streets in the sun would make me sick. I have also taken the notion to refuse all the invitations which people have made me, which are not very easy because the visits and the [consolations] make us cry on both sides.[13]

LONG BRANCH

During the summer, Vic's limited engagement with society included friends and relations of the Bauduys. The depressing shadow of Ferdinand's death still lingered over each of these close-knit families. At one such gathering, John Keating, who was related to the Bauduys by marriage,[14] suggested that a two-week trip to the seashore might do everyone some good. Keating said that he knew of a Mr. Bennett who ran a large hotel along the shores of Long Branch, New Jersey, and offered to book rooms for the entire party at his own expense. Victorine felt she could not refuse their pleas to join them.

From August 4 to 18, Victorine stayed at the Jersey Shore with various representatives of the Bauduy, Garesché, des Chapelles, Eyre, and Keating families. They had departed Philadelphia by steamboat and enjoyed a peaceful trip up the Delaware River to Bordentown, New Jersey. From there they traveled overland by stagecoach to Long Branch. Later nicknamed America's "first seaside resort," Long Branch in 1814 consisted of little more than a couple of isolated hotels situated upon a long stretch of sandy, desolate coastline. Victorine's first impression was not a positive one. To further dishearten her, she discovered that the mail arrived only once a week, a situation that caused "no little matter of distress."[15] The only other options for sending and receiving correspondence was by the hand delivery of a trustworthy guest, or by "the fish waggons," which made daily trips back and forth from the shore. During her two-week stay, she received only a few letters from home.

Reflective and sobered by the disquieting companionship of sorrow, her letters to Evelina depict a person who is amidst a crowd, yet emotionally apart. To the degree that social graces permitted, she kept to herself by writing letters, reading books, and walking alone along the shore. Literature was her primary form of escape, and she thought she had brought a sufficient supply, having raided the Philadelphia bookstores with Mimika Bauduy the day before their departure. At Bennett's hotel, the widow spent many private hours reading in a chair on the hotel's wraparound porch, which provided a splendid view of the sea. In less than a week, she fretted, "I see with sorrow that our store of books is nearly exhausted. I don't know what I will do when I have nothing to read."[16]

She occasionally bathed in the ocean with Mimika and Cora, a sensation she had not previously experienced but came to enjoy—unless men happened to be present. "They never miss taking a good view of us in our green gowns & caps," she complained.[17] Socializing primarily with Ferdinand's sisters, Victorine liked to watch the gregarious Mimika play billiards with the men. She had initially tried the activity but quickly gave it up: "It is a game much too difficult & I do not relish exhibiting my awkwardness before so many gentlemen, as the billiard room is the general rendezvous of all the loungers."[18]

She attended a few socials in the evenings, where music was provided for the guests, but usually did not linger. She confided to Evelina that she was grateful her chamber was not directly above the rooms where the events were held. "I spent the evening with feelings far different from those who were amusing themselves below. Fortunately our *wing* of the *castle* is very far from the assembly room, therefore the sound of the music did not reach my ears. I need not tell you that it could only have augmented my sadness."[19]

She was attracted to the changing moods of the sea, but found that it, too, accentuated her sadness. Roaming the beaches tended to produce the same effect in her: "We saw several wrecks in the sand. I went into the cabin of one of those vessels. It was filled with sand; and seemed to be decaying fast. Many pieces of timber were strewn along the beach, and presented a scene of desolation. Although the weather was perfectly calm, what must it be during a storm when the sea dashes against the shore with fury! I cannot think of any situation more calculated to inspire melancholy than one on the sea coast, as you are constantly exposed to witness misery which you cannot relieve."[20] Seven months had now passed since January's tragedy, and Victorine was slowly resigning herself to a future without Ferdinand. Although she was healthier physically and mentally, her Long Branch letters reveal her muted spirits.[21]

At one interesting point during their visit, the lodgers witnessed a minor incident in the War of 1812. Victorine recorded the event:

> There are here two English frigates always in sight. Yesterday they chased a poor schooner, and we were all very much [concerned] for her as you may suppose. We stood on the shore watching her movements. At last we had the satisfaction of seeing her escape. She came very near us, and as she hoisted up the American colours in triumph, she saluted us as she passed. Some of the gentlemen returned the compliment with a common hunting gun, & we furnished our pocket handkerchiefs to make a flag. You cannot think how I dislike those English frigates which seem to be there merely to do as much harm as they can to our weaker vessels.[22]

Six days after Victorine's departure from Long Branch, the British attacked and burned large sections of Washington, DC, including the presidential mansion and the Capitol building.

The young widow also referenced God several times in her letters. She had been reading her Bible, and the works of authors such as William Cowper. "I wish I could get a letter from some of you," she wrote to Evelina on August 14, "but Alas! What signifies *wishing*, Cowper says, . . . [is] that 'wishes in this world are never realized, and in the next we shall make none.' That we may one day meet in that blessed abode of the righteous is, my beloved sister, the foremost hope of your ever affectionate, Victorine."[23]

Overall, the trip to Long Branch proved to have had the restorative effect for which her friends and family had hoped. Although her first impressions had been negative, the "melancholy sea" had won the forlorn widow as a friend. For the first time since Ferdinand's death, she was summoning her creative powers, an indication that she was once again *seeing* beauty in the world around her.

> Yesterday morning I rose before 5 o'clock, being determined to see the sun rise as we were to set off early in the afternoon. I felt ashamed not yet to have beheld the orb of day majestically rising out of the sea, after having been told it was one of the greatest curiosities of the place. Therefore I stood on the gallery to witness the magnificent spectacle. Nor did I return to my chamber until I was nearly blinded by the stream of living gold which dyed the surface of the water when the sun, like a globe of fire, suddenly emerged from its watery bed. . . . I was sorry to think it was the last time I should, like the nerieds of old, enjoy the cool waves as they dashed around me. . . . How changeable is human nature! It was with extreme reluctance that two weeks ago I consented to bathe in the sea, and it was with regret that I went out of it yesterday morning![24]

Victorine arrived back in Wilmington by stage in the late afternoon of Tuesday, August 23. Although her experience at Long Branch had marked a turning point in her journey of grief, she still suffered its lingering despondency.

As winter's darkness advanced, Victorine's most traumatic year was drawing to a close. Having begun with the nightmare that took her husband's life—and nearly claimed her own—1814 ended with a subdued sense of resignation, and a hint of hope. On New Year's Day, 1815, Anna Smith wrote the following lines and sent them to Victorine. Her intention was to provide her friend with extra encouragement as she entered the month that would mark the first anniversary of Ferdinand's death.

> Another year is gone!
> May each succeeding one
> Find our hearts the same,
> And bind us closer still;
> Till in obedience to his will,
> Who guides this ethereal flame,
> We leave this tenement of clay
> For realms of everlasting day![25]

CHAPTER 8

Departures and Arrivals

Although war with England kept demand for gunpowder high, the U.S. government was slow in its payments to the Du Pont Company: by mid-1814 it owed the company $20,000. Irénée's credit was good, but he now owed $60,000 to the banks. He had purchased the lower yards at Hagley to expand his production capabilities during the war but was still making payments on the initial purchase. He had also been forced to borrow in order to keep Victor's textile mill afloat.[1]

Despite the mutual compassion that Irénée and Peter Bauduy had expressed in the wake of Ferdinand's death, the season of tenderness between the two men proved unsustainable. Still vexed by what he perceived to be Irénée's "piece of madness" in purchasing the Hagley property, Peter Bauduy began to stir up trouble with the company's investors. He sent several letters to the investors in the spring of 1814, charging Irénée with stealing their money, wasting the company's profits, and making foolish purchases for expensive machinery and uncultivated land. His accusations had the effect of striking a beehive with a stick. Several of the investors had attained their shares through Du Pont de Nemours Père et Fils et Compagnie and, without consulting his youngest son, Pierre Samuel had converted their investments to an equivalent value in Irénée's company, assuring them of generous returns. The proud father had made the somewhat forgivable error of bragging about the accomplishments of his son and his successful powder company. The investors, he promised, would be guaranteed high profits through the receipt of regular dividends. The dividends, however, were slow to arrive. Irénée was determined to reinvest the profits into the company's infrastructure and to repay his debts, believing that both steps were essential to Du Pont's future success. He had counted on the willingness of shareholders to participate in his long-term strategy and assumed that investment in an enterprise that was surpassing everyone's expectations would more than compensate them for their short-term sacrifices. His error was not one of dishonesty but of poor communication.

Jacques Bidermann, an influential banker and one of the company's key investors, decided to send his son, Jacques (James) Antoine, to personally investigate

Bauduy's charges. When he arrived, the young man not only found the books to be in order, but he was so impressed by what Irénée had accomplished that he asked his father if he could remain in America as an employee of the manufactory. Both fathers were pleased with this arrangement and young Jacques took up residence at Eleutherian Mills. It was not long before his familiar face at the du Pont table led to an attraction between him and Evelina, Victorine's raven-haired sister. The two were married a year later on September 14, 1816.

Bauduy's complaints had not only stirred up the investors, but had succeeded in outraging Irénée's father as well. In what certainly became the elder states-man's most regrettable letter, he penned a scathing note to both of his sons, accusing them of dishonesty and deceit that could "destroy our reputation and our honor," and encouraged them to "repent."[2] Mercifully, it was the father who quickly repented and confessed that he had been mistaken in underestimating the extent of the hard work and sacrifices his youngest son had made in establish-ing his company.

When Bauduy saw that his attempts to discredit du Pont had ultimately failed, he approached Irénée with the offer of selling his shares, and the offer was readily accepted. On February 15, 1815, both men publicly declared that the association between Bauduy and du Pont was officially terminated. Peter Bauduy then set about establishing his own powder company in Wilmington, using horses instead of water for power.

For a time after the relationship between their fathers had officially disinte-grated, Ferdinand's sisters, Mimika and Cora Garesché, maintained their associ-ation with Victorine. They continued to exchange several affectionate letters with Victorine, as did their mother, Juliette Bauduy, who saw no conflict in commu-nicating with her son's widow: "I pray God to give you all the consolations that we can have on this earth and I like to think that a daughter as good as our Victo-rine will receive from Providence a reward for her virtue. Will you, my dearest, give your mother and Lina my best regards and wishes of happiness."[3] The omis-sion of Irénée's name in Juliette's valediction was probably not accidental.

Mimika saw Victorine frequently through the first four months of 1815. Peter Bauduy had regularly sent his carriages to Eleutherian Mills to facilitate rides for his daughter-in-law but, by May, the transports had ceased appearing. An exam-ple of Mimika's ongoing concern for her sister-in-law was conveyed on June 8, when a fierce explosion rocked the Du Pont powder yards, taking the lives of nine men— the first fatalities to be recorded at Irénée's young company.[4] "Dear Sister," wrote a frantic Mimika, "I have been started out of my bed this morning by a dreadful shock. . . . I found a heavy volume of smoke rising from your mills. Since then sev-eral reports of the most serious kind have reached us, they tell us that several lives are lost. Do let me know, dear Victorine, the truth, and if you have not suffered very much from the shock."[5]

By the end of July, however, a seemingly innocuous incident revealed that the icy relationship between the fathers was beginning to affect their families. Due to the public's awareness of the schism, Victorine grew increasingly wary of appearances. Overly sensitive to her father's feelings, she feared that a public display of intimacy with Peter's daughters might be construed as support for their father. On this particular occasion Mimika had made an appointment to call on Mrs. Briggs, a woman who lived in the village near Irénée's lower yards. She sent a note to Victorine detailing her itinerary, in the hopes that it might provide an opportunity for the two women to meet. Victorine, fearful of how it might look to her father's workers, declined to go, but expressed the hope that her sister-in-law was not offended. Mimika, however, did feel the slight, and thought the excuse an overblown notion of "filial duty."

> I am not offended, my dear Victorine, because as long as I shall think you love me, I shall be inclined to excuse you, but . . . at the [first opportunity] of meeting on the banks of the Brandywine, you refuse walking five steps to meet me and represent your conduct as dictated by duty alone. . . . I love my parents as much as you do yours; there is not a sacrifice which I would not make for their happiness; but I should fear making them appear in the eyes of the public as tyrants, if from exaggerated ideas of filial duty I should abstain from pleasure so innocent and dear to my heart.[6]

Vic was hurt and embarrassed by Mimika's response. The suggestion that her overly cautious actions might reflect negatively upon her parents made her wince.

Usually fluid and confident in her letters, she had great difficulty in crafting a response. The surviving draft is heavily edited and contains several crossed-out lines.

> My Dear Mimika . . . You say I have given up a family I once considered as my own, but is it my fault if I have done so? Was it to be expected that I should abandon the cause of my father? No, not one in your family would for a single moment suppose such a thing. . . . I continued to behave as an affectionate daughter and sister to you all. But when at last it became necessary for me to choose whose part I should take, I did not hesitate an instant, although at the same time I felt the bitterest anguish at being forced to break this which I once cherished as my greatest consolation. . . . I never can think of making a parade of my feelings and . . . I would not have borne the idea of making all the work people in the factory a witness of our interview. . . . You should consider this request of mine as a proof of my desire to continue an intimacy which has lasted since our childhood, and of my being very far indeed from wishing a *rupture* to take place.[7]

Despite their intentions, the "rupture" did take place. The sisters-in-law would never again return to the intimacy they had shared for most of their youth. Nor was the break a clean one, as they could not avoid running into each other in social settings with mutual friends. Families who knew both the Bauduys and the du Ponts tried (at least outwardly) to remain neutral, but the unspoken tension was often palpable. Even Rebecca Ralston's family had remained on good terms with Peter Bauduy, bringing some discomfort to Victorine. Writing from her bedroom at the Ralstons, Victorine confessed to a pregnant Evelina in early 1817, "What puzzles me a little is that everyone in this house appears to have the same high opinion of Mr [Bauduy] as ever, & still they are as friendly as possible to me."[8]

Cora, and eventually even Ferdinand's mother Juliette, ceased writing. Although Victorine's father had never suggested that she break ties with the Bauduys completely, "she saw [for] herself it was best to withdraw."[9] The fallout from the feud had been painful for the women of both families. Each in her own way had felt deeply betrayed. The Bauduy and du Pont daughters had known each other since childhood, and Juliette Bauduy had lost the companionship of her son's greatest happiness. Years later, Victorine would express surprise that she had "recovered any tranquility . . . on a subject which once was so extremely painful to me."[10] Apart from the commitment to carry her husband's name, by which she would henceforth be known in her community, Mrs. Victorine (du Pont) Bauduy was determined to put the painful saga behind her.

AND BON PAPA, TOO

The War of 1812 came to an official end on Christmas Eve 1814, with the signing of a peace treaty in the Belgian city of Ghent but, while hostilities between the United States and England were coming to a close, troubles were stirring again in Europe. Napoleon escaped from Elba in late February 1815 and began his victorious return toward Paris. As the Corsican's swelling army advanced, Victorine's politically minded grandfather, Pierre Samuel, decided it would not be prudent to wait for him. As Secretary-General under Tallyrand's provisional government, it was du Pont de Nemours who had signed Napoleon's abdication papers. Pierre's exit from Paris on March 20, 1815, preceded Bonaparte's triumphant return by only three hours.[11] Accompanied by Cardon de Sandrans, a young relative of his wife who posed as his secretary, Pierre made a hurried journey to the port of Le Havre by horseback. Ten days later, the indefatigable patriot departed his beloved France for the last time.

He sailed aboard the *Fingal* on March 30 and arrived in New York City on May 3. A few days later, he was reunited with his ecstatic sons at Eleutherian Mills, who had not seen their beloved father since his departure from the Brandywine thirteen years earlier. His wife Françoise was unable to accompany him, having slipped on an icy Parisian street a few weeks prior, sustaining a serious injury to her hip. It was agreed that she would join Pierre when the hip had healed, but it was a journey she would somehow never make.

Pierre was provided his own room, and a desk from which he eventually penned numerous essays and letters on a wide variety of topics. Du Pont biographer Ambrose Saricks reported that "an almost unbelievable quantity of manuscripts flowed from his desk in the next two years."[12] Pierre also maintained a long correspondence with Madame Germaine de Staël,[13] the literary lioness of Paris, and explained to her that America was "the only place where I can still be useful to the world and end my career as I began it. America is necessary to *the unity* of my life."[14]

On the evening of July 16, 1817, Pierre was gravely injured helping to extinguish a fire at Eleutherian Mills. A powder worker named Ritchie was hurrying to wind things up at the charcoal house. In this building, wood stripped from willow trees was burned to charcoal in large cylinders and, after cooling, emptied into wooden barrels for later use. Victorine recorded that Ritchie: "emptied a cylinder one hour after it was burnt and left the charcoal in hogsheads; of course it was kindled again, and no one perceived it till the whole house was a blaze."[15] Alarms were sounded and the entire workers' community joined forces to put out the flames, but when the water pumps failed, it became necessary to form a bucket brigade from the river to the charcoal house. Victorine wrote to Alfred early the next morning that "no person was dangerously hurt, though there were many scratches and bruises."[16] What she didn't yet know was that her seventy-six-year-old grandfather, whose health had not been good of late, would pay a penalty for his role in putting out the fire.

Although various family members had tried to dissuade him from participating in the brigade, it was not in the older man's nature to sit idly by when a need was so great. As a result, Pierre's biographer Ambrose Saricks wrote: "He became desperately ill; for two weeks he suffered horribly. . . . Early in August he lapsed into a coma and never regained consciousness. With his sons and eldest grandson at his bedside, he died in the early morning hours of August 7, 1817."[17] Unfortunately, more than two months passed before his wife Françoise heard the news; she wrote to him on September 8 to let him know that his friend Madame de Staël had died. Ironically, the last letter she had received from her husband was dated July 16—the very night of the fire. It might have comforted the poor woman to know that of the many thousands of pages the venerable old man had penned in his lifetime, she had been the recipient of his final words.

In a lengthy condolence written to Irénée on September 9, Thomas Jefferson described the obituary he'd read as, "but a modest sketch of the worth of M. Dupont; for of no man who has lived could more good have been said with more truth. I had been happy in his friendship upwards of 30 years, for he was one of my early intimates in France. . . . No man ever labored more zealously or honestly, of which he has left abundant monuments."[18] Washington's former aide, the Marquis de Lafayette, expressed to Irénée: "You know me so well that I need not tell you how I am suffering. You have known the tender, deep and grateful friendship that I have felt for your noble father for many years."[19]

Pierre Samuel's death was most keenly felt by his wife in France and his family on the Brandywine—especially his youngest son. Now forty-three, Irénée felt that he had lost one of the two supporting pillars of his life; his dear Sophie, of course, yet remained. But it was to his father that he had always turned for guidance and counsel and, perhaps more importantly, for an authentic sense of self-worth. Although he had not always agreed with his father's opinions (especially in matters of romance and business), he had needed the older man's approbation.

The family home, Eleutherian Mills, is built atop a steep cliff overlooking the powder yards, but it is not the highest point of the surrounding landscape.

The house itself is situated at the lower end of a broad, gentle slope that begins its descent about a quarter of a mile away. At the brow of that hill was a copse of trees and a sand pit, known as Sand Hole Woods. It was here that Irénée and Victor decided to lay their father's body to rest and, with that simple decision, they dedicated the ground for what eventually became the Du Pont family cemetery. It remains such to this day.

For the remainder of his life, Irénée would make frequent trips to the top of the hill to have quiet "talks" with his father. His eyes would invariably fall upon the words inscribed in the white gravestone, which declared some of the accomplishments for which the patriarch had been most proud: "Sacred to the memory of Pierre Samuel Du Pont De Nemours. Knight of the order of Vasa, of the Legion of Honor and of the order du Lis. Counsellor of State, member of the first Constituent Assembly, President of the Council of Ancients and member of the Institute of France. Born in Paris December 14th A.D. 1739. Died at the Eleutherian Mills August 7th, A.D. 1817." It seems a bit incongruous to find such words decorating a tomb on a rural hillside north of Wilmington, Delaware; but prior to sailing from France for the last time, Pierre had confided to Germaine de Staël that: "America pleases me, because I prefer liberty to influence . . . I hope that I shall go to die in the land of those men who do not bother each other, who do not bother me, who do me the honor of paying me no attention, and of leaving me with my children and my work."[20]

Victorine deeply felt the sorrow of the old man's passing. Ever since their early excursions into the golden fields behind Bois-des-Fossés, a unique and enduring bond had been forged between them. She had remained his favorite grandchild, not only because she was his first, but also because he thought she was most like him. No other grandchild had placed such a high value on learning or attained such an academic mastery of subjects. To Victorine, the death of her grandfather marked a break—not only in her family circle—but with something much larger. She knew that her grandfather had been instrumental in recent French affairs, not only in the realm of politics, but also in the realm of ideas.[21] Pierre himself had written voluminously on a wide variety of topics. Most of his works had been left in the hands of his wife in France but were still largely intact. In the distant future, Victorine would play a significant role in preserving that intellectual legacy.

CHAPTER 9

Life and Spirit on the Brandywine

"Home" had always meant the Brandywine Valley to Victorine du Pont. Sylvan wonders abounded there—all beckoning Victorine to explore their hidden mysteries. Her father, who had identified himself on his passport as a *botaniste*, continued to trade multiple varieties of plants, seeds, and tree seedlings with friends across the sea, most notably Count Louis Lelieur, director of the royal gardens in Paris.[1] That love for horticulture, which both he and Sophie possessed, was passed to their children and is still evident among du Pont descendants today.[2] It was from her father that Victorine learned the names and scientific identifications of hundreds of plants and shrubs, along with their associated uses. Potted varieties abounded in multihued displays both inside and outside the family home, and could be seen in the parlor, on windowsills, or by the front door where the lemon tree was placed during winter months.

Music was a familiar sound along the wooded banks. The family of émigrés had sailed from France with no fewer than three pianos. The Dalmas side of the family had imparted the love of music to both Sophie and her brother Charles, who could play the piano with proficiency. The latter also played the violin and guitar, and he was often called upon (with minimal urging) to contribute to an evening's gaiety, though he himself "could not be prevailed upon to dance."[3] The melodic notes that floated through du Pont windows were often accompanied by a choir of feathery creatures as well. The family (for the most part) enjoyed their chorus of colorful birds all singing from cages that hung like so many wooden chandeliers in the warmer rooms of the house. Victorine was their primary caretaker and maintained a winged menagerie of songbirds throughout her adult life.

A variety of useful barnyard animals, such as goats, horses, cows, and chickens, were a common sight in du Pont yards. The numerous cats limited (but never eliminated) the mice and rat populations; and the dogs provided additional security against the occasional straggler who wandered onto the property. Pets of every kind found sanctuary at du Pont homes, including deer, squirrels, turtles, and fish.

Figure 19. *Samuel Francis Du Pont,*
1803–1865. Unknown photographer,
photographic print, 1840.

As a boy, Alexis (also known as "Lex" or "Lil" by his siblings) had kept a white rat
suspended in a cage from one of the piazza posts (to prevent the numerous cats
from putting an early end to his proprietorship).

Nicknames among the du Pont children were common. Victorine, for instance,
was "Vic," "Tini," "Tene," "Sister," or "Aunt Vicky." She herself often closed her
letters with a simple "V." In the surrounding mill community, however, it was the
full version of her first name that was most admired. Over the next several
decades, a number of neighborhood children would bear Victorine's name. Cardon de Sandrans, the relative who had accompanied Pierre in his flight from
Paris, and who now managed the tanning mill on Irénée's property,[4] requested
Victorine as his newborn's godmother, an honor that included the bequeathing of
her name. Victorine told her seafaring cousin Samuel Francis that "Miss Victorine Cardon de Sandran . . . came into the world about six weeks ago and is
already a great beauty; but as her ladyship will probably alter very much in a short
time, I do not think it necessary to give you a very particular description of her at
present."[5]

Victorine had tutored young Samuel Francis ("Cousin Frank") when he was a
child, and later became one of his most faithful correspondents throughout his
naval career. Unlike most of his relations who went to boarding schools, Frank had
enlisted in the Navy at the tender age of thirteen. With the help of a recommenda-
tion from Thomas Jefferson to President Madison, his father Victor had succeeded
in procuring a midshipman's berth for him aboard the newly built, seventy-nine-
gun *USS Franklin*. Bound for Spain and Italy, the *Franklin* eventually became the
flagship for the Mediterranean Squadron and did not return to America for two
and a half years, concluding her first mission at the New York City piers on April 24,
1820. While home on leave, Frank resolved to increase his opportunities for

advancement in the Navy and sought out Victorine's tutelage in mathematics to prepare him for the exams.[6]

Victorine's letters to Frank, especially in the early years, were playful, light-hearted, and filled with local Brandywine news. The young midshipman was grateful to hear from home and replied as often as he could. Victorine, an avid reader of history, enjoyed his firsthand accounts of the places he had visited, and even her younger sisters showed an interest in their cousin's travels. In the summer of 1818, Vic mentioned to Frank that "Sophy begins to write small, or rather *middling* hand, learns her multiplication table and at last knows how to read in French. . . . She has a great deal of *bonne volante* and, upon the whole, is a very good little girl. She has learned on the map the names of Gibraltar & Messina 'because cousin Francis was there' but her skill in geography goes no further."[7] In 1818, little Sophie was eight years old. She and Cousin Frank shared September birthdays and were almost exactly seven years apart in age. Vic's observation that Sophie's limited interest in geography was "because cousin Francis was there" is perhaps the earliest recorded hint that the youngest daughter held a special place in her heart for the older cousin. Fifteen years later, they would marry.

By the end of 1818, Sister Vic was also teaching four-year-old Henry to read and write, while she continued to give Eleuthera and Sophie their lessons.[8] On the first of May each year, she would pack a picnic lunch and take her siblings and cousins "a-Maying," an annual excursion through the woods and fields that was intended to be both recreational and educational. She used these outings to teach them the names and species of the early flowers and plants they encountered. Victorine walked everywhere and was often seen with her two youngest sisters in tow; even when visiting with Becky and Anna in Philadelphia, her thoughts were never too far from the girls. The frequent letters she wrote them from Philadelphia spill over with more than a hint of motherly guidance. "You have written me another charming little letter," she wrote the nine-year-old Eleuthera in 1816:

> I want to know how you come in your studies. Do you follow exactly the directions I left for you? I am quite anxious to see my two little daughters again. Tell Sophy that when I come home I hope she will be very good and make haste to learn to write & read. . . . You must be very attentive indeed to your sister Lina, my dear Eleuthera, try to make up for my absence as much as possible & when she is alone I wish you would try to entertain her as much as you can. You will find, my love, that we are never so happy as when we can contribute to the happiness of those around us. . . . I hope you are always very obedient to our dear mama. I am sure you would not fail in that duty willfully on any account, but my dear, I know that you are sometimes very impatient and not quite as gentle & submissive as I would wish you to be.[9]

Childless and widowed, the responsibility she felt for her "daughters" filled her life with purpose. Denied the dream of building a family with Ferdinand, she found herself fulfilling a portion of that maternal role within the home of her youth. Her wide mastery of subjects found an outlet as she served as first educator not only to her siblings, but also to her Brandywine nieces and nephews. While these duties extended to all her relations, it was clear that her investment in the females of the family carried an extra bit of enthusiasm.

The Second Great Awakening

Another influence upon the direction of Victorine's life at this time was the Christian faith. In this, however, she was not alone. The country itself was in the middle of the Second Great Awakening, a broad movement of religious fervor that swept the land from the mid-1790s to the 1840s. During those fifty years, church attendance doubled, from one in fifteen Americans to one in seven.[10] Wilmington itself experienced a series of revivals in 1813–1814, 1819–1820, and again in 1827, when the evangelist Charles Finney came to the city.[11] The movement spawned the establishment of philanthropic enterprises, such as hospitals, orphanages, shelters, and homes for widows. Foremost among these new institutions were Sunday schools, the product of a movement that began in Philadelphia in 1790. In 1817, an organization called the "Sunday and Adult School Union" was established in the same city. Protestant and evangelical in nature, the new entity quickly grew into the nation's largest supplier of Sunday school materials in less than ten years. Writing in 1835, the young Frenchman Alexis de Tocqueville noted that "Upon my arrival in the United States, the religious aspect of the country was the first thing that struck my attention. . . . There is no country in the whole world in which the Christian religion retains a greater influence over the souls of men than in America."[12]

Victorine's closest friends (and their families) were devoted Christians. At Anna Smith's home in the Frankford section of Philadelphia, Victorine was exposed to a warm and pious family who thoroughly enjoyed the tall Delawarean's presence. "It is impossible," she wrote to Evelina, "to be more kind and attentive than Mrs Smith & all Anna's sisters were to me. . . . Were I leisurely seated with you in our room I could give you a most interesting description of the time I spent with this amiable family. . . . Yesterday of course we went to church."[13]

The greater portion of her time in Philadelphia was usually spent at the Ralston home. Victorine's relationship with this family, now spanning a dozen years, was surely the strongest influence upon Victorine's religious progress. Although Robert Ralston was well known for his civic achievements and philanthropic initiatives, it would be from Becky's mother, the entrepreneurial and devout Sarah Clarkson, that Victorine would receive her greatest inspiration. Mrs. Ralston, employing the influence she carried among Philadelphia's merchant class, labored ceaselessly on behalf of the less fortunate. At a time when women were expected to focus solely on their families, Sarah Ralston succeeded in launching three major initiatives on behalf of the city's women and children. She founded the Female Bible Society of Philadelphia and the Indigent and Single Women's Society, which included a refuge for widows.[14] In 1814, she launched plans to establish Philadelphia's first orphanage. Built upon land purchased by her husband and a group of like-minded businessmen, a home was successfully erected "at the north-east

corner of Cherry and Schuylkill Fifth street [now 18th Street],"[15] and received its
first children in 1815. Biographer Page Miller wrote that: "Prior to Ralston's leadership, women in Philadelphia had not undertaken major building projects. . . . In
selecting deserted children and neglected women as recipients of her orga-
nizational efforts, Ralston focused on domestic concerns. . . . Thus while pioneering in new modes of women's charity work, Ralston concentrated on traditionally
feminine responsibilities."[16]

At least three of Sarah's daughters, Rebecca, Elizabeth, and Abigail, participated
in the affairs of the orphanage and taught classes for the children. "I must tell you
of a society we have just established for the relief and education of orphans," Becky
wrote to Vic in December of 1814. "If you resided in the city, I should be delighted
to have you for a fellow worker in this new undertaking. . . . I have received more
pleasure from the recollection that I have contributed to the relief of a suffering
family than I ever did from the remembrance . . . of any party I ever was at."[17] Such
altruistic language inspired Victorine. She decided to accompany Rebecca to the
orphanage and was deeply moved by what she saw. Being in the actual presence of
parentless children brought the reality of their plight into focus. As she watched
them playing in the large, fenced-in yard during recesses, she was impressed by
the scope of Sarah Ralston's vision and faith. Witnessing the impact that this selfless goal was having upon the lives of these needy children, left an indelible impression upon Victorine.

Sarah Ralston died on December 29, 1820, at the age of fifty-four. Her eulogy in
a Philadelphia paper stated: "By her decease, Religion has lost a firm defender and
zealous advancer; society a valuable member; the poor and afflicted a constant
friend; her husband and numerous offspring an affectionate wife and mother.
Matrons! Follow her example."[18] The orphanage she established in 1814 would
survive for another 150 years.[19] Enabled by the social and economic influence of her
husband, Ralston stood out among the women of her time in terms of her ability to
initiate social and institutional change. Through Victorine's intimacy with the
Ralston family, she had a front row seat to these accomplishments. She was learning
that leadership opportunities for women, which did not seem possible in her mother's
time, could be achievable in America—under certain circumstances.

Victorine's biblical understanding continued to expand throughout the years
1816 to 1820. She read the writings and commentaries of popular theologians and
heard sermons from some of Philadelphia's most prominent ministers, all of which
helped to shape her theology.[20] By age twenty-five, her religious growth could be
clearly observed through two notes written exactly one year apart. Precipitated by
an accident that had resulted in the death of a young father in the Brandywine community, Victorine sat down at her desk on February 3, 1817, and confessed:

> Were it some beloved relative who had been snatched thus suddenly away, could
> I say from my heart *Thy will be done*? Alas, I fear not. I have a weakness about
> me that whispers, no, I should [complain]. O Lord pity my frailty, and support me,
> for thou alone art the rock on which it is safe to lean! . . . One most dreadful

lesson have I had already. Let it suffice, O gracious Lord, I beseech thee. . . .
O Lord, what shall I do to prove my gratitude for all thy goodness? From this
day I shall endeavor to live according to thy Holy commandments, and to per-
form to the uttermost of my power, the duties of my station as a daughter, a
sister, but above all a Christian![21]

Exactly twelve months later, she assessed her progress.

One year has elapsed since I formed the above resolution, and this evening I sit
down to examine how I have fulfilled it. . . . My heart tells me that I have wandered very far from that sacred covenant which in a moment of awakened reflec-
tion, I had made with my heavenly Father. And how has He, the righteous
judge, requited me for my willful neglect and disobedience? Has he not constantly showered his choicest blessings upon me, while I, careless of my promise, have too often neglected to return thanks for his unmerited goodness? I am
not unconscious of all the blessings which are my portion, and I would offer up
my thanks tonight for them. I have the best of parents and of friends; I enjoy
good health, and while the storm rages without, I am near a comfortable fire
surrounded with all the conveniences of life. Glory be to thee O Heavenly Father
for all these precious gifts. I never can sufficiently praise and love thee. "Praise
the Lord O my soul and forget not all his benefits!"[22]

Overall, the comparison of the two pages had disappointed her. The reality that
death could strike so suddenly was now empirically rooted in her consciousness
after losing Ferdinand: "One most dreadful lesson have I had already. Let it suffice, O gracious Lord, I beseech thee."

From the point of view of her spiritual development, however, these notes reveal
that the eldest daughter of Eleuthère Irénée du Pont had traveled a considerable
distance from the ambiguous deistical beliefs of her father and grandfather. Her
fluid incorporation of biblical language makes it clear that the Bible had become a
frequent and familiar source of reading. Her growing religious convictions had not
gone unnoticed by her family, particularly by her grandfather. Writing to his wife
in January of 1817, only months before his death, Pierre Samuel somewhat unhappily observed that "Victorine has intelligence and courage but she is English and
above all Christian, enough to make you shiver."[23]

CHAPTER 10

The Brandywine
Manufacturer's Sunday School

Knowledge creates an obligation.
—Pierre Samuel du Pont de Nemours to Françoise
(Poivre) du Pont, September 6, 1816

On a Sunday morning in early 1816, Eleuthère Irénée du Pont crossed the Brandy-wine Creek and traveled south along his brother's side of the river. His destination was Simsville, a newly developed worker's community about half a mile below his own. From this side of the river he could survey his lower yards, which were still referred to as "Hagley" by the locals.[1] With a sense of accomplishment he could view his stone-gray rolling mills, the machine shop, the quarry, and the graining mill—all lying conspicuously deserted on the Sabbath. Halfway up Slitting Mill Road on the left, he could see the blacksmith shop (John Gregg's old forge),[2] and as his blue-gray eyes traveled to the peak of the promontory on the right, he would have had an excellent view of the gleaming white house he had built two years pre-viously for the director of the lower yards. "Hagley House," as it quickly became known, was a magnificent three-story dwelling, complete with root cellar and attic. Its first occupant and director was Irénée's brother-in-law, Charles Dalmas.

Desiring to speak to the textile manufacturer John Siddall about a matter of business, Irénée stopped at the man's home. His wife answered the door and told him that John was at the mill conducting a Sunday school class. Intrigued by this news, Irénée decided to investigate. His youngest daughter, Sophie, later recalled: "My father went over the mill and there he found on an upper floor a space that had been cleaned of machinery, stock, etc., and in this rough room many men, women and children who were employees in the factory were being taught."[3]

Du Pont discovered Siddall in the company of his nephew James, and about thirty-five men, women, and children crowded about an open space. Fascinated, he sat quietly and respectfully until the conclusion of this rustic "factory school." When the class disbanded, Irénée pressed Siddall for further details about what he had just witnessed. John, a devout Christian, informed him of the work of Robert Raikes, a newspaper printer in Gloucester, England, who had started the

Sunday school movement in 1780. Mr. Raikes, observing that factory children were often poor, uneducated, and unruly, had decided to establish a class on Sundays where the youth could be given a basic education and strengthened in the tenets of Christianity. Siddall's nephew James had participated in such a class on a recent trip to England.[4]

Another of Siddall's workers was later described by Victorine as "a weaver of the name of Daniels, an illiterate but pious man, who was well acquainted with the manner in which Sabbath schools are conducted in England. He offered to organize a Sunday school on the Brandywine, for instructing the children employed in the manufactories."[5] Siddall took Daniels up on his offer and began to teach a small class in his own parlor every Sunday morning. Attendance grew so rapidly that he was soon forced to relocate the class to the mill. Organic in its vitality and fueled by evangelical enthusiasm, the dual goals of literacy and biblical instruction were sufficient motivations for the Siddalls' and Daniels' school.[6]

Standing on the fourth floor of Siddall's mill, Irénée had a quick appreciation for the humanitarian and educational components of Siddall's endeavor and foresaw that its benefits could be expanded to engage a wider audience. The Lower Brandywine in 1816 was home to one of Delaware's fastest-growing manufacturing communities but, with the exception of a few "grog shops" and general stores, public amenities were sparse.[7] The nearest access to either churches or schools was in Wilmington, nearly four miles away. Many of the workers were, like Daniels, illiterate; they had learned a trade but had never received the benefits of even a basic education. Victorine would later observe that the parents of the children were, "in general" uneducated and "wholly unable to give them any instruction. At the Sunday school they are taught the precepts of Christianity, their duty to their Maker and to their fellow creatures; they moreover acquire a love of neatness and regularity extremely gratifying to their teachers who take the deepest interest in their welfare."[8]

Convinced that here was an endeavor worth undertaking, not only for the benefit of his own employees but also for families throughout the entire valley, Irénée returned home with a renewed sense of enthusiasm. He spoke with his friends Robert McCall and Raphael Duplanty, who operated the textile mill at the lower end of the Hagley yards. They, in cooperation with Siddall, moved the class to the fifth floor of the Duplanty–McCall building before the year was out, resulting in greater access for larger numbers of young people on both sides of the river. Word went out quickly that the children of any worker in the local manufactories (including those of tradesmen and farmers) who could make it to the mill on a Sunday morning were welcome to attend at no cost. The school met at Duplanty's for the remainder of 1816 and the greater part of 1817, while John Siddall and his nephew continued to superintend its operation.

As attendance at Siddall's school increased throughout the second half of 1816, Irénée and other merchants met more frequently to discuss its future. The net result was that a sort of unofficial "school committee" began to take shape, with each participating manufacturer contributing to the school's financial needs through means of an annual subscription. To help supplement expenses, their goal was to have the Sunday school incorporated with the State of Delaware, thereby making it possible to receive a ten-cent subsidy per student. A constitution was drawn up, and the necessary paperwork submitted to the state legislature in Dover. Since the school was a collaborative effort of manufacturers and businessmen, its name was entered as the "Brandywine Manufacturer's Sunday School" (BMSS).[9] The legislature wasted little time in processing the request and, on January 29, 1817, an act of incorporation was passed by both houses.[10]

Back at Hagley, the trustees of the school released a statement to the public that read, in part, "Be it known that a Sunday school is established on the Brandywine. Designated by the name of the Brandywine Sunday School for the improvement of Children or Adults of all denominations and sects and for the better dissemination of knowledge by which means the rising generation may be made good and enlightened Citizens and become useful members of Society."[11] The proclamation was accompanied by a list of the subscribers, with Victor du Pont's name at the top. (The participation of Victor, who was popular among the local merchants and a member of Wilmington's newly formed Masonic lodge,[12] encouraged others to contribute.)

Shortly after, the trustees decided to move ahead with plans to erect a building for the dedicated use of the Sunday school. Irénée donated a piece of land on Slitting Mill Road about 150 yards above the blacksmith shop and assigned the project to his company carpenter, William Boyd, and stone mason William Cleaden. By early October, the beautiful thirty-by-fifty-foot stone building was completed.[13] Inside the large one-room structure, the white ceiling and horsehair plaster walls combined with tall, recessed windows to provide maximum light.

An opening ceremony had been arranged and, on Sunday, October 19, 1817, a large crowd of curious adults and children entered through the tall white doors for the first time. Dr. Thomas Read, an elderly Presbyterian minister who had assisted George Washington during the War of Independence,[14] gave a short message of dedication, and concluded by praying that God would bless the endeavor to the benefit of the children and community. Among the celebratory crowd stood the tall, attractive widow, known to many in the community by her married name, Mrs. Victorine Bauduy, with her two younger sisters in tow. Eleuthera, now eleven, and Sophie, seven, watched the event with wide-eyed curiosity. Along with their twenty-five-year-old sister, they had little idea on that crisp autumn morning just how large an impact this inauguration would have upon their futures.

One result of the school's opening (that Irénée had not expected) was that Protestant clergymen were invited to use the building in the afternoons to provide worship services for the local community.[15] Presbyterian pastors Read and Rev. Thomas Love[16] were among the earliest preachers there. Victorine traditionally invited the ministers to Eleutherian Mills after services, to share a meal with the family. Clergymen were typically among the best educated of their communities, and the granddaughter of du Pont de Nemours enjoyed the lively discussions that often ensued.

Victorine felt proud that her father had elected to have the schoolhouse built on his property. Due to the community's lack of educational or religious entities, she viewed the school's establishment in much the same way she had perceived Sarah Ralston's orphan asylum—as a bold and compassionate enterprise that met a great social need. Although she fully supported its establishment, her involvement at the school was initially sporadic, and included minor assignments, such as assisting the Siddalls with administrative tasks or filling in for an absent teacher. Later, sister Sophie remembered: "I have heard my sister Mrs Bauduy relate how her father came to her, then a young widow in her 24th year, (but just recovered from the long ill health that followed the loss of her husband 2 years before) & taking her by the hand asked her for his sake to become a teacher in the new school & endeavor to rouse herself from her affliction—to take an interest in it."[17]

In 1900, a former scholar named Samuel Brown, was asked to write his recollection of a conversation he'd had with Sophie du Pont just prior to her death in 1888. He recalled her as saying:

> As [my father] walked home [from Siddall's mill] it occurred to him that if he could get his oldest daughter, Victorine, then a young widow, interested in that school, it would help to take her mind off her great sorrow, . . . [her husband] had only lived a few months after their marriage and she was terribly depressed and almost inconsolable. The more my father thought about it the more convinced he became that it would tend to turn her mind away from her despondency, improve her health and at the same time be a splendid work in that region where there were no schools of any kind at that time.[18]

However, Sophie was only six years old at the time of these events, and Victorine herself would later explain her father's motivations somewhat differently to her brother Henry: "The great good which it would do to the children of the workmen, & to gratify his daughter who took a warm interest in the scheme, were the motives which induced your father to build the school house."[19]

SHIFTING PATTERNS

By early 1818, three emerging realities had begun to alter the patterns of Victorine du Pont's life. The first of these was her increasing engagement with the Sunday school. By summer, she had agreed to take weekly charge of a class of boys and to assist the Siddalls in their administrative oversight.

The second reality was a notable shift in the balance of time spent with each of her sisters. When Evelina gave birth to James Irénée Bidermann in the fall of 1817, she became engrossed with caring for her baby—an orbit that her older sister could not easily share. The sororal intimacy between Evelina and Victorine had begun in France, but that exclusive relationship was beginning to experience encroachment. When the twelve-year-old Eleuthera was sent to Mrs. Hughes' boarding school in Philadelphia, it prompted Victorine to send numerous missives to encourage the homesick girl through her first term. As their correspondence increased and the years piled up, so did their confidences. On Eleu's heels was eight-year-old Sophie, a creative little sprite with a flair for pen and crayons. Thus, as Lina grew more preoccupied with her baby, Victorine grew more involved with the rearing of her "two daughters."

Third, the familiar patterns of friendship with her closest friends were also experiencing metamorphosis. The years of love and loyalty between them had been a contributing force to her development, and a guiding light through her darkest days. But all this was changing. Antoinette Brevost had departed for Pittsburgh in 1815, and though the two friends continued to exchange letters and small gifts, they were to never meet again.[20] Rebecca Ralston had introduced Victorine to a new visitor at her Germantown home—a young minister from the state of New York named John Chester, the son of one of her father's acquaintances. John and Becky began a warm correspondence that eventually led to romance. On June 1, 1818, Victorine and Anna Smith joyfully witnessed the wedding of their dearest friend in the parlor of the Ralston home. The saddest note for Victorine, however, was that the bride immediately departed for New York State, where her husband would go on to pastor two churches.[21] At first the new Mrs. Chester tried to visit Victorine whenever she returned to Philadelphia, but their correspondence dwindled over time and eventually ceased altogether.

Eighteen months after Becky's wedding, Anna Potts Smith, the independent and spirited class poet, married the wealthy textile manufacturer Daniel Lammot. Moving into the widower's stately home at 716 French Street in Wilmington, she became an instant stepmother to his four young children, one of whom (Margaretta Lammot) later married Victorine's brother Alfred. The remarkable union between Anna and Daniel lasted for over fifty-five years, during which time Anna birthed nine children and lived to the age of eighty-one, passing away on July 25, 1875. Given that Anna became Alfred's mother-in-law, her lifelong friendship with Victorine was assured.

In addition to these shifting patterns, it was becoming more evident that the dangers posed by the black-powder mill were likely to be an ever-present—and unpredictable—threat to Victorine's peaceful life along the Brandywine. At nine o'clock on the morning of Thursday, March 19, 1818, while Victorine was schooling her siblings, the catastrophic event known in DuPont Company chronicles as "The Great Explosion" occurred. Thirty-four people were killed and seven others wounded in the calamity.[22] Victorine's sister Eleuthera recalled:

> My sister Sophie, myself, & Brother Henry, were preparing to commence our lessons, under our loving and excellent teacher, sister Victorine Bauduy. I was taking an atlas from the window seat when the first explosion occurred! The window, sashes, glass and all shattered to pieces, flew in my face & cut me in several places but not seriously. Our Sister [Victorine] took Henry by the hand & told us to follow her quickly. In the entry (upstairs) we met Mama rushing out of the door of her room which was exactly opposite to that of our school room. She held in her arms our little brother Alexis, just two years of age. She told us to get out of

the house as quickly as possible. . . . My sister Victorine wrapped a shawl around [Evelina], seized little James Bidermann with difficulty from the terrified nurse and got her to take charge of her sister and followed her.[23]

The family then fled up the hill toward Sand Hole Woods: "We were just about half way out of the Sand Hole when the magazine blew up with the most tremendous report I ever heard. Looking up, we beheld an immense cloud of white, thick smoke filling with dark objects, stones, beams, etc., the debris of the building and its contents. Mercifully none fell on us!"[24] Uncle Charles was not as fortunate. He had been struck by a large stone that broke his arm and dislocated his shoulder, an injury that would take several months from which to recover.

A subsequent investigation revealed sufficient evidence to allege that Augustus d'Autremont, the yard foreman, had been drinking at the time of the accident and had ignored a worker's caution that an unusual sound had been heard in the glazing mill's machinery. Moments later the entire building exploded, setting off the nearby magazine, in which, it was said, there was more than thirty tons of powder stored.[25] Volunteers undertook the unpleasant task of recovering the broken bodies and fragments of charred flesh for decent burial. Biographer J. F. Wall records that "The du Pont women . . . did not flinch from the services demanded of them. Louviers [Victor and Gabrielle's house] was turned into a temporary hospital and morgue, and the women tended the wounded and laid out in shrouds what remained of the dead."[26] The unidentified remains of powder workers would be laid to rest in ground directly abutting the family cemetery.

Irénée was devastated to hear that so many had perished, and that his own wife and brother-in-law had been seriously injured.[27] Although he knew that a black-powder business must accept the risk of explosion, it deeply affected him whenever a life was lost in his employ. Despite the huge operational loss, he immediately issued an order that every widow was to be pensioned at the rate of $100 per year, a generous sum for the time. In addition, they were permitted to remain in their lodgings without charge and could rent out rooms if they wished to supplement their income. These provisions were especially helpful for women like poor Mrs. John Brady, who lost both her husband and son in the explosion.

Alfred was recalled from school in Philadelphia and immediately replaced the discharged d'Autremont as director of the upper yards. Evelina's husband, James Bidermann, replaced Uncle Charles as foreman of the lower yards, and he, Evelina, and little James moved into Hagley House. In the 119 years from its founding in 1802 to the closing of the yards in 1921, the black-powder company started by Eleuthère Irénée du Pont experienced a total of 288 explosions. From sixty of these, 228 people lost their lives.[28] Victorine, who struggled occasionally with anxiety, lived to experience over eighty of these blasts during her lifetime.

CHAPTER 11

A New Superintendent

It is no unsubstantial good to dwell
In childhood's heart,
On childhood's guileless tongue;
To be the chosen favorite oracle,
Consulted by the innocent and young:
To be remember'd as the light that flung
Its first fresh lustre on the unwrinkled brow.

—Bernard Barton

Not usually impressed by Bernard Barton's works, Victorine had been so inspired by these lines that she copied them down on two separate occasions. Like the Quaker poet, she was cognizant of the far-reaching implications of the teaching profession. Education in the du Pont household, as defined by her late grandfather, had always implied a responsibility commensurate with its attainment. He believed that for those who had been endowed by the Creator with a good mind and the privilege of a robust education, efforts to better the conditions of their fellow man were an obligation. Since her childhood days in the gardens of Bois-des-Fossés, Victorine had inherited a thirst for knowledge that was seemingly insatiable. She absorbed history, science, botany, biology, medicine, chemistry, languages, geography, music, and astronomy like a thirsty sponge. Literature, across a wide spectrum of genres, was especially delicious to her. The only standard she held for herself (and others) was that the writing had to be of high quality—informative, entertaining, well-written, and morally excellent. "A judicious choice of books," she told Eleuthera, "is what I consider of the utmost importance in education. Nor is it . . . sufficient that no bad books should be put in the hands of young people, but it is highly important that *good ones* should be given to them at the time when they will prove the most useful."[1]

Historian Mary Johnson noted the connection between literature and morality, as passed down by Pierre Samuel. "Du Pont de Nemours," she wrote, "took a special interest in his granddaughter's development since he had very precise notions about the role of women and the upbringing necessary for the fulfillment of their role." Pierre, she added, believed that mothers should be "capable of inculcating their children with sound moral principles, respect for reason, and patriotic

69

sentiments."[2] What the venerable old man had not foreseen, however, was the extent to which his granddaughter's morality would be shaped by the tenets of her Christian faith.

During 1819 and 1820, Wilmington experienced a series of revival meetings that extended to the Brandywine neighborhood. When Victorine's father discovered that the Siddalls had permitted a few of the evangelistic preachers to use the schoolhouse for evening meetings, he immediately countermanded the order; he felt it violated the school's nonsectarian philosophy. Irénée had also not envisioned the Sunday afternoon services as part of the original intention for the schoolhouse, but Victorine defended the practice as an additional benefit to the workers. She reminded her father that with no churches in the immediate area, families had little access to congregational worship. Although Protestant ministers were the only ones participating in the worship rotations, she affirmed that the services were conducted by clergymen from more than one denomination. Yielding to his beloved daughter's logic, Irénée reluctantly accepted the status quo.

Victorine's involvement at the Brandywine Manufacturer's Sunday School (BMSS) increased significantly during 1818. In addition to her class of boys, she had taken on a group of young girls. In general, she found girls easier to teach and more attentive than their male counterparts. A few years later, she would admit to Eleuthera that "I like little girls better than boys. This, you will own, is an admirable conclusion."[3]

Victorine found herself increasingly drawn to the children, many of whom seemed so earnest in their desire to better themselves. Determined that they should continue to have the opportunity to pursue an education, she became a permanent member of the teaching staff. The Siddalls continued to oversee the school's operations, but it is clear that by 1819 they considered Victorine an equal partner in its administration. Her name appears on several school documents during this time, including receipts for purchases and supplies. While James Siddall kept an account of expenses into the early 1820s, Victorine gradually assumed responsibility for the school's records and class books.

———

The winter of 1821–1822 had been unusually severe. The combination of cold temperatures and excessive precipitation meant that snowfall depths remained high across the countryside. As warmer weather arrived, everything began melting at once. Inhabitants along the lower Brandywine had grown accustomed to seeing their creek rise significantly each spring; they knew the river was an untamed lion that was not always caged by its steep banks, and the threat of flood was a perennial possibility. Known as "freshets" by the locals, these springtime torrents, if formidable enough, could sweep away an entire building as easily as a dollhouse.

The Brandywine drops 120 feet in its last five miles, creating a surge of waterpower that was a natural advantage to every manufacturer along its banks; but that which was an asset during most years proved to be a disaster in 1822. Few had remembered seeing a deluge like the one that cascaded down the valley on Thursday,

February 21. As the waters rose, men on both sides of the river could be seen scampering about in a wild array of activities, doing whatever they could to protect their homes and properties. Victor's son, Charles Irénée, who now ran his father's textile mill, ordered his men to pull to higher ground any equipment that could be threatened. On Irénée's side of the river, workers could be seen pulling the boats up behind Fountain's store, which was located between the upper and lower yards. Historian J. Thomas Scharf recorded that "the Brandywine rose twenty feet above its banks, took away the dam, [and] destroyed the races."[4]

Victorine had never seen the creek so high. Conveying the threatening sight to Eleuthera at Mrs. Hughes's school, she reported:

> You cannot form to yourself an idea of the height of the Brandywine on this occasion. It exceeds anything that ever happened before. The water came up into the piazza of the store, and on the other side it covered over all the gardens of my Uncle's workmen. . . . I never saw anything look so desolate as the shore on this side; I could hardly recognize it. All the poplars have been uprooted and the ground itself gave way leaving nothing but bare rocks and precipices. At Mr Young's [paper mill] there was one family in eminent danger for a whole night. Their dwelling was surrounded by water. It rose to the very garret where eleven persons had retired for shelter—part of the building even gave way. But the rest stood and they were saved![5]

Joshua and Thomas Gilpin's paper mill was also damaged, and just upriver from them stood the Simsville Mill operated and leased by John Siddall. Historian Roy M. Boatman reported that the 1822 freshet "flooded part of the Simsville Mill, and John Siddall & Co. 'suffered considerably, as a considerable part of his machinery was new, and is very much injured.' . . . [Eventually] their creditors overtook them and a public sale of the machinery was announced for October 23, 1823."[6] John Siddall was ruined and his mill was eventually leased to others. Forced to seek his fortunes elsewhere, he left the neighborhood shortly after.

With its overseer gone, the question on the minds of many parents was the future of the Sunday school. Its continuation would depend on finding a superintendent who could fulfill several daunting requirements. These included someone who was familiar with its operations, had an academic background, possessed the religious commitment to advance its cause, could subsist with little to no reimbursement, and had the necessary time and skills to devote to its oversight. Not surprisingly, most of the neighborhood's residents were aware that such a person already existed. The school's trustees approached Irénée, asking him to convey to his daughter that the position was open to her if she wanted it.

This was a crossroads moment in Victorine's life. The young widow knew that a decision in the affirmative would result in the immediate surrender of a significant portion of her time. Since the BMSS was open every Sunday of the year without break, taking the job would greatly limit the freedom of her social activities. Administrative oversight of staff, operations, and the preparation of curriculum would consume hours of responsibility—much of them before the doors even opened on Sundays. On the other side of the equation, however, she knew that an extended absence of leadership could place the entire endeavor at risk. Her father was committed to the project for the present, as were the shrinking number of subsidizers, but every worker in the community knew that a spacious building in the middle of a quickly expanding manufactory could surely be used for other purposes.

For the older generation of du Pont women, however, it was likely that quite another train of thought had occurred to them; they may have marveled that such an offer had even been extended to a woman. In France, Victorine's mother Sophie had not foreseen such possibilities. When her daughter was still a toddler at Bois-des-Fossés, she had lamented to Irénée that the child's intellectual capabilities would be wasted because she had been born a girl.[7] Here in America, however, male business owners—with the consent of the entire community—were prepared to let her daughter take the helm of an institution traditionally reserved for men. While many churches permitted female oversight of their Sunday schools, it was with the traditional understanding that they were under the auspices of their male pastors; but an independent Sunday school backed by a male-dominated community of manufacturers was another story. The literature of the American Sunday School Union (representing several denominations) in the 1820s reveals that their general assumption for the role of superintendent was that he would be male.[8]

Surely the pioneer example of Sarah Ralston came more than once to Victorine's mind. Ralston had utilized her social status in Philadelphia to undertake the establishment of three major institutions in the city at a time when women were neither expected nor encouraged to take on such entrepreneurial roles. But neither Ralston nor her protégé, Victorine du Pont, were driven by the need to make history; they were simply driven by the need of the community. Their socioeconomic circumstances provided the wherewithal to pursue their endeavors, but the sacrifices they were willing to make to accomplish them were fueled by compassion and a sense of calling.

Victorine du Pont Bauduy assumed the superintendency of the BMSS in the fall of 1823, and systematically began to bring order and vision to its operational structure. One of her first administrative acts was to grant young Sophie, now thirteen, the charge of a class of girls—thereupon fulfilling one of her sister's greatest wishes. But the new superintendent did not stop there. Victorine was a born organizer, a keeper of lists, and a recorder of details. The powderman's daughter preferred order in nearly all things. "[Baltimore] is handsome," she once remarked to Evelina, "[but] you know I am not fond of crooked streets, and it shocked me quite to see the finest streets turn in different directions."[9] When a local farmer once harvested his crop of peaches a fortnight too early, she labeled it "the acme of barbarism."[10]

That same year she affiliated the school with the Sunday and Adult School Union in Philadelphia, which, in May of 1824, changed its name to the American Sunday School Union (ASSU) in order to more adequately reflect its national scope. A friend of Alfred's named John Farr was the first to alert Victorine of the ASSU's resources. Victorine "took steps to have the school [become] an auxiliary to the Union. From that time its religious character & influence grew apace."[11] Auxiliary membership in the Union did not, however, mean anything more than affiliation. The ASSU provided guidelines and sound doctrine through their teaching materials but did not dictate the operational aspects of member schools. Each entity was to remain autonomous in governance.

The ASSU and the BMSS had a particularly strong relationship, primarily because both entities shared similar goals and the same nondenominational approach for reaching them. Although both institutions wished to provide a free education to their students, it is no secret that the Christian message was deemed the highest good that could be implanted in the lives of their scholars. In Victorine's day, the term "religion" was synonymous with an individual's personal faith. When, for example, she reported to the ASSU in 1830 that "Our great aim is to convince our pupils that Religion is the one thing needful,"[12] the pious widow did not mean that the children should embrace a particular denomination, but God himself through an act of personal faith. This, she believed, would inevitably result in the demonstration of a pious life if one's "religion" were authentic. A quote she copied from Baxter's *The Saint's Everlasting Rest* supports this conviction: "Let the world see, by your heavenly lives, that religion is something more than opinions."[13] Historian Margaret Mulrooney points out that "Victorine supervised the curriculum, and her correspondence, coupled with that of her sisters, who also taught at the school, reveals an overt desire to awaken their little charges."[14]

The BMSS and the ASSU both refrained from promoting any particular sect. At this, the little school along the Brandywine was remarkably successful in that its students consisted of both Protestants and Roman Catholics. Since it had been started by a local businessman, and not a church, it had presented a nondenominational face to the community from the outset. Victorine was able to maintain Siddall's nonsectarian approach by instructing her teachers "to dwell chiefly on those doctrines in which all Christians agree."[15] Families throughout the area, both Catholics and Protestants, became convinced that the school's leadership was committed to this policy, and sent their children without fear of violating their consciences.

Throughout the years that followed, Vic's appreciation and loyalty to the ASSU for the success of the school would remain firm. On one occasion in 1830, when a Wilmington paper was about to print an article stating that E. I. du Pont did not think the school was affiliated with the ASSU, she immediately sat down and wrote to the editor, Ziba Ferris: "Sir, . . . My father was mistaken when he told you that our school was not joined to the American Sunday School Union. We have been united to that institution ever since the year 1823. . . . After reaping for several years the benefit of this institution it would be very wrong in us to deny it, or to countenance anything that might be said against the said Sunday School Union."[16] Considering Victorine's devotion to her father's honor, it is noteworthy that she would take the initiative to correct such a seemingly innocuous comment. But her own sense of the family motto *Rectitudine Sto* (Upright I stand) would not allow the misleading statements to be printed, even if it was her own father who had unwittingly made them.

In 1823, when Victorine allied herself with the ASSU, seventy-five children were in regular attendance on Sunday mornings. Within the space of two years, the number had doubled to 150; and by 1829, just six years later, the number had nearly tripled to 219 scholars. It soon became clear to the entire Brandywine community north of Wilmington that the leadership of the new superintendent was an educational triumph for their region.

TEARS, GROWTH, AND ANXIETY

Eleuthera had been enrolled at Mrs. Hughes's school in Philadelphia since February of 1821. Initially, it was not a trip the fourteen-year-old had wanted to make, as was tearfully evident for several days before her departure. Victorine had no intention of allowing the "poor child" to make the journey alone, so she arranged to stay with Anna Smith until Eleu felt comfortable enough to remain by herself. The girl had great difficulty adjusting to her first extended time away. Homesick, downcast, and constantly on the verge of tears, her misery was compounded by a severe head cold. Victorine obliged her by extending her stay at Anna's, but after two weeks the older sister was beginning to feel the weariness. She told Evelina that Eleu was beginning to adjust, but that

> The poor child looked very sad at the thoughts of my going away and declared with tears in her eyes she wished she could come home with me. Indeed Evelina, I scarcely know how I shall leave her. . . . I try to cheer myself with the hope that this temporary separation will be of use to her in other respects. She will learn to think and act for herself in many little circumstances where she was wont to depend on me—and perhaps she will learn to estimate that love which has led me to devote so great a portion of my time to her. . . . I am weak and foolish this evening my dear Sister and would need yours or our dear mother's sympathy.[17]

To while the time away, she read Walter Scott's latest novel, *Kenilworth*, which had been released two months earlier. "There never was a more interesting tale, nor more delightfully told, but the catastrophe is too painful and I think it has also had a share in producing the fit of the *blues* above alluded to. I advise you not to read it till the bright month of May when all nature will be laughing around you."[18]

Three weeks later, Vic was back home and writing to Eleuthera almost daily. Expecting the same from her correspondent, she urged her sister to tell her everything, no matter how seemingly insignificant. Her letters run the full spectrum of motherly advice, covering everything from health and study habits to Eleuthera's choice of books ("Scott's novels are certainly among the very best," she reminded her).[19] She worried constantly about Eleuthera's health, her social experiences, study habits, choice of friends, and her excursions about the city. It became evident that while the younger sister was adjusting to her new situation, the older was growing more anxious: "I expect the arrival of the post with great impatience to get your letter. I feel so uneasy about you that your letters are the only comfort I can have."[20]

Although fourteen years separated them, the interdependent nature of their personalities only served to augment their attachment. The love that Victorine felt for her sister was deeply maternal. "You are indeed my own *dear daughter*," she effused, "and I question very much if Mama herself can love you better than I do. I certainly enjoy through your means my dearest child, a degree of happiness which I once thought never would have existed for me on this earth—Oh how thankful I feel for this [and] for *all* the blessings which I enjoy!"[21] Eleuthera, for her part, seemed to welcome her sister's motherly attention as much as Victorine took pleasure in supplying it. On a social level, Eleu tended to be more timid than her sister, and less assertive. Both were gentle by nature, but Victorine seldom allowed that to inhibit her opinions; Eleu, on the other hand, usually chose the path of silence in conversations heated by strong points of view.

Despite her conviction that the separation would be character building for Eleuthera, the older sister found herself missing the homesick girl more than she had anticipated. "I am here quite alone in my room after supper & you have no idea how very lonesome I feel without you," Victorine confessed. "It is a great trial my dear child to be thus parted after living so many years together, but let it turn to your advantage and I shall become reconciled to the sacrifice."[22] In another note she confided: "Your improvements in music & drawing (two accomplishments for which you have natural talents) will alone make me some amends for all the anxieties I have suffered on your account during our temporary separation."[23]

By the beginning of her second year, Eleu had adjusted to the school, but Victorine's "fretting" had not improved: "Whenever I am more than two days without hearing from you, I feel very uneasy. Last night I dreamt you were sick and I awoke quite sad."[24] Other letters express the depth of her fears: "The house seems so gloomy without you that I feel quite at a loss what to do to keep up my spirits. And then I awake regularly at three o'clock in the morning and I begin to indulge a thousand fears for you, which I know are very weak and useless but that nevertheless annoy me extremely and effectually prevent me from sleeping anymore."[25]

These admissions reveal a significant level of anxiety; yet her conviction that the separation would reap long-term benefits in Eleuthera's development was a price she was willing to pay. Like her father, Victorine seemed able to keep future rewards in view while enduring discomforting levels of present hardship. From her mother, she inherited the sacrificial ability to persevere for the sake of love. When Vic saw indications that Eleu was beginning to develop those same traits, it emboldened her to maintain the present course of action. Writing to her friend Antoinette Brevost in April 1821, she reflected:

It is singular how much we outgrow our juvenile tastes. I do not yet feel myself growing old [she was twenty-eight], but I find I am greatly weaned from my fondness for public amusements of all kinds. I see the vanity of them and rejoice at it. But I can make full allowance for the feelings of young people in that respect, and for that reason I am truly thankful that Eleuthera last week willingly gave up going to a ball and to the play because she thought I would be better pleased she should stay at home. I know these were great sacrifices at her age and I give her full credit for them. . . . Is she not a good girl Antoinette?[26]

Eleuthera also demonstrated a willingness to make changes at home, beginning with her sisterly spats with little Sophie. Vic responded to one of her letters, "When I read to Sophy the part of your letter where you say that you will never quarrel with her, she burst out a-crying. Indeed my dear Eleuthera, she loves you very dearly and I am sure she will also be more careful, when you meet, not to have any more little disagreements with you."[27]

Unlike Eleu, little Sophie was of a more independent nature, and playfully willing to resist her big sister's authority. Sophie accepted the bond between her older siblings, and later acknowledged that Victorine and Eleuthera had always been "everything to each other."[28] Although she loved Victorine dearly, she was not as eager to receive her sister's oversight in every area of life. Eighteen years separated the two, and the difference had been sufficient for Sophie to seek camaraderie from others closer in age.[29] At home, the youngest sister could often be observed hunched over her writing desk. "I have begun to draw," Sophie told Cousin Frank in the fall of 1821, "with the crayons Victorine brought home and I like them very well."[30] This announcement launched a twelve-year period during which Sophie would paint or sketch numerous (and often humorous) caricatures of local people and events, which she referred to as her "caricks."[31]

After two years at Mrs. Hughes' establishment, Eleuthera returned home in 1823, the same year Victorine had assumed the superintendency of the Sunday school. The eldest sister immediately assigned her to a class of girls, thereby ensuring that three of the four du Pont sisters were now firmly entrenched as teachers at the BMSS.

Victorine's reign had begun.

CHAPTER 12

Second Mother

My early friends are all gone, but I do not feel the want of them, because I have you & Sophia to replace them.

—*Victorine to Eleuthera, March 3, 1826*

In the autumn of 1823, Victorine and Eleuthera decided to initiate a sort of family newspaper, a weekly publication intended to provide amusement during the winter months. They entitled their enterprise the *Tancopanican Chronicles*, borrowing the Lenni-Lenape term for the Brandywine Creek. Drawing a tongue-in-cheek parallel to the French and English literary societies of the day, they referred to themselves as editors of "the Blue Stocking Club." They wrote articles in the third-person style of detached journalists and enhanced the two-column pages with their own ink drawings. Included were humorous accounts of everything from family events, politics, poetry, and literature, to barnyard antics and local Brandywine news. The famed literary attempt lasted only two winters. Its final edition, released on January 15, 1825, predicted its own demise. Their first issue announced:

> Several of our readers have, we understand, manifested their surprise, nay even their disapprobation, at the title of our paper. Some find the word Tancopanican harsh and unharmonious, and wonder that we preferred it to the more simple Brandywine; while others, who are not given to antiquarian researches, remain to this day in ignorance of the word. . . . We can prove that Tancopanican was a most appropriate appellation, bestowed upon the romantic stream by the native inhabitants of the soil. It signifies literally, "The large river where potatoes grow."[1]

Nothing was safe from the prying eyes of the reporters—and everyone was fair game. One example entitled "Daring Outrage," targeted Evelina and James Bidermann's traumatic experience with a butterfly in their bedroom. Evelina gave the alarm and, after a ferocious battle, James laid the "ferocious animal low" with the help of a cane. "This should serve as a caution to housekeepers to guard carefully their doors & windows lest such dangerous animals should enter."[2]

For Victorine, the *Tancopanican Chronicles* had served as a temporary outlet for her intellectual creativity, which teaching children seldom provided. Had she chosen a different path in life, she had the skills to lend her voice to the literary world she both loved and inhabited. Her uncanny ability to read newly published

works and critique their value long before future editors would confirm her judg-
ments evidenced her contemporary insights. But such a path would not have
inspired her. Vocationally, Victorine was born to be a teacher. While literature
stimulated her, teaching fulfilled her. The joy of casting that "first fresh lustre" of
knowledge upon "the innocent and young" was unsurpassed by any other pursuit.[3]
The subheading she had chosen for the the *Tancopanican Chronicles* had been *Inest
sua gratia paduis*, which she translated as "Even little things have their particular
grace."[4]

WEDDINGS, HEROES, AND FUNERALS

The year 1824 recorded the marriages of no fewer than three du Ponts. On Irénée
and Sophie's side of the river, their son Alfred wed Margaretta Elizabeth Lammot
on October 28. "I am more happy than I have been since many years," gushed Vic
to Evelina, "although I do not go as far as Eleuthera who declares she is more
delighted than the parties themselves."[5]

Irénée had ordered the construction of a handsome, two-story house for the
newlyweds, just a short distance from Eleutherian Mills, which Alfred named
Nemours.[6] Completed in 1824, the happy pair took occupancy shortly after their
wedding. Their first child, born in August of 1825, was named Victorine Elizabeth.
The tiny niece endeared herself to her namesake immediately. "I cannot tell you
how fond I am of her," glowed the senior Victorine Elizabeth to Lina. "My affection has increased tenfold since I have her so constantly with me."[7] Born in the
same month of the year, the two Victorine Elizabeths would maintain a lifelong
friendship. At her death, it would be to "little Vic" that "big Vic" would leave the
largest, noncorporate portion of her will.

Across the creek, two of Victor's children were also wed that same year. Frank's
sister Julia was married on May 12 to a young naval officer named Irvine Shubrick.
And in the fall, their brother Charles Irénée du Pont married Dorcas Montgomery
Van Dyke on October 5, 1824. Her father was a senator in the Delaware legislature
and her grandfather, Nicholas Van Dyke, had served as a Continental Congress-
man during the time of the nearby Battle of the Brandywine. It was in this capacity that he had first met the Marquis de Lafayette, who was currently in America
upon the invitation of President James Monroe to take part in the country's fiftieth
anniversary celebrations.

On September 28, 1824, the Marquis delivered a speech at Independence Hall
in Philadelphia, where a grand ball was held in his honor. Victorine, Eleuthera,
and Sophie, who had been visiting in the city with Mr. and Mrs. Richard Somers
Smith, were among those in attendance. Vic confided to her mother on September 23, "I think, dear maman, that we will go to the great ball. Mrs. Smith is going
and urges us to go with her. I should like Eleuthera to have the pleasure of seeing
so beautiful a fete."[8] A week after his speech in Philadelphia, Lafayette attended
the wedding festivities of Charles and Dorcas du Pont, which were held at the Van
Dyke home in New Castle, Delaware.[9] The Marquis had been given the privilege

of giving the bride away, and the wedding was later described as "one of the most important" social events that the old town of New Castle had ever witnessed."[10]

Lafayette returned to France aboard the USS *Brandywine* in late September 1825 but, before departing, Bessie Gardner du Pont recorded that he "spent the night of July 25 at E. I. du Pont's house; while there he wrote in Eleuthera du Pont's album: 'After having seen nearly half a century ago, the banks of the Brandywine a scene of bloody fighting, I am happy to find it now the seat of industry, beauty and mutual friendship.—Lafayette.'"[11] The next day, Irénée and Victor accompanied the Marquis and his son, George Washington Lafayette, to Chadds Ford, Pennsylvania, where the old warrior revisited the scenes of the Brandywine battle. Before departing Eleutherian Mills, however, Lafayette stopped the carriage at Sand Hole Woods to visit the grave of his old friend, Pierre Samuel du Pont de Nemours, where he paid his silent respects. At the time of the General's visit, his old compatriot was still the only occupant atop the quiet hillside.

But he was not to be alone much longer. On January 30, 1827, Victor Marie du Pont suffered a heart attack on the streets of Philadelphia and was carried to his room at the United States Hotel. He died within hours. Victorine broke the news to her brother Henry: "It appears that a blood vessel broke near the heart which caused his death in a very short time, even before the doctors could arrive. . . . Our dear father has met with a very great loss."[12] Irénée made the somber arrangements of having his brother's body transported to Eleutherian Mills and, since Victor was their father's eldest son, he had him buried to the right of Pierre Samuel. The blow was a heavy one for Irénée. It seemed to him that those ties which had moored him most closely to his past were, one by one, releasing their strands.

Thankfully, Irénée still had the one person in life who had been his strongest support—his beloved wife. But this knot too was beginning to slip. Sophie had struggled with a variety of health issues for several years. Some historians believe they originated from the injuries she had sustained during the Great Explosion of 1818 at the powder mills. "Our dear mama's indisposition has been more serious," Victorine had written in 1822, "for she has had headaches which returned every day at the same hour, and nothing appeared to bring her any relief."[13] By the winter of 1827, Sophie's periods of wellness were being measured in terms of intermittent days, rather than months. "Our dear Mother was not so well as she had been. . . . Today she is better, but I cannot feel easy while she is subject to these frequent relapses."[14]

While Victorine felt a fierce loyalty and love for her father, it had always been her mother to whom she could bare her heart. As a toddler in Bois-des-Fossés, it had been *Maman* who was her constant companion; and in young adulthood, Sophie's quiet strength had nursed her daughter through her greatest trial. By the summer of 1827, Sophie's back pains had returned and she also struggled with recurrent bouts of redness and discharges from both eyes. By December, a chronic swelling in her legs had become more severe, making it painful to walk.[15] She confessed to Victorine that she missed the sunshine, and the ability to sit in the garden during pleasant weather, but most of all, she confessed, she regretted being unable to come down to the family parlor, the social center of their home. "The cold weather prevents her still from leaving her room," noted Vic.[16] To compensate, Irénée and the children assembled upstairs and spent the evenings in her company, transferring the warmth of the parlor's amenities to her bedroom.

Spring and summer of 1828 did little to alleviate her discomfort, and by the first days of August, everyone feared the worst. In a short note to Antoine Girard, one of the company's agents, Irénée wrote "I am not able to attend to business affairs as I should. My only thought is for my wife, who is painfully and dangerously ill, and has been so for several weeks."[17] On August 3, he told his close friend and Philadelphia agent Francis Gurney Smith that Sophie's health was getting "considerably worse."[18] Her condition consumed his thoughts and fed his fears. "Mrs. du Pont is so ill today that I hardly know what I am writing."[19]

Smith responded by sending the renowned Walnut Street physician Thomas Hewson to Eleutherian Mills the very same day.[20] Dr. Hewson took measures that relieved much of Sophie's discomfort, and as early as the following day, Irénée wrote a letter of gratitude to his friend declaring that his wife was showing distinct signs of improvement.[21] Sophie's rally continued for a couple of weeks. "When she began to be a little better," wrote Vic to Cousin Frank, "I could not persuade myself that it was indeed the case, so much did I fear that our hopes would be delusive. Happily it did not prove to be the case; our beloved patient has continued to improve."[22]

Although Irénée told Smith that he could now "confidently hope" in his wife's recovery, Victorine found it difficult to surrender to her father's level of optimism. She had witnessed such things before—most notably Ferdinand's brief improvement just prior to his death. Still, like the others, she was cautiously optimistic, but late August 1828 was extremely hot, and the torrid days exacted a heavy toll upon Sophie's weakened system. By early September, the swelling in her legs had increased. As Victorine and her father tended to her daily needs, they noted that Sophie's former gains had all but evaporated by early October. In quieter moments, Irénée simply sat beside his wife's bed, alternately holding her hand or adjusting her pillows. The girls took turns reading to her whenever she felt up to it, and Vic made sure that fresh flowers adorned the desk and windowsills in the room each day. On November 22, Irénée described her situation as "severe and almost hopeless."[23]

Five days later, Irénée watched helplessly as Sophie Madeleine Dalmas, the belle of Metz and strength of Bois-des-Fossés, surrendered her last breath. The grief-stricken family stood on the consecrated ground of Sand Hole Woods once more, and laid to rest the first member of the family to be placed on grandfather's left. Irénée had lost the center of his world, the children their mother, and Uncle Charles his sister—the last link to his family in France.

Maternal Succession

Sophie's death affected family dynamics in ways that were, at first, not so obvious. One such subtlety was the measure in which it increased Victorine's maternal role. Due to her status as eldest child, she had been granted—at least by perception and

French family tradition—a measure of unspoken authority over her siblings. This perception was augmented by three realities: Victorine's daily administration over the household, the early tutelage of her siblings and cousins, and age disparity. Although only a few years separated her from Evelina and Alfred, the difference in ages between Victorine and the "second family" (the American-born du Ponts) was more substantial. Alexis, for example, was twelve years old when his mother died, but twenty-four years separated him from Victorine.

The American-born members of the family were too young to question this role of "second mother" in their lives. Though she was their first tutor, her influence did not diminish when that tutelage was ended. Even their absences from the family home provided no respite from her counsel, as her countless letters followed the siblings into adulthood. Although her teachings of a moral nature were imparted with an air of gentle authority, there was, in the gentleness, an expectation of compliance.

In the case of Eleuthera and little Sophie, Victorine functioned as a mother guiding her daughters through puberty into young adulthood—a relationship acknowledged even while their mother was still alive. On one occasion, while Sophie was away at Mrs. Grimshaw's school in Wilmington in 1825, she assured her youngest sister that "Mama and I feel your absence more than I can tell you; . . . but then these few months will soon be over and we shall both be proud to see our Sophia improved in all her studies!"[24]

Victorine's grandfather, like most of his Enlightenment peers, embraced the concept of noblesse oblige, the belief that those born with exceptional abilities or privileges were obligated to use them toward the good of their fellow man. "I am perfectly convinced," he had written to Irénée in 1812, "that every personal advantage we experience is a motive and an obligation for us to do our duty to our fellow men."[25] This ideal surfaces frequently in the writings of the elder du Pont, and it is evident that he desired his sons and descendants to be especially remembered for it. "Let us be among men a race apart—that the world may say *The Du Ponts de Nemours* as they say the Catos, the Aristides, the Epaminondases, the Marcus Aureliuses!"[26]

Although expressed in the grandiose fashion to which the elder statesman was inclined, these basic ideals were, nonetheless, impressed upon his sons. Irénée, particularly, displayed these values in the manner in which he treated his employees. Programs he implemented that benefited the workers and their families, such as higher wages, safety innovations, and savings accounts, were uncommon practices in most manufactories of the day. This environment of paternalism, which characterized many of the company's later policies, could not have survived if its ideals had failed to be adopted by succeeding generations. While Irénée, Alfred, and the capable James Bidermann would maintain them for a time, the continuing influence of these values upon Henry and Alexis would need to be reinforced by someone who initially held far greater sway over their development.

Everyone knew that Victorine was guided by strong moral convictions but, unlike her father and grandfather, she did not ascribe their source to what she

considered the ambiguous philosophies of a deistical worldview. For her, the teachings of Jesus Christ were not vague in matters of morality. She could, for example,
find grounds for supporting her grandfather's views of noblesse oblige, because she
had seen its basic principle clearly stated in the Bible: "For unto whomsoever much
is given, of him shall be much required."[27] While the brothers were being groomed
to handle the affairs of the company, the moral environment of the home was influenced, in large part, through the role that Victorine played in their lives. In his
Guide to Manuscripts at the Hagley Museum, John Beverley Riggs described her as
"a woman of great perception and force." He affirmed that Victorine, according to
French custom as the eldest member of her family, "exerted great influence in all
matters concerning their affairs."[28]

When ten-year-old Henry first attended Mount Airy College in Germantown
in the fall of 1822, his siblings wrote to encourage him through his early bouts of
homesickness. But by 1827, a more settled Henry had created new problems for the
family: he and some of his friends had engaged in prankish behavior that resulted
in the issuance of a disciplinary warning. Victorine's first response was to gently
remind the fourteen-year-old of his familial responsibilities: "Recollect my dear
Henry, that you must contribute your share; you are no longer a child, your character as a man is forming itself for life, think of it seriously, and recollect that the
good example which you received from Alfred must be given by you to Alexis. We
have good hopes of you, let them not be disappointed. You must do your best to
become worthy of your papa and grandfather."[29]

Eight months later, another negative report was received from the school, indi-
cating that young Henry had yet to learn his lesson. The older sister immediately
sat down and wrote a searing letter to her brother, incensed that he should so self-
ishly hurt his parents and dishonor the family name. The admonishment reveals
as much about her own sense of paternal devotion as it does about Henry's apparent neglect of it at the time. From Victorine's chagrined perspective, his behavior
was incomprehensible.

> My dear Henry, I little thought last spring when you appeared to repent of your
> ill conduct at the examination, that you should so soon misbehave again and give
> us so much sorrow. Judge of what we felt this morning when a letter came from
> Mr Roumfort[30] to papa containing an account of your very reprehensible con-
> duct! Our dear mother . . . has been very unwell all day, owing I am sure in a
> great measure to the shock the news your bad conduct gave her. Papa is in Phil-
> adelphia, and I am going to have the very painful task of informing him that
> one of his children is not worthy of him. If ever [a] parent ought to have good
> children, it is surely our dear father, whose whole life is devoted to do what is
> good and useful and who never thinks of himself. Are you not sorry Henry to
> make him unhappy instead of doing your best to repay his unvaried kindness?
> I really don't know what to say to you, because I cannot comprehend the motives
> which have led you to such a course as that you appear to have adopted since
> the last holy days. Is it bad advice from some of your companions? Surely you

ought to know better than to be activated by it, and you are of an age to make use of your reason. I should have hoped that the lessons you have already had on the score of obstinacy would have been sufficient, to show you the *evil* and the *folly* of rebelling against the authority of your teachers. When you neglect your duties, do you punish them or yourself? Will not the disgrace be all your own in the end—and the sorrow ours?[31]

Henry repented, and in the spring of 1829, four months after his mother's death, he was enrolled in the U.S. Military Academy at West Point. He initially expressed some disillusionment with his new institution, but Victorine suspected that he had come under the influence of disgruntled cadets and cautioned, "My dear Brother, I would warn you not to nourish a discontented spirit. . . . Be determined to do your best to conform to the rules and to get on well with your studies. If you do this I am certain . . . you will inevitably recommend yourself to the notice & . . . good opinion of your superior officers. Remember that the more difficulties you encounter, the more merit there will be in overcoming them."[32]

When it is remembered that in twenty-one short years Brother Henry would become "Boss Henry," the head of the entire Du Pont enterprise, it makes the unseen effect of his sister's early influence more palpable. Twenty years his senior, Victorine had established the expectation that while others may play around or settle for mediocrity, a son of Eleuthère Irénée du Pont could not. The precise degree to which the lad inculcated her advice may be a matter of debate, for he too had inherited some of his father's qualities—including bulldogged stubbornness. But there is little doubt that few others, if any, would ever again attain the degree of moral authority over Henry du Pont that Victorine exercised during these formative years. Her influence inevitably waned as the young man grew older, but the granddaughter of du Pont de Nemours continued to be the family's moral standard-bearer. Driven more by *amour oblige* (love obliges) than noblesse oblige, Victorine's considerable influence was woven daily into the family tapestry.

CHAPTER 13

A Growing Family,
a Thriving Community

Eleutherian Mills in the 1830s was now a full-blown workers' community. The granite rolling mills stood like three-sided sentinels along the water's edge, while the hillsides behind them were dotted with the numerous buildings necessary to the powder-making process. Scattered above and beyond the steep hills were rows of communal stone houses that served as homes to the workers and their families. During the daytime, the grinding, creaking, hammering sounds of machinery demonstrated that the prophecy once made by Pierre Samuel about his son—that Eleuthère Irénée du Pont would become one of America's most prominent industrialists—had been fulfilled.

The loss of his beloved Sophie had been a severe blow to Irénée, but his correspondence indicates that he was as indefatigable as ever. The company was in the strongest position it had been to date and, in 1834 alone, his mills produced over one million pounds of black powder. Financial obligations to original investors like C. M. Talleyrand[1] and Antoine Lavoisier's widow, Marie-Anne, had been settled, and the company was in the process of buying the remaining shares from the last of the original investors. The operation was soon entirely in the hands of the du Pont family.

In August 1834, sixty-three-year-old Irénée mentioned to F. G. Smith that he wasn't feeling his best. "I am not sick, but weakened by the heat and tired from too much exertion."[2] September's cooler breezes resuscitated him, however, and he departed on a business trip to Philadelphia on Wednesday, October 29, feeling quite well. Around four o'clock the following afternoon he suffered what was probably a heart attack while returning to his hotel.[3] In what most agree was a striking coincidence, the event occurred on the same street where Victor had succumbed to a heart attack seven years earlier; some even claimed it was the identical spot. Like his brother before him, he was carried to his room at the United States Hotel, where he died in the early morning hours of Friday, October 31, 1834.

Four days later, the *Delaware State Journal* carried an extensive account of his death, stating that when the good citizens of Wilmington first heard the news,

The deepest sorrow was manifested by the by-standers, which was reflected from every countenance. . . . His remains were brought from Philadelphia on the steamboat *Wilmington* and were met at the wharf by a large number of citizens in carriages and on foot, who accompanied them to his residence, five miles from this place. On Saturday afternoon, they were removed to their last resting place in the private burying ground of the family, attended by an immense assemblage of friends and neighbors . . . and by the widows and orphans whom his bounty sustained. . . . We saw these objects of his benevolence follow their benefactor to his grave . . . the heartfelt sorrow speaking in their countenances, the silent tears coursing down their cheeks. . . . No appeal of benevolence passed by him unheeded—his heart, his hand and his purse were always open to promote every kind intent, every generous impulse, every charitable and public spir-ited enterprise.[4]

On November 7, the Washington-based newspaper, the *National Intelligencer*, printed an abbreviated version of the same article. That this national paper should publish his obituary with the assumption its readers were familiar with his name, testifies to the impact the man had made during his own lifetime. The loss of her mother, and now her father, was heartbreaking to Victorine. Not long after Iré-née's death, the ink from Victorine's quill bled the following words by Felicia Hemans onto the pages of her journal:

Our morning star has vanished
and the tomb throws its deep lengthened shade
o'er distant years to come.[5]

———

The decade also witnessed the wedding vows of each of Irénée's American-born children. Sophie was married to Cousin Frank on June 27, 1833. The following year, Eleuthera married the young physician Thomas Mackie Smith, son of Irénée's Phil-adelphia agent Francis Gurney Smith.[6] In what must surely have been a great relief to Victorine, her "two daughters" would not be leaving the neighborhood. Sophie and Frank moved across the creek to "Upper" Louviers, completed in 1833 for their wedding, and Eleu and Dr. Tom Smith moved into Jacob Broom's old house, above the lower yards. In 1836, Victorine's youngest brother, the twenty-year-old Alexis, also married into F. G. Smith's family when he married Joanna Smith on December 15. Seven months later, his brother Henry tied the final knot in the family when he married the pretty Louisa Gerhard on July 15, 1837. All of her sib-lings' spouses would become pivotal figures in Victorine's life, and one male in-law would become a vital participant in the Du Pont company.

Within days of his father's death, Alfred du Pont asked Evelina's husband, James Bidermann, if he would consent to become the acting head of the company for an interim period. As the eldest son, Alfred was the legitimate successor to the position, but he understood that he did not yet possess a sufficient grasp of the administrative side of the business. More adept at working with his hands, Alfred had been interested in the operational aspects of the mill since he was a boy; he knew how to run every piece of machinery the company utilized and frequently made improvements to their designs. Having studied under Thomas Cooper at Dickinson College for two years, Alfred was a fine chemist in his own right. Spending countless hours in his laboratory, he tweaked and improved the quality of the family's products and the safety of their processes.

Bidermann, on the other hand, had been Irénée's business manager ever since the departure of Peter Bauduy in 1815. He understood the business, was familiar with its financial and administrative arrangements, oversaw the salesmen, and knew all of the company's agents, territories, and customers. Thus, beginning in November 1834, Bidermann assumed the founder's responsibilities and proceeded to manage the firm for the next thirty-three months. Simultaneously, he was able to keep it on a promising trajectory, familiarize Alfred with its operations, and achieve the personal satisfaction of paying off the last of the original shareholders. At the conclusion of his interregnum in the summer of 1837, he sold his own shares back to the company and left it (for the first time in its thirty-five-year history) entirely in the hands of du Pont heirs.[7] Perhaps the greatest tribute to his brother-in-law's accomplishments was demonstrated when Alfred named his seventh and final child Antoine Bidermann du Pont, born October 13, 1837.

One of the first things Alfred did as the company's new president was to build an office that was separate from the family home. Prior to this, Irénée had run the entire operation out of two rooms on the ground floor of Eleutherian Mills. Thus, for Victorine, the death of her father essentially marked the end of her informal secretarial role within the company. While this role had already diminished to a great degree as the business expanded, the fact that the company office was still in the family home meant that it was simply a matter of convenience for Irénée to make requests of his daughter. Alfred completed the stone office by December 1837.[8] As early as the following month Victorine could say, "I scarcely ever hear anything about the business now except through [Cousin] Frank, for neither Alfred nor Henry are very communicative & I seldom converse with either of them."[9]

After the transition of leadership to Alfred, James and Evelina Bidermann stayed in the neighborhood long enough to attend Henry and Louisa's July wedding and then departed for two years abroad. James wished to reconnect with his loved ones, most of whom he had not seen since he had left France twenty years earlier. He and Lina especially desired to reunite with their son, James Jr., who was completing his engineering studies in Paris. Before departing, "Brother Bidermann" arranged for the construction of a new house which he hoped would be completed by the time of their return in 1839. He had purchased the farm Irénée had acquired in 1810, a lush property of gently rolling hills and fields where the founder had grazed his flock of Merino sheep. Located on the Kennett Pike about two and a half miles from Eleutherian Mills, Bidermann laid plans for a twelve-room, Greek Revival house that he intended to call "Winterthur," after his ancestral home in Switzerland. The couple sailed for France on Monday, July 24, 1837, vacating

Hagley House where they had lived for nearly two decades. Alexis du Pont, now superintendent of the lower yards, moved his young wife into the stately home even as the Bidermanns were packing up to leave.

Evelina's departure was bittersweet for Victorine. She missed her sister but comforted herself in the knowledge that the absence was to be temporary. Three months after the couple had sailed, however, Vic thought it necessary to remind Lina that France was no longer a competitor for their hearts—or their patriotism. "My dear sister," she began, "you don't know how glad it makes me to think that you look forward anxiously to the time of your return to this country. . . . I only hope that dear Brother and James will also continue to love this Country well enough to come back to it. As long as James is studying hard, I should think he will not become too fond of Paris. But I think that you will bring him with you. It would be too great a trial to separate yourselves again from him."[10] Unfortunately, it would become a trial Evelina would have to endure. Young James never returned to America. Like his father before him, he fell in love shortly after leaving the country of his birth, marrying the lovely nineteen-year-old, Camille Begue, on July 8, 1844.[11] As Evelina's only child, James's absence became an abiding sorrow for the lonely mother.

Sister Sophie, meanwhile, suffered a series of debilitating symptoms shortly after her marriage, including weakness, back pain, fatigue, and bleeding. There is also evidence that she had suffered a miscarriage in 1835. Anthony F. C. Wallace recorded that among Sophie's effects at the Hagley Museum was "an infant's cap labeled in her hand, 'My baby's cap Sept 25, 1835.'"[12] A couple of Victorine's letters also seem to support this tragic premise.[13]

The relationship between Victorine and her new sister-in-law Louisa was mutually affectionate—much to Henry's gratification, since Louisa was coming home with him to Eleutherian Mills. Although knowing very little about each other previously, the two women formed an enduring friendship. For example, Louisa referred to Victorine so frequently as "Darling Vicky," that one of her toddlers began to mimic it.[14] For her part, Vic confided to Sophie that

> I am more and more pleased every day with our sweet new sister. Henry has, I believe, drawn a high prize in the *lottery* of matrimony. She is lovely, gentle and refined in the highest degree. Her influence must be a happy one when exerted on our brother. He is at present perfectly delighted if one may judge from appearances; it is a different sort of happiness from the *laughing loves* of Joanna & Alexis, which I told you of last winter. This pair is much more sedate and sentimental, but they are also, it is evident, all the world to each other. . . . Louisa appears to take an interest in everything. She goes with Harry to the powder yard, to the harvest fields, and will, I do say, soon be quite a good farmer.[15]

Louisa's arrival at the family home proved to be a smooth and complementary transition for both women, as Victorine continued to oversee the operational affairs of the house, and Louisa settled down to the joys of being a young wife and soon-to-be mother. Over the next eighteen years she would present Henry with nine children. Her firstborn was a son, as was her last. Sandwiched between the two boys, Louisa gave birth to seven girls in a row. Irénée and Sophie's three sons would eventually raise twenty-four children between them. Ironically, their four daughters combined to produce but one heir—little James Bidermann du Pont—and he settled in France.

Although Victorine was a widow, her letters reveal no hint of envy toward others over their marital felicity. When Henry wed Louisa, for example, she told Sophie that "I am charmed to see it, for . . . I always enter into the feelings of those around me & love to see people happy."[16] As her cadre of nieces and nephews steadily increased over the years, the proud aunt's letters bubbled over with numerous anecdotes of the "youngies." Victorine noted each of their arrivals with her usual first-hand commentary. When little Henry Algernon was born on July 30, 1838, Vic observed his cooing parents and noted that "Louisa is charmed with her little son although she was disappointed it was not a daughter. . . . Henry appears very happy, too. I prophecy that in a few months he will be prouder of his son than he ever was of his puppies. That is not saying a little."[17] When Alexis and Joanna's first-born arrived, they named her Frances.[18] "Fanny" would become one of Victorine's most admired nieces, but at her birth the aunt remarked: "Alexis' little daughter is decidedly much more like Joanna than like her father . . . ergo she is not very pretty, but she is a sweet little baby and grows finely. She would be very well if it were not for the sharpest chin you ever beheld, which gives her an odd look."[19] Meanwhile, brother Alfred's wife Margaretta ("Meta") was nursing little Antoine Bidermann, but she frequently suffered from spells of fatigue. Victorine's pediatric advice was to reduce the period of breastfeeding: "Margaretta's health is good, but morning fatigues her so much that I hope she will wean her baby in the spring. He drinks milk like a young calf."[20]

With each addition, the interior of the old family home was beginning to get crowded, as its structural dimensions had changed little since 1803. By the time Henry Algernon turned sixteen, he had been joined by seven lively sisters. Victorine was pleased by this. Shortly after the delivery of Louisa's seventh daughter, she commented, "I am very glad it is well over & not too disappointed it is not a boy. You know I love girls."[21] Sadly, the daughter to which Victorine was referring, her brother's final girl, died of a fever at not quite seven months.[22]

Outbreaks of typhus, yellow fever, and scarlet fever were a recurring threat throughout the nineteenth century, and infant mortality rates were especially high in port cities like Wilmington. "We see so many young ones early cut off by disease in various families," observed Victorine sadly.[23] Death knocked on the door of Charles and Dorcas du Pont on February 25, 1833, claiming their two-month-old daughter. "I have bad news to tell you of little Emily," wrote a sorrowing Victorine to Eleu, "Our hopes have proved vain and the dear child expired this afternoon at five o'clock. I was in the room at the time with all the family. At dusk I left Dorcas much more composed and resigned than we could have hoped."[24] When little Emily was buried exactly twenty-four hours later, her aunt noted: "It was a sad scene as you may think. Poor Sophia [Sophie] was very much overcome at her meeting with Dorcas."[25] Five years later, little Emily was followed to the grave by her much beloved mother. Dorcas Montgomery du Pont succumbed at Louviers to a lingering illness at the age of thirty-two.

Oaks along the Brandywine

The du Pont influence in America was steadily growing. Ever since the days of Pierre Samuel's early connections with Franklin and Jefferson, the family had been making its mark on the politics of the budding country. The proximity of Irénée's powder works to the nearby hubs of Washington and Philadelphia had enhanced the du Ponts' contact with some of the country's most influential merchants and politicians. Although Alfred was beginning to show signs that he was a far better chemist than businessman, the family was nonetheless making steady inroads into the upper social strata of American life.

By the 1840s, the du Pont residences of Eleutherian Mills, Winterthur, Louviers, Hagley House, and Nemours all required the employment of several servants. These included cooks, gardeners, handymen, cleaning staff, seamstresses, washing women, and, in the case of the three brothers and their wives, nursery staff and governesses. Due to her experienced oversight of Eleutherian Mills, the family home, Victorine was usually consulted when other relations were in need of domestic

Figure 20. *Eleutherian Mills: Residence with Powder Yards*. Bass Otis, oil on canvas, c. 1840.

help. For example, because Winterthur was even more remote from Wilmington than were the du Pont homes along the Brandywine, Evelina found it difficult to entice young girls to move so far from their families to work there. Vic
loved her sister, but occasionally voiced disapproval in the way Lina related to
her staff. In one instance, after suggesting yet another young lady for her sister,
she hinted:

> There is a simplicity & honesty about the girl which are uncommon & make
> me think she would attach herself to her place & to her mistress; and after all it
> is only from love that we can be well served. I always thought that Eleu had so
> much comfort in her girls, because, she is always so kind & considerate for
> them, that they love her, & would do more for her than any other girls would
> for their employers. My own experience has taught me the same thing, and
> I find that the less I scold & find fault, the better I come on with mine. When
> we scold we excite bad feelings, which must throw a distaste upon everything.
> On the contrary, when people are happy they are disposed to do a great deal
> better.[26]

Of those who wound up working inside du Pont homes, most were young women
who performed various household duties. Young men were usually assigned as
handymen, or given outdoor tasks such as gardening, cutting firewood, or
driving.

One fellow who filled this latter role for many years was James Mullen (or "Mullen," as he was referred to by the sisters). Frequently employed as the family's carriage driver and errand-runner, Victorine appreciated his faithfulness—if not
always his driving. On one occasion when she and Eleu had been picked up at the
schoolhouse during a tremendous downpour, she quipped: "James Mullen rattled
away on the stones at such a fearful rate that our bones were almost broken &
I told Polly in French it was a pity we did not share in our conductor's belief that
the mortifications of the body were beneficial to the soul!"[27] Whenever possible,
Victorine provided opportunities for some of her poorer scholars to earn money:
"I had the school house white washed by Spencer and scrubbed by Mary Mullen
this week. So we shall have it very nice for church tomorrow."[28] Expense records
show that she paid Spencer $3.37½ cents for the whitewashing and Mary Mullen
$1.75 for the scrubbing.[29]

Victorine's nonsectarian approach at the Sunday school paralleled the manner
in which she respected the religious convictions of her household staff. "I should
never let it be supposed that we had any preferences in point of religion in our servants," she told Sophie in the summer of 1845. "I have always avoided it in my own
case."[30] Years later, however, Sophie would recall that although Victorine avoided,
"making any public profession of her faith, she continued patiently & devotion-
ally to labour for years spreading true religion thro the population of this valley
in whatever way the Lord gave her the opportunity."[31]

MADAME BAUDUY, VISITING NURSE

Eleuthera and her new husband, Dr. Tom Smith, purchased from the Du Pont company the elegant Jacob Broom house, which stood atop the rise where old Slitting Mill Road dipped directly down to the lower yards at Hagley. As the young physician set about developing a local practice, he occasionally invited his sister-in-law to accompany him. Victorine had an interest in medicine, and Tom found her knowledge (both homeopathic and conventional) amazingly robust for a laywoman. Her nursing skills were already well known in the workers' community, however, and families often sent for "dear Mrs. Bauduy" whenever a doctor was unavailable, and often in lieu of one.

Such was the case when local millworker Joel Swayne wrote Victorine saying that his wife was "very desirous" to see her: "She has been confined to her room with an exceedingly painful hand, for seven or eight weeks; the family physician has given up hopes of effecting a cure. A number of neighbors, among whom is Joel Hollingsworth have advised her to apply to M[adame] Bauduy, as possessing great skill in such complaints and as it is impossible for M[ary] Swayne to leave her room, she would feel under great obligations to you for a visit."[32] On another occasion, when an eleven-year-old Sunday school lad named Joseph McGarvey burned his hand with gunpowder, Victorine was immediately summoned. Upon arriving at the home, she deduced that the young scholar had stolen the powder from the mills and, after properly scolding him, commenced to treat him. "So you see," she pronounced to Eleu, "that I am *practicing* as usual. I hope there will be nothing to dissect in the hand or I shall have to summon my *confrere* Tom to my assistance."[33]

One of the most dreaded diseases of that time was smallpox, known locally as "cow pox" due to its early association with diseased cattle as the source of infection. Through the work of men like Bernoulli and Jenner,[34] it was learned that by making a serum from the scabs or lesions of infected calves and transferring small amounts by needle into the arm of a healthy person, an immunity to the disease could be created. Though many families remained fearful of the process, vaccination had become more widely accepted by the time Victorine came of age.

The Brandywine nurse tended to welcome such discoveries with enthusiasm, and with apparently little fear. She instructed Eleuthera to tell her husband that "I am determined to practice vaccinating with him on all the urchins of the place when he comes down, & that I beg he will come provided with a suitable quantity of *scabs* for the purpose. Vaccinating is an accomplishment I am determined to acquire & with our good old Doctor's [Didier's] lancets I shall do wonders in the neighborhood."[35] Outraged that local physicians were charging poor families the exorbitant sum of one dollar per child for vaccinations, she was determined that her Brandywine neighbors would be treated more kindly: "Tom & I . . . will proceed along more liberal principles I hope. Sophia says provided we can find anyone who will consent to be *massacred* by us."[36] Working under Dr. Smith's guidance, Victorine du Pont was very likely the first woman in the rural communities north of Wilmington to vaccinate adults and children against smallpox.

CHAPTER 14

National Recognition

Little Annie Holland was among a handful of children who entered the Brandy-wine Manufacturer's Sunday School (BMSS) at the tender age of three and a half. Enrolling on that same September day in 1830 was her neighbor, Mary Toy, who was a year older. Both girls lived in the workers' cottages of Squirrel Run, a short distance through the woods from the Sunday school. Their fathers, Patrick Holland and Daniel Toy, had immigrated from County Donegal in Ireland, and both men had secured employment at du Pont's powder mill. Although Irénée's mills had suffered ten additional explosions in the fourteen years since the Great Explosion of 1818, none had added to the total of worker deaths. On the morning of August 25, 1832, a powder man working in the upper yards observed two men leave the dust mill and then turn abruptly on their heels to rush back into the building. Seconds later the entire building exploded. The two men the worker had observed were Patrick Holland and Daniel Toy.

Eleanor Holland had just given birth to little Patrick Jr. when her husband was killed, leaving her with an infant and two young children. Annie was five and a half at the time, and although she remained in school for the next eight years, there are indications that her need for a father figure never waned. The class books show that she married a "J. Brady" in 1840, when she was but thirteen years old. Brady, who was twice Annie's age, was the nephew of the same Mr. Brady who was serving as a school master at the BMSS.[1] The uncle, however, knew more about his nephew than the latter had revealed. When the senior Brady heard that the couple had approached Father Reilly at St. Peter's in Wilmington to unite them in holy matrimony, he went to the priest and informed him that his nephew still had a wife in Ireland.[2] Reilly, who had just replaced Father Kenny upon the latter's death in March, refused to marry the couple on grounds of potential bigamy. Undaunted, the junior Brady convinced his future mother-in-law that his uncle's charges were untrue and, for reasons known only to her, Eleanor supported the younger man's claims of innocence.

Victorine was disgusted by the whole scandal and broke the news to Sophie: "Annie Holland is actually married. . . . Everyone thought the match broken, but the ill-advised couple went to Philadelphia and were married there. Everyone blames Mrs Holland, who encouraged her daughter & said she did not believe the man had another wife."[3]

The sad affair reminded Victorine of Cousin Amelia's unhappy episode with bigamist William Clifford, and it angered her that unscrupulous men could so easily escape their responsibilities in old Europe to begin afresh in young America—a sad reality, she conceded, that had become all too common.

The explosion that took the lives of workers Holland and Toy served as a grim reminder that working for Mr. du Pont in the powder business carried a significant degree of risk; the locals knew it was the major reason for the higher wages he paid. Although many Du Pont employees spent years "in the powder" without serious injury, others viewed the risk as too high and departed after a brief period of employment. Irénée's youngest son, Alexis, would later agree that "The man who follows my business should be ready at any moment to meet his God."[4] For the Brandywine superintendent, however, tragedies could potentially carry an educational value: "A few words spoken at the right time often make an impression never to be eradicated."[5] Such an example occurred during the summer of 1827, when one of her scholars suffered a fatal accident. The following Sunday Victorine addressed the sobered children of the school:

> You, no doubt, have all heard of the dreadful accident which has happened this week to one of your companions. I am certain you feel very sorry indeed for the loss of that amiable child who was here with us last Sunday, in as perfect health as any of you are at this moment. . . . There are many among you surely that are far from being so ready to die as he was. Therefore, my dear children, let this event, I beseech you, have a useful effect upon you. . . . Resolve to be better than you have been, to love God above all things, to keep his commandments and to abstain from all evil. Make good use of the time which is allotted to you and never forget "that in the midst of life we are in death."[6]

A "Flourishing" School

In a manner of speaking, it might be said that Victorine married the Sunday school. She engaged the position of superintendent with determination and order, launching a detailed system for keeping student records in 1827. Although the previous records had contained the sparest of information, Victorine now included each child's biographical background, place of residence, and the names, occupations, and religious faiths of their parents. Class books recorded each scholar's academic performance and behavior. In 1828, Victorine instituted a community-wide library, stocking it predominantly with American Sunday School Union (ASSU) publications.[7] It amassed over one hundred titles within its first two years. Two decades

Figure 21. *The Missionary's Visit.* Sophie M. du Pont sketchbook, c. 1825.

later she would declare that "Our chief & greatest help was the books of the American Sunday School Union, which by means of the libraries & rewards ['premiums'] given every 3 months to the children, proved to them an unfailing source of enjoyment and improvement."[8] Sophie later remembered that the library was established "at a time when books were very scarce & newspapers very few & dear, [which] afforded a valuable fund of reading for parents as well as scholars & its influence over all the people was felt for good."[9]

A portion of the school's interior was sketched by Sophie, probably in 1825,[10] and entitled "The Missionary's Visit." The ASSU employed agents ("missionaries") who were responsible for visiting each school within their designated territory or state. The gentleman who can be seen inspecting the contents of the window desk with Sophie is probably the ASSU agent for Northern Delaware. In perusing the annual reports from their six thousand auxiliary schools in 1830, the ASSU leadership in Philadelphia soon realized that there was much to like about the vibrant little enterprise along the Brandywine River in Delaware. An example of this interest appeared in the first issue of a newspaper the union launched in 1830, which included a glowing report of Victorine's Hagley-based school.[11]

Nine years later, Frederick A. Packard, secretary of the ASSU, authored the book *The Teacher Taught*, a 396-page volume of instruction for teachers, still regarded today as a definitive resource for students of the Sunday school movement in America. Laying out his defense for the importance of "Sunday-schools in manufacturing villages" (one of six groupings identified by the ASSU),[12] Packard highlighted this section with a singular example:

> One of the most flourishing schools of the kind under consideration was established twenty years since upon the Brandywine (Delaware). It was first suggested by a poor, illiterate, but pious weaver, and was kept in the upper story of a cotton-mill. The proprietors of the works, aware of the utility of the school, gave it every encouragement, and it was soon incorporated as "The Brandywine Manufacturer's Sunday School for the improvement of children and adults of all sects and denominations." . . . As many of the pupils had no opportunities of instruction elsewhere, writing and reading were taught in the Sunday school, while all the children received instruction in those principles of the gospel upon which the great body of Christians agree. Such catechisms were taught as the parents or friends wished, and the Scriptures were used as the great and only source of religious knowledge.[13]

The Teacher Taught became a handbook for Sunday school teachers across the nation, and the honor of being highlighted in its pages was even more impressive when one considers that the number of ASSU schools in 1830 was: "probably above 6,000, teachers 60,000, and scholars at least 400,000, [with auxiliaries] in all parts of the country."[14]

The passage of Delaware's Free School Act in 1829, providing for public schools, had little immediate impact upon rural areas. Several years passed before any of these "free schools" were established along the Brandywine. As a result, most of the local children were keenly aware (as were their parents) that apart from the little schoolhouse at du Pont's mill, access to a proper education was all but closed to them.

During the BMSS's peak years (1827–1845), enrollment numbers exceeded two hundred in every year but two.[15] Victorine's records for 1835 cite an average attendance of 140 to 170 children every single Sunday. The remarkable appearance of so many young people, several of whom were surrendering their only day off from work, is a vivid example of their desire to learn. "Some of the children live nearly two miles from the school," observed Victorine in 1835, "but it does not prevent them from coming very regularly all the rest of the year."[16]

Another factor that impressed the ASSU was the rate of community participation at the Brandywine schoolhouse. When they requested that their auxiliaries describe their recruitment strategies, Victorine could reply as early as 1830 that "There is no need of employing any means of increasing the number of our scholars. All the children in the neighborhood attend the school & are much attached to it. The teachers visit them frequently to give them advice & to converse with their parents about them."[17] Her reply not only points to the popularity of the school, which experienced 100 percent attendance, but also provides an example of the social network that often prevailed in isolated manufacturing communities. By visiting the homes of her scholars, Victorine became acquainted with every member of their hardworking families and gained a perspective into their lives that even their employers seldom possessed.

The school's curriculum remained virtually unchanged throughout its first forty years. In the early 1830s, Victorine described her schedule as:

1st: Prayer and a chapter of the Bible read at the opening of the school.

2nd: Writing—on Slates & the best scholars in copy books.

3rd: Reading—two chapters in the old or new Testament, with questioning by the Teachers on the contents.

4th: Recitation—Union Questions—Catechisms and Hymns.

5th: Spelling.

6th: School is closed with Prayer and another Chapter is read.[18]

The influence of the Christian religion in this curriculum is self-evident. Thomas Gaw, a missionary for the ASSU, reported that even the "writing" class required the children to "copy a tract, or their scripture lesson for the day."[19] Literacy goals were considered met when a student could read "indifferently" out of both the old and new testaments. Of the four primary subjects listed, the most overtly religious content was supplied during the session described as "Recitation." In this class, a nondenominational Christianity was taught; all children received the same Bible lesson of the day, which was conveyed at the comprehension level for each class.

There is scant evidence that arithmetic (sometimes referred to as "ciphering")[20] was included in the curriculum. Since teaching literacy (reading, writing, and spelling) and the basic tenets of Christianity were the school's primary goals, it appears that the limited four-hour period, once a week, did not include mathematics. "Besides regular tuition in reading & writing, children of every denomination receive instructions in those principles of the gospel about which all Christians agree," explained Victorine in 1830.[21] By the mid-1850s, Vic recalled that, in the school's earliest days, under Siddall and Daniels, "Reading and writing were taught, and religious instruction imparted from the Bible alone, in addition to which each child was to learn the catechism named by its parents. . . . It has continued during thirty seven years, with very little deviation from its original plan."[22]

For years, the school maintained a ratio wherein one in four students belonged to the Roman Catholic faith, with the remaining three-quarters consisting of various Protestant denominations. Although herself Protestant, Victorine had a good working relationship with Rev. Patrick Kenny,[23] the Catholic priest who had presided over her wedding to Ferdinand in 1813. "Mister Kenny," as she referred to him, had dedicated St. Peter's, Wilmington's first Roman Catholic church, on September 12, 1818. The building had been designed by her father-in-law, Peter Bauduy. (There were some at the time who speculated on how much influence the architect had exerted over the choice of that particular saint's name.) Victor's wife Gabrielle, a lifelong Catholic, often invited Father Kenny to Louviers. It had been in their parlor in 1828 that the good priest celebrated "the first Mass held in the neighborhood of the Brandywine Banks."[24] Their son, Charles Irénée, continued to support the diocese and, following Kenny's death in 1840, became the largest individual contributor to the construction of St. Joseph's on the Brandywine, the neighborhood's first Catholic church.

Victorine reported to the ASSU that "A great improvement is observable in the children of this neighborhood; they are generally fond of reading and eager to avail themselves of every opportunity of obtaining information. Many of them who work in manufactories, always keep their Testaments & hymn books open near them, and every minute that can be spared from their work is devoted to their lessons. In this way they commit from 20 to 30 verses of Scripture to memory every week."[25] If even the smaller number was attained, it would mean that nearly every child could, by year's end, have memorized over one thousand Bible verses. In this aspect, the BMSS was very much like other such schools across the country. Anne Boylan states that "All Sunday schools provided an education centered on Christian belief, the founders of the evangelical schools placed paramount emphasis on the religious aspects of teaching. . . . For them, teaching reading and writing was only a means to an end, not an end in itself. That greater end [was] an evangelical interpretation of the Bible."[26] When considering Alexis de Tocqueville's observation in 1835 that "there is no country in the whole world in which the Christian religion retains a greater influence over the souls of men than in America,"[27] one must certainly include the weekly impact that thousands of Sunday schools across the nation were making upon the minds and hearts of these young citizens.

Victorine's class books, which meticulously recorded every child's progress, were organized under the headings of "Conduct, Writing, Reading, Spelling, and Recitations."[28] Her philosophy had always been to engage the minds of her scholars by fueling their excitement for learning, a motivational style both her father and grandfather had instilled in her. She hinted at this in an 1832 report to the ASSU:

> The mode of instruction which we prefer is by conversation with the class. The teacher should seize every opportunity of impressing important truths on the minds of his pupils, whether from the lesson they have been reciting . . . or any event that has just occurred from which a moral may be drawn. A few words spoken at the right time often make an impression never to be eradicated. We do not require our scholars to commit long lessons to memory. We prefer that they should learn short lessons every week and understand them thoroughly.[29]

A tool Victorine found particularly useful for this purpose was the *Union Questions*, a series of small booklets published by the ASSU that contained direct passages from the Bible, "suited to compel attention to every minute point, to excite and draw forth thought and to awaken the moral sensibility of the heart."[30] The *Union Questions* remained at the heart of the Recitation class until the 1850s.

On January 16, 1831, Victorine recorded that "our school was closed for the first time since fifteen years, owing to the great depth of snow which rendered the roads impassable."[31] Twenty years later, she would report that only one additional Sunday had been denied an opening—creating an astonishing record of only two school

Figure 22. *The Brandywine Manufacturer's Sunday School today.* Photograph by the author.

closings in forty-six consecutive years.[32] When it is remembered that the BMSS operated every Sunday of the year, this accomplishment is particularly noteworthy. Victorine's love for the children and her conviction that the school was a noble endeavor, were strong motivations for her to keep the doors open. Inspired in her youth by the altruistic example of Sarah Ralston, it was now she who was inspiring others. Although she would not have thought of herself in those terms, little else could explain why such a long train of volunteer teachers would follow her leadership for so many years, all without remuneration.

As the neighborhood's religious and educational hub, the Sunday school often provided the first point of social contact for those children who lived at some distance from each other. Over time, the BMSS class books would note the marriages of several former scholars. "There are grand news in the matrimonial line my dear," confided Vic to Eleu, "two marriages in less than a week, and both secret ones too, without leave of friends on either side! . . . One is the marriage of David Connell to Mrs. Belin's girl Maryanne—to the great vexation of the Connells who think him much too young. The other you had long anticipated, Mullen & Mary Green. This was also done without the knowledge of her family, so all the Greens—great and little—are furious!"[33] Playing upon the ASSU's name, Vic referred to these marriages as "Sunday School Unions."[34]

Due to the closeness of the tight-knit mill community, Victorine and her sisters were familiar with most of its residents. Among her earliest students were the

Lowery children, John and Mary, who enrolled in 1823, the same year she had assumed the superintendency. After graduating, John found employment as a clerk in Wilmington, and Victorine made a point of visiting him one day. "I went to Mr Corke's store to see John Lowery who knew me at once, & was delighted to see me. He had tears in his eyes all the time he spoke to me of old times. I was quite touched to see it."[35] His sister Mary wed James Patchell in August of 1833, and John followed the newlyweds to New York, where he found employment. But the siblings never forgot their teacher. Each year, they mailed Victorine a pair of handsomely bound Bibles to be used as premiums (rewards) for the best male and female scholars. For nearly thirty years, it was their way of expressing gratitude for the love and education they had received at the old schoolhouse.

CHAPTER 15

Legacies and Conflicts

When the United States annexed Texas in 1845, it precipitated a war with Mexico that raged from 1846 to early 1848. Sharing their family's Whig sentiments, the du Pont sisters disapproved of President Polk's expansionist decision to send troops to occupy the territory between the Nueces and Rio Grande rivers, displacing, as Sophie put it, "Mexicans residing quietly in their own possessions."[1] In a letter to Cousin Frank in 1847, Victorine announced that "We have heard today of another victory won by General Scott over the Mexicans. If it could bring us peace I should rejoice, but if it only induces our government to pursue the conquest of Mexico, all right-minded people ought to regret it. I have lost all my early enthusiasm for military glory, and I only feel how dreadful it is to have those near & dear to us exposed to the dangers of war. I need not tell you how sincerely I sympathize with poor Julia in her affliction."[2] Cousin Julia was Frank's sister, and the "affliction" was the death of her first-born son, Thomas Shubrick, at the battle of Vera Cruz six weeks earlier.[3]

The Mexican-American War became a fiery theater in which the courage and tactical abilities of Commander Samuel Francis Du Pont were put on full display. Frank's command of the USS *Cyane* off the Pacific Coast led to the defeat of over two dozen warships and control of the Gulf of California. In early 1848, he was given command over the naval blockade of California and, in October, the distinguished but weary husband returned home to a relieved Sophie. Three weeks later, the du Pont sisters celebrated the Whigs' return to power with the election of "Old Rough and Ready," General Zachary Taylor, as president.

Along the Brandywine, it was not the health of the military that was the sisters' primary concern, but that of Eleuthera's husband, Dr. Tom Smith. He had been experiencing heart palpitations, tired easily, and found himself out of breath while making his rounds. As a result, he prescribed a medicinal regimen for himself that had such good effect that he and Eleu made plans to spend a sabbatical year in Europe, visiting as many countries as time would allow. On Sunday, April 26, 1846, Eleu said goodbye to her class of weeping scholars. As Vic described the tearful event to Sophie, she lamented, "We had a very sad time after school. All Eleuthera's girls cried when she told them goodbye. They even sobbed, & I saw several girls in the second and third class crying also. Dear Eleu, she well deserves to be loved!"[4] The Smiths departed a week later, arriving in England by the middle of May. After spending a few days sightseeing in London, they traversed the rolling English countryside, went up into Scotland, and later crossed the Irish Sea to Dublin.

The sisters exchanged several lengthy letters during the absence. "It will be so painful not to see you," moaned Vic, "and to think how very distant you are!"[5] Although she never felt sufficiently inclined to sail abroad herself, Victorine was immensely curious to hear firsthand accounts of the places Eleu and Tom visited. When she received news that the Smiths had been to Loch Katrine in Scotland, the setting for Sir Walter Scott's *Lady of the Lake*, she was unable to contain her excitement: "I could scarcely believe I was not dreaming and that you were actually in the midst of the scenery W. Scott describes in the Lady of the Lake! . . . So graphic are your descriptions, it seems almost as if I had visited the different places myself!"[6]

Interestingly, it was something Victorine had read about a Scottish clan that had prompted her to give an assignment to Eleu before departing. She desired her sister to attempt the retrieval of their grandfather's writings—if, indeed, they still existed. These papers had remained in the possession of Pierre Samuel's second wife, Françoise Robin Poivre. After Pierre's death, his widow had moved into the home of her daughter, Madame de Pusy, faithfully carting her husband's documents along with her. Victorine viewed Eleuthera's trip to Europe as a rare opportunity to recover them. Although de Pusy had died the previous year, Victorine hoped that contact with her relations might yield results:

> When you are in Paris, don't forget if you see any of the Pusy family to inquire about grand papa's papers and letters. I wish we could have them, and it would be so good an opportunity if they could be put under your care. What put me in mind of it is a most interesting article I read in the Quarterly with Sarah [Gilpin] about the Lyndsays [*sic*] of Scotland,[7] and although our family is not so illustrious, still to ourselves, it would be very interesting to have everything relating to our grandfather's history if we could get it.[8]

Victorine recalled how frequently her grandfather had voiced anxiety over his papers, having been forced to leave them behind when Napoleon returned from Elba. Fearful of their loss, he had suggested that Françoise have his documents bound like books, so that vindictive agents from Napoleon's court might not easily discover them.

Victorine, in harmony with the ancestral *mentalité* of her fathers, felt an urgency to recover Pierre's works. The article she had read of the Scottish Lindsay clan put in mind the thought that Irénée's children should begin to gather these documents into one secure depository, if for no other reason than the family's historical interest. She knew that her grandfather had written extensively on a wide variety of topics, and that his life had intersected with prominent individuals on both sides

of the Atlantic. The granddaughter's sense of urgency suggests a budding awareness that the family's history (though not meriting the status of a famous Scottish
clan) could, perhaps, be morphing into something larger than the isolated tale of
a moderately successful family of French immigrants.

Compounding the fear that the papers might already be lost, stood the possibility that the de Pusy family might deny their release. When Bureaux de Pusy died
in 1806, the shares he owned in Irénée's company had passed to his wife, Julienne
de Pusy. Stirred up by Peter Bauduy's false reports of alleged mismanagement, and
fearful of losing any pecuniary benefits from the dividends, she had commenced
a long and perennial series of demands for additional payments from her step-
brother. After Irénée's death, Alfred and Henry angrily remembered the anguish
her frequent requests had caused their father and felt she had received far more
from the original investment than she deserved. Both were glad when the final dis-
position of her shares had been settled under Bidermann's effective interim as
president.

Not sharing the same levels of bitterness toward Madame de Pusy as their
brothers, the sisters had maintained an ongoing, if infrequent, correspondence with
her. "Though a very fine woman," Eleuthera was later to recall, "[She] was of a quick
and impulsive character. And Mr Peter Bauduy's insinuating manners had
already . . . acquired much influence over her."[9] After Julienne's death the previous year, no guarantees existed that her daughter Sara would be amenable to surrendering Pierre Samuel's papers. But whatever the previous interactions between
her mother and Irénée may have been, Sara de Pusy did not begrudge the request
of his daughters. She was, in fact, of a mind that the papers belonged more rightfully
to them than to her. After a delightful afternoon spent in the parlor of her Parisian
home, sharing old memories, Sara instructed her servants to prepare the documents for transport. Thus it was, that in April of 1847, thirty years after the death of
du Pont de Nemours, Eleuthera returned home triumphant—with all of his writings
safely ensconced in her luggage.

It is difficult to overstate the importance of this recovery. Elizabeth Fox-
Genovese, in her introduction to Pierre's autobiography, notes that "The subsequent history of du Pont's manuscripts and papers constitutes a detective story in
its own right. Only in 1847 did Irénée's daughter, Eleuthera du Pont Smith, retrieve
the papers from the heirs of Françoise Poivre du Pont. She brought the core of the
present collection back from France."[10] Unknown to most is the role that Victorine du Pont played in securing those manuscripts. Had she not been cognizant of
her grandfather's works and launched the plan to have Eleu retrieve them, much
of what we know today about the du Pont saga may have been lost to history.

By the time Tom and Eleu returned to Delaware, they had visited much of
Europe, including the British Isles, Italy, Belgium, Holland, and Switzerland. The
majority of their time, however, was spent in France, where they visited their son
James and his wife Camille in Brignon, and du Pont de Nemours's former estate
at Bois-des-Fossés. When reading of their visit to the old family home, Victorine
excitedly remarked, "I was so touched by all the memorials of our dear parents, &

it so revived all my own early impressions of that first abode of my childhood! How very kind it was in Tom to take a sketch of the house. I exclaimed aloud with joy when I came to that part of the letter."[11] The Smith's sabbatical had proven therapeutic for the doctor. Tom returned home tanned and healthy, and resumed his practice with renewed energy.

Schism

Victorine and Sophie considered St. Andrews Church their Wilmington congregation of choice, where presided Rev. Alfred Lee, the first Episcopal bishop for the Diocese of Delaware.[12] Responsibilities at the Brandywine Manufacturer's Sunday School (BMSS) required the sisters to cover for each other if either wished to make the four-mile trek to the city for services, but more often than not, they attended afternoon services at the schoolhouse. Clergymen who agreed to conduct worship services at the schoolhouse were paid one dollar per Sunday.[13] The longest serving of these ministers had been Rev. Thomas Love, the pastor of two Presbyterian congregations.[14] Recruited by Victorine the first year she became superintendent, he faithfully administered this task until 1851. When a complaint was later made to Bishop Lee that a Presbyterian was still teaching at the schoolhouse, Victorine quickly retorted: "The school is an incorporated Union school, & that the house where we hold service belongs to it, & that the Presbyterian clergyman preached here before any others & had done so for 30 years."[15] Needless to say, Rev. Love kept his position in the rotation. Since 1838, two of the Sunday rotations there had been filled by Dr. John McCullough, the rector of Trinity Episcopal Church, making that local Brandywine option more amenable to the growing number of Episcopalian du Ponts for their home church.

The first three churches to be built in the Brandywine neighborhood (one Roman Catholic, one Methodist, and one Presbyterian) were established in the decade between 1841 and 1851. As each one launched their own Sunday schools, most of their members withdrew their children from the BMSS. The exodus of these denominations resulted in an Episcopalian majority at the old schoolhouse, leading to speculations that a church of that ilk might soon follow. When Dr. McCullough's health forced him to step down as rector of Trinity in the spring of 1847, the ailing minister managed to keep his final commitment to his Brandywine congregation on Sunday, March 21. Julia du Pont's husband, Irvine Shubrick, organized a collection for the faithful pastor, who was retiring with little means to support himself. "More than $200 have been collected," rejoiced Victorine.[16]

Several names were bandied about as possible candidates to replace Dr. McCullough at Trinity, including that of niece Ella's brother-in-law, Rev. Charles Breck. Victorine hoped that a Rev. Bronson would be chosen, partly because his wife was a close friend of Joanna's: "I am sure his influence over Alexis would be good, thrown together as they would by the intimacy of their wives."[17] In the end, however, Bishop Lee accepted the candidacy of one Rev. Edwin M. Van Deusen, installing him as the new rector of Trinity in late November 1847.

It was a decision the evangelical bishop would come to regret when his appointee, Van Deusen, proved to be an avid supporter of a controversial new movement within the Anglican Church. The "Oxford Movement," a term used to describe this new influence, was the essential cause of the rift. A small group of Church of England members (meeting at Oxford University) felt that the influence of Puritan Reformers had rendered the Church too "plain" and were guilty of throwing away too much of its ecclesiasticism. As a result, they advocated for the return of several Roman Catholic rituals to Anglicanism. Disseminating their "high church" views in pamphlet form, they were dubbed "Tractarians" by their opponents, who viewed them as attempting a syncretistic attack on their faith.

This debate landed in America with some force in the 1840s and 1850s, pitting many Episcopalians against one another—including the du Ponts. Victorine, Sophie, and Captain Samuel Francis Du Pont favored the former evangelical practices, aligning themselves with the "low church" beliefs of Bishop Lee and Trinity's Dr. McCullough. However, Dr. Tom Smith, his wife Eleuthera, and his sister Joanna, would eventually come under the Oxford influence.

In the spring of 1848, the arrival of another stranger to the valley would sharpen the theological divide between the du Ponts. Rev. Samuel Crawford Brincklé, an Episcopalian minister, preached his first sermon at the little schoolhouse on May 28. Recording the event in his new diary, he wrote: "Bishop Lee made an appointment for me to preach at Du Pont's school house this afternoon at 3½ o' clock. So accordingly I preached for the first time to a tolerable congregation. House large. Much pleased with what I saw. Trust that God may make me the instrument of good here."[18]

Born in Dover, Delaware, in 1796, Brincklé graduated from Princeton in 1815, later enrolling as a divinity student under the tutelage of Bishop William White of Philadelphia.[19] Following his ordination, he served Pennsylvania churches for the next thirty years. In 1848, he established a connection with the Protestant Episcopal Church of Delaware, and Bishop Lee agreed to sanction him as a "missionary" of the diocese. His duties were to assist Lee at St. Andrews in Wilmington, and to provide pastoral assistance to churches throughout New Castle County. One of his first assignments was to cover the Episcopal vacancy in the rotation at the BMSS. After a gratifying meeting with Mrs. Victorine Bauduy, to whom he submitted his request to conduct services, he not only received the coverage of Dr. McCullough's two Sundays per month but was also granted an additional week by the forward-looking superintendent. The veteran Presbyterian pastor Rev. Love still had one Sunday a month.

Brincklé believed from the outset that he was embarking upon a church-planting mission. So convinced was he of the hand of Providence upon his efforts, that he commenced a journal to record his progress. Due to his frequent encounters with members of the du Pont family, his diary opens a new window into the life of Victorine du Pont at a time when her Christian faith had largely matured. As a layperson, her theological understanding was fairly robust; she studied the Bible frequently and read numerous religious articles, books, and sermons. Spending hours at her desk, she copied extensive selections of works by theologians such as Adam Clarke,[20] whose commentaries were popular in her day.

Rev. Brincklé brought onsite pastoral care to the rural mill valley, something that neither Victorine nor her sisters had yet to experience in any consistent fashion. The Catholic priest, Rev. Kenny, had filled this role for Aunt Gabrielle in his day, but here now was someone who could make an ongoing contribution to the evangelical du Ponts. Vic was encouraged by what his presence meant for the community. She knew that the religious views of a woman—be she du Pont or not—carried little weight in the minds of her male neighbors. In the personage of Mr. Brincklé, however, was the presence of an ordained minister with ecclesiastical experience and authority. Her enthusiasm was evident, for example, when recounting one of his sermons, in which she heard him challenge the fathers to lead family worship times in their homes: "Both Eleu & I were delighted to hear all he said on the subject."[21]

In "good Mr. B,"[22] Victorine saw a man of integrity, whose life clearly demonstrated the sincerity of his devotion: "I admire his straight forward simplicity of character more than I can tell you. I never knew anyone, who seemed so determined to do what he thought right and leave the event in God's hands. It is a beautiful example; I hope I shall profit by it."[23] For the minister's part, he found in Victorine an early supporter of his ministry and a key ally within the tight-knit du Pont family, whose good graces would be necessary in any effort to plant a church in their neighborhood. He wasted little time getting to work. On July 18, 1849, Brincklé baptized five of Henry and Louisa's six children (little Victorine Elizabeth, an infant of but four months, was not included). The minister recalled that Henry was

> present and standing up, though the mother and Mrs. Bauduy acted as sponsors. Mrs. B[auduy] regretted very much that the education of her brother had been at West Point at a time when the religious influence was of the worst kind, and that it was really ignorance in him. I told her there was great ground of hope in the examples he had about him. . . . She took my hand, & expressed the satisfaction I had given them. Her eyes filled with tears. I cannot but think that God will bless my labors here, tho' as yet there are no visible fruits. O if He would but give me souls for my hire![24]

The "tolerable congregation" Brincklé had observed on his first visit convinced him that the number of people in the neighborhood was sufficient to plant a church, but two major hurdles confronted him. The first was that the operational times of the BMSS were fixed squarely in the pre-noon hours of Sunday morning—the traditional slot for worship services. The minister felt that being forced to hold his services in the afternoon to work around the school hindered his attendance numbers. "I am convinced, if our services were in the morning instead of afternoon they would be much better attended. There are some difficulties in the way of this at present, which in His own good time I trust God will remove. The chief is Mrs. B.'s [Sunday school] which has been conducted about 30 years, occupying all the forenoon. Out of this school has grown the present effort."[25] The irony of Brincklé's dilemma, as he duly acknowledged, was that his present congregation existed because the school had predated *him*. Victorine's early championing of ministerial services at the BMSS had, in fact, gathered the nucleus for every one of the four denominational churches along the Brandywine.[26]

The minister's second obstacle was finding a suitable piece of land upon which to erect a building. Running into each other in Philadelphia one Friday afternoon, he and Victorine shared their mutual enthusiasm for the establishment of a new church. "I spoke of my favorite site," recorded the minister, "contiguous to their family burial ground—of its picturesque beauty."[27] Victorine made no comment, but she could not have forgotten how adamantly her brother Alfred had refused the Catholics when they, seven years previously, had requested to build their church on du Pont land. However, Mrs. Bauduy was not the minister's only ally. Sophie and her respected husband, Commander Samuel Francis Du Pont, were enthusiastic about the church-building effort, as were Dr. and Mrs. Tom Smith, Henry's wife Louisa, and Alexis's wife Joanna. Initially, all three of Irénée's sons were supportive of the idea, and even suggested various sites to build the church. None of which, of course, were on du Pont property.

Despite the two obstacles, attendance for worship services in the afternoons was steadily increasing, and by 1849, numbered one hundred persons. On the first Sunday afternoon of September, Victorine made an unexpected suggestion to Rev. Brincklé that changed the minister's perspective in terms of waiting to incorporate. He noted that "[Mrs. Bauduy] spoke of organizing a church [and] suggested whether it would not be best to do it at once without waiting for a building other than the one we have."[28] The suggestion to establish a church was put before the congregation that very afternoon and unanimously approved.

Vic said she would inform Dr. Tom Smith of the decision and, although Brincklé did not object, doubt drifted across his mind. Over the course of the past year, Victorine's brother-in-law had become increasingly influenced by Van Deusen's high church views. Ever since Tom's recent appointment as head vestryman at Trinity, his desire to help the Brandywine church had waned in proportion to his involvement in Wilmington. "I am constrained to fear his interest has very much declined," observed Brincklé, "that being now warden of Trinity Church and in communication with Mr. [Van Deusen], he has been brought up to a pitch of churchmanship not favorable to our interests here."[29] As Trinity's rector, Van Deusen had been resolute in his opposition to the new Episcopal church just four miles north of his own, especially since it was established by Rev. Brincklé, whose low church positions did not sit well with him. Trinity's rector never acknowledged that Brincklé's role in the diocese had carried any genuine authority. "Mr. Van Deusen," wrote Brincklé, "denied that I had any missionary station [and] said I was preaching in parts of two parishes, his own & the Bishop's."[30]

Nevertheless, plans to rearrange the schoolhouse to more adequately serve the new church's long-term purposes went ahead. Victorine supported the idea of adding a vestry room to the school building so that Mr. Brincklé could have a dedicated place to pray and make his Sunday preparations. When her brother-in-law, Dr. Smith, heard about the plans to use the schoolhouse as a worship location, he replied, "Well, you may do as you please, but I can tell you the ordinances cannot be administered."[31] The "ordinances" consisted of the authority to administer the Lord's Supper (communion) and to conduct baptisms. Under Van Deusen's influence, Tom had become convinced that unless the new church was sanctioned by majority vote at a diocesan convention, it could not function as a church with full ecclesiastical privileges.

For Victorine, the most unsettling aspect of the matter was the growing wedge these differences were beginning to create between family members. Eleuthera, gentle soul that she was, felt increasingly uncomfortable whenever these "church discussions" arose, but she, like her husband and her sister-in-law Joanna, had also been influenced by Van Deusen's Tractarian views. Victorine's first impression of Mr. Van Deusen had not been positive. When Trinity's pastor had been urged by some of his friends to take a turn preaching at the "Du Pont school," he had reluctantly agreed. But upon his arrival, he had not been pleased with the rustic arrangements. "I learned," said Brincklé later, "that prior to my coming, [Mr. Van Deusen] had preached but once in our school-house, & that he objected to the position of the pulpit, saying he would never preach there again till its position was changed. Mrs. Bauduy took him at his word, & never asked him again."[32]

Despite Van Deusen's chronic opposition, support for an Episcopal church along the Brandywine continued to gather strength. When the aging Presbyterian minister Thomas Love decided to retire from the rotation after twenty-eight years of service, Brincklé observed: "This will obviate a difficulty in the way of our making a church of this place. This Providence seems to be gradually preparing a way for us."[33] Mr. Love's departure meant that the Episcopalians were now in full possession of the rotations, thereby ensuring that the building would be available every Sunday afternoon for the sole use of their congregation.

Among those supporting Brincklé's position were Sophie and Frank. The naval man's zeal was beginning to rival his wife's and even extended to his life at sea, where he initiated worship services and Bible studies aboard the ships he commanded. When a door-to-door survey was taken in June of 1851 to determine the level of neighborhood interest in a church, Sophie reported that the list was "signed by near 70 people, all Episcopalians."[34] Her husband added that he fully expected "a large body of people, farmers & others" to join them as well.[35] The next step was to appoint vestrymen to share the leadership. Among those selected were Frank; Henry Hedrick Belin, the Du Pont Company's chief accountant; John Brincklé, Samuel's brother; and Andrew Armstrong, whose six daughters had all been educated at the BMSS and of whom three still continued as teachers. All that now remained was to provide an official name for the church. Rev. Brincklé suggested that naming privileges should be extended to the three du Pont sisters in appreciation for their work. The ladies were honored by the offer, and it was to the youngest that inspiration came first. In her diary, Sophie recalled, "The name that had first suggested itself to my heart and mind, Christ Church, was approved by the majority of those consulted, and given to the Parish."[36]

The pioneers were ready to present their church to the diocese for a vote. Its next convention was to be held in May in Newark, Delaware, and although Captain Frank had to be away in Washington, Bishop Lee felt the time was still ripe to submit the proposal to the assembly. Despite Mr. Van Deusen's strong objections and procedural impediments, which greatly prolonged the debate, the proposal was finally accepted by the majority of officers present. Dr. Smith declined to cast a vote by withholding his name. On Thursday, May 29, 1851, Christ Church Christiana Hundred[37] became the newest member of the Protestant Episcopal Diocese of Delaware. A year later, Van Deusen resigned his post in Wilmington and took an assignment in Pittsburgh.

Although Christ Church was now a joyous reality, it had come at a price. Personal feelings had been hurt and divisions highlighted. Victorine, now fifty-nine, felt badly about the awkward tensions it had created between some of the family's members, and hoped the rift wouldn't get worse. She would be disappointed.

CHAPTER 16

Loss and Restoration

Alfred and Meta hosted the wedding of their eldest child, Victorine Elizabeth du Pont, on January 18, 1849. "Big Vic" stood tearfully by as the woman she had tutored since the age of two gave her hand to young Peter Kemble.[1] Two weeks later, the young bride traded the Brandywine for Brooklyn, where her husband resumed the helm of the iron foundry his father had established. When Mrs. Kemble gave birth to the first of her five children in September of the following year, she invited her Aunt Vic to New York to attend little William's christening. The older woman did not hesitate to make the trip and was humbled to learn that the couple had surrendered their first-floor bedroom so that she would not have to mount the stairs to the third floor. Of the numerous relations she had instructed over the years, Little Vic had always been her aunt's favorite. Even after the younger woman moved to New York City, the two Victorines maintained their close relationship through visits and letters.

Six weeks after Little Vic's departure to Brooklyn, her namesake replacement arrived. On March 1, 1849, Henry and Louisa added *their* Victorine Elizabeth to the crowded family home. Big Vic told Sophie that "Louisa . . . has named the youngie *Victorine*. She says Henry would have liked to call her Sophia, but that as there are already two in the family, they concluded it would be better not to have so many alike, and this little one will only take over niece Vic's place. I am very much pleased that she is called after me, for it always creates an additional interest in the child."[2]

By midcentury, only Uncle Charles had possession of a single-occupant room at Eleutherian Mills. In addition to Henry's large family, the cramped quarters were shared with Sarah, the cook, and Mrs. Waterman, the head housekeeper. Louisa's eldest two daughters shared Aunt Vic's room. While Sophie was visiting friends in Alexandria, Vic reported: "Lina and Ellen both sleep in my room now. I do not find them at all annoying for they go as soon as they are up into the nursery to get dressed and I can be alone to bathe &c until breakfast. Little [Louisa], who is chattering at my side, wishes me to tell aunt Sophy she must come back from *Alexander* as she wants to see her!"[3]

Figure 23. *Victorine Elizabeth (du Pont) Kemble with one of her children.* Unknown photographer, photographic print, 1852.

In the spring of 1850, Louisa discovered that she was expecting her seventh child. Although Henry was fully aware of the need to expand the family home, his mind was on more pressing matters. The company was now half a million dollars in debt—an astounding figure for the middle of the nineteenth century. By autumn, the three brothers agreed that Alfred would step aside and allow Henry to take the helm, a decision that proved to be one of the most advantageous the company would ever make. For the next forty years, Irénée's second son would put the company on a profit-making trajectory from which it would never look back. On the very day his brothers handed him the leadership of the company, his wife handed him his seventh child—little Sophie Madeleine—born on January 1, 1851.

———

Although renovations to alleviate the space issues at Eleutherian Mills had stalled, two major projects were underway at the schoolhouse to accommodate the new church. The first was the installation of a large wood-and-coal furnace, requiring a partial cellar to be dug and the entire floor to be raised eighteen inches. The second was the addition of a vestry to the east side of the building, a fieldstone structure measuring fourteen by sixteen feet.[4] Access to the new addition was to be through the east window which was made into a doorway. Several other improvements were made in 1851,[5] including the installation of two mahogany chairs to be positioned in the chancel area for Rev. Brincklé and his head vestryman. The four du

Pont daughters had donated these in honor of their mother, who had brought them to America on the *American Eagle* in 1799.

On August 17, 1851, a sort of "quasi-consecration" took place, which was presided over by Bishop Alfred Lee. The event was attended by several local clergymen, including Rev. Van Deusen, "notwithstanding his opposition," noted Brincklé.[6] Although defeated in his attempt to bring the Brandywine church under his jurisdiction, Van Deusen still had considerable influence in the community. In April, half a dozen girls from Sophie's class were confirmed at his Trinity Church, along with twenty-five-year-old Williamina Cavender, a former Brandywine Manufacturer's Sunday School (BMSS) scholar. The news stung Rev. Brincklé, who had formerly baptized "Willie": "I confess I heard it with concern," he acknowledged.[7] Sophie expressed a similar concern for the newly confirmed girls and wrote them separately to encourage them. Since confirmation was considered a public avowal of one's faith, she wished to "express my solicitude for your stability and growth in grace, by sending you a few simple suggestions. 1st—Cherish a spirit of affectionate gratitude to God . . . for his grace in awakening your soul to a sense of the importance of eternal things, and inspiring you with willingness to follow Christ. . . . 2nd—Enter into the inestimable privileges of your new relationship. The Scripture exhorts us to 'walk worthy of God, who hath called us to his kingdom and glory.'"[8]

While Sophie's words demonstrate how far the youngest sister had progressed in her faith, the same could not be said of her youngest brother. When under Victorine's tutelage as a boy,[9] Alexis had shown an early receptivity to the principles of Christianity that was later reinforced when he attended Yale University between 1830 and 1834. During those years, this interest grew through his acquaintance with Joanna Smith, spending social weekends at the Philadelphia home of her devout family, and attending St. Peter's Episcopal Church with them on Sundays. By his eighteenth birthday, however, Alexis had become "indifferent" to matters of religion.[10] In spite of his marriage to the pious Joanna, he continued to show little interest in spiritual things. Although Hagley House, where he and Joanna lived, was perched just seventy yards above the Sunday school, his attendance at Rev. Brincklé's services was sporadic at best. Alexis thought the minister a good preacher, but he was more interested in the music. When his wife donated a melodeon to Christ Church, Brincklé's daughters Anna and Margaret practiced the new instrument at Hagley House with thirteen-year-old Fanny du Pont. On one such evening, when the minister arrived to accompany his girls home, Alexis mentioned an interest in the men's choir. Brincklé invited him to practice with them. "Should this be the means of leading him to attend church," he noted in his diary, "and to such a knowledge of the truth as may lead him to the Saviour, it will indeed be a matter of heartfelt joy."[11]

"This Treacherous Month"

January 21, 1852, probably began like most wintry evenings in the parlors of the du Pont homes.[12] At Eleutherian Mills, Victorine could be found consulting with

Mrs. Waterman over supplies for the coming weekend, while across the creek at Upper Louviers, Sophie would be preparing lessons for the girls of the fourth class. At Jacob Broom's old house, Tom and Eleuthera Smith were seated near the crackling warmth of their parlor fireplace. Whether it was from the heat of the room, or some other source, Dr. Smith began to feel ill, and asked his wife to bring him a mixture of the medicine he requested. When Eleu returned, Tom drank the mixture but knew immediately that the taste was wrong. Recognizing its source, he rushed to the cabinet for an emetic and took several large gulps. In very small dosages, aconite was used to treat ailments like anxiety, high fevers, severe colds, and headaches, and was a common passenger in a doctor's bag. In higher dosages, however, aconite was almost always fatal. Known by such appellations as "Monkshood," "Wolf's Bane," and "Devil's Helmet," immigrants from England had long called it the "Queen of Poisons." Dr. Bush was immediately summoned and, after a few agonizing hours, Tom's agitation suddenly quieted. Hope stirred briefly— but in vain. Dr. Thomas Mackie Smith slipped into unconsciousness and died later that same evening.

Eleuthera went into shock. To have a tragedy of such magnitude befall the gentlest of the du Pont sisters alarmed everyone. Victorine remained by her sister's side and immediately set up temporary quarters in her home. Eleu never left the house and, like her sister thirty-eight years before, ate little, wept much, and stared sightlessly into the long black hours of despair. By the end of the first week, Victorine spoke to Eleuthera about moving in permanently. The younger sister wept in assent—she wanted her mother with her.

Leaving Eleutherian Mills, the home Victorine had lived in for nearly fifty years, was not going to be easy. She had run its affairs since before her mother's death and wanted to ensure a smooth transition for Louisa's sake. "I agreed to give up the housekeeping to Louisa the first of next month," she told Sophie, "but I shall not move till we make the summer arrangements."[13] Mrs. Waterman, who had been Victorine's head housekeeper since the days her mother had run the household, found the news of her impending departure unbearable. The good woman's health had been steadily declining for the past five years, and the thought of adjusting to a new Lady of the House (even one as kindly as Louisa) seemed insurmountable. Victorine was visibly moved by Mrs. Waterman's response: "I spoke to her today about my removal and before I could say anything more, she burst into tears and said 'Oh Mrs Bauduy, I can never live here without you!' I was deeply touched by the good woman's devotion. She said she clung to me as to all that remained to her of our dear parents & old times."[14]

If Mrs. Waterman viewed her mistress as the last link between herself and the "old times," she certainly had the empathy of the nostalgic Victorine. Only a sense of duty kept her from dwelling too deeply upon what it meant to leave her father's house. She had witnessed nearly every event that had taken place at the house since, as a girl of ten, her father had led his family across the threshold for the first time. She could still remember when Uncle Charles had put the finishing touches on the white rocking horse he had carved for her and Evelina[15] and hear the echoes of winter laughter as the *Tancopanican Chronicles* were read aloud. She had witnessed the marriages of both her "daughters" in the parlor, and when she too had stood upon the braided rug in the center of the room and given her hand to a beaming youth who could scarcely believe she was his. Just twelve feet away was the room in which he had died seventy-three days later. In the bedroom directly above her head, *chère Maman*, too, had released her last breath.

Had it not been for a grieving sister and an inexperienced sister-in-law, Victorine may have indulged the spirit of nostalgia, but at that moment there was too much that needed to be done. Her first task before moving out was to convince the servants not to leave Louisa in the lurch. "I need to speak to the other girls . . . & tell them to make up their minds if they will stay with Louisa or not. . . . I have not quite determined, however, what to say to them. All this is very painful to me. The sooner it is over the better it will be."[16]

Tom's death left a pall over the entire neighborhood. The doctor had been well liked and many in the community had been recipients of his medical attention. Rev. Brincklé, like everyone else, was shocked by the news and was forced to reflect upon his tense relationship with Dr. Smith: "We differed on church principles but differed kindly. . . . His last attendance on public worship was in our church."[17] Brincklé's visits to du Pont homes in the weeks that followed were appreciated by the grieving family members. On one occasion at Henry's, the solicitous minister had been pleased to hear Louisa say that Tom had been spiritually prepared for "a death so sudden & mysterious."[18]

Knowing how close Joanna and her brother Tom had been, the faithful minister found her visibly shaken, but her faith quite strong. Joanna had found additional solace by writing and publishing a tract that listed her brother's many accomplishments as a doctor and a "churchman." The pamphlet also portrayed him as a leading figure in the establishment of Christ Church. Although his role had diminished since his involvement at Trinity, Joanna was determined to memorialize his contributions to the Brandywine church. Among the three du Pont brothers, the tragedy had its greatest impact upon Tom's brother-in-law Alexis. Within days of the doctor's death, he requested that Brincklé meet with him at his home. Unfortunately, just before their scheduled appointment, he was called away by Mr. Van Deusen to attend a funeral service. He dutifully complied but asked Joanna to keep the meeting with Brincklé anyway. When the minister arrived at Hagley House, Joanna told him how very much her husband had wanted to meet him: "She said that as soon as [her brother] Dr. Smith breathed his last, her husband, taking her into another room, asked her to kneel down & pray for him, & she saying she could not, he said, 'O Yes. You must call on the Lord Jesus!'"[19]

By April, the minister noticed that Alexis was kneeling in church for the first time. The youngest brother was soon referring to Christ Church as "our church" and participating in the distribution of the communion plates. After Sunday services on June 13, Rev. Brincklé found him "in a most tender frame of mind, & ready to give himself to the Saviour. . . . His wife shed tears of joy."[20] A week later, Alexis invited the man to his home and, "deeply affected," told him he had determined to "make the Lord his portion."[21] Brincklé rejoiced and on Sunday, July 4, 1852, Alexis I. du Pont was baptized by the faithful minister in front of a large congregation. As for Henry and Alfred, Eleuthera told Brincklé that she had spoken to both brothers, and "had pressed Henry to attend to this subject, & come to church, & that if anything could comfort her under her affliction it would be that it might be blessed for their good."[22]

Tom's death had rent such a tear in the fabric of Eleuthera's life that she believed it could never again be mended. Victorine understood her sister's grief and confided to Sophie that "I am very well aware of all that dear Eleu suffers, though she does not tell me anything of it. . . . I am very anxious that Eleu should make up her mind to come to church, but she has repulsed hitherto everything I said on the subject in the most positive manner. Do you not think there is no use in putting it off? The longer she waits, the worse it will be, and it is dangerous I think to indulge habits of seclusion at such times."[23] Ironically, this was the very advice her friends had implored *her* to follow in the days following Ferdinand's death.

Although intimate with her sisters, Victorine had grown accustomed to a degree of emotional distance from her brothers. After their marriages, the men had busied themselves with families and business, and the eldest sister was aware that they had grown apart in various ways. One afternoon in March, while packing up a few of her remaining books at Eleutherian Mills, she was surprised by a visit from Alfred: "Yesterday afternoon, Alfred spoke to me about my removal here in the kindest manner. He introduced the subject himself. He appeared to understand fully what a trial it must be to me, said that if I could make up my mind to do it, it was the best thing for poor Eleu. Altogether, he showed an interest and friendliness I seldom experience from any of my brothers and I was deeply touched by it."[24]

In April 1852, fifty years after the du Pont family's arrival in Delaware, Victorine left the home of her youth and moved in with her sister at Jacob Broom's old house. Ever since she had named Eleuthera forty-six years ago, Victorine had felt a strong attachment to her younger sister. When the girl had reached fifteen, Vic could express, "Indeed my dearest child I love you more and more every day. I sometimes think you engross too large a share of my affections."[25] By the time Eleu turned twenty-two, Victorine confessed that "I certainly enjoy through your means my dearest child, a degree of happiness which I once thought never would have existed for me on this earth."[26] And now—through the pain of yet another tragedy—the two sisters found themselves living under the same roof again. The mutual comfort they received from one another was palpable, and perhaps more so whenever January 21 rolled around each year. They must have thought it a strange and sober coincidence that each of their husbands had died on the very same day of the year.

On New Year's Day, 1853, Vic informed Evelina that "Our dear Eleu is pretty well this morning but very sad indeed."[27] It would, in fact, be seven more years before Eleuthera could bring herself to participate in the family's traditional holiday festivities. But the gentle daughter brightened visibly whenever her sisters-in-law stopped by with their children. Victorine observed that "The youngest ones, Vic & Sophy, come often carried by their nurses and Eleu appears to enjoy their visits."[28] Joanna would bring Eleu's namesake, little Eleuthera Paulina (soon to be five), and the cheerful Francis Gurney, who would be two in May. Usually assisting her mother was the serious Irene, who had turned seven in the fall. For Eleu, who loved children of every age, their happy countenances were better than a thousand medicines. Joanna's newest arrival, little Thomas Mackie du Pont, was born exactly seven months after the death of the uncle for whom he was named and, at only four months, the child had endeared himself to the grieving widow.

Victorine loved Joanna, and thought her sister-in-law both caring and pious, but she also thought her headstrong at times. She felt that Joanna's conversations with Eleu dwelt too much upon the past. She knew that "Joan" (as Joanna was alternately called) was grieving the loss of a brother as much as Eleuthera was grieving the loss of a husband, but Victorine couldn't help feeling that their constant discussions about Tom were unhealthy. Confiding to Sophie, she fretted: "Joanna was here with dear Eleu, . . . [but] I don't think those long conversations they have together, always on the same subject, are good for either of them. Yet I don't know how to prevent it. I fear Joan might not like my asking her to refrain indulging in these retrospections, which are but too natural. So it is best, I suppose, to let matters alone."[29] Although she understood the need, Vic feared that the excessive indulgence in memories of Tom hindered her sister's recovery. Ironically, this had been the very concern Antoinette Brevost had held for her, forty years before.

Eleu's grief over Tom's death likely stirred emotions in Victorine that were associated with her own loss. Perhaps it is what motivated her to ask Alexis if he would see to the restoration of Ferdinand's monument at Old Swede's Church, which had fallen into disrepair over the years. To her great pleasure, Alexis had seen to it immediately and the completed work had been much to her satisfaction.[30] She noted that near the bottom of the monument, like a humble footnote requesting no distraction from the larger story, was the short Latin phrase that translates simply, "Restored by wife, A.D. 1853."Although Ferdinand's epitaph has experienced nearly two centuries of erosion since the repairs were made, it is still legible today. Following his name, it reads: "His soul pleased the Lord, Therefore hasted He to take him away. He was the pride and joy of tender parents and of a numerous family. The earthly happiness and hope of an affectionate wife are buried in his grave." This last sentence is perhaps the most definitive testimony as to why Victorine never remarried.

A Time to Tear Down

In the autumn, fifteen-year-old Henry Algernon left his "nest of sisters"[31] for Dr. Lyon's school in West Haverford, and then went on to West Point after graduation. As Victorine had encouraged his father through frequent letters, so she did for him, keeping up a faithful correspondence with young Henry throughout his military career. When compared with the letters she had written to his father, the pages to the son carry an echo of maternal déjà vu. On one occasion, when informed that her nephew had slipped in his academic standing from first to fifth in his class, Aunt Vic inquired, "What is the cause of this dear Henry? Pray do not relax your efforts to do your very best. . . . You will find difficulties vanish if you persevere in study. Do not let the examples of any of your companions induce you to act differently, I entreat you my dearest nephew."[32] Seven years later, Henry Algernon du Pont graduated at the top of his class at West Point.

Over at Eleutherian Mills (which Vic now referred to as "Louisa's"), the crowded conditions knew little respite. In addition to Henry's family of nine, four other souls occupied the family home—Uncle Charles, Sarah the cook, Mary Bradon (the children's nurse), and a new head housekeeper. Although lack of space for his growing family was a strong incentive, Henry's decision to finally renovate the family home was not based upon that motivation alone. Eleutherian Mills was celebrating its golden anniversary in 1853 and, although half a century was a relatively young age for such a well-built house, few structures had endured the trauma of more than fifty close explosions in as many years. The blasts had taken their toll. Damaging cracks, chinks, and weakened beams had resulted in multiple repairs from the cellar to the roof. Plans for a total renovation were drawn up, and reconstruction began in earnest by late May. The timing was propitious; Louisa discovered in early June that she was pregnant with their eighth child.

Characteristic of Henry, his plans for reconstruction were not modest. Ultimately, the entire back wall of the house, which included the former piazza, was totally removed and fourteen extra feet added to the depth of the house, which now rose to three floors. The third level, which housed the garret rooms, was raised to full height, and a new roof—complete with dormers—was laid on top. An entire new wing was added to the north side of the house, and the south side (which already had a partial wing) was raised to match the height of the other. The optimistic Henry had hoped the work would be completed by late summer, but the project would take nearly a year and a half to complete. "The house is in the greatest confusion," reported Vic to Sophie. "The back part is all laid open, so that they have only the two front rooms upstairs for all the family. Little Henry slept in the library."[33] Victorine fretted about the danger the exposed walls posed to the children. Their father had built the house near the edge of a cliff in order to have a clear view of his operations. When standing on the piazza, visitors often felt the sensation of being precariously high. With nothing now between oneself and the valley below, she felt the danger was all too real. "It is a wonder to me how Mary Bradon can prevent our two youngest nieces from breaking their necks," she said. "There are precipices on every side. Happily by this weather they can be out of doors nearly all the time."[34]

As it turned out, Henry would be the only member of the family to suffer an accident during the renovations. In August, he fell through the attic floor. "Our Brother Henry had a very narrow escape on Tuesday," wrote a relieved Victorine, "falling through the garret floor into the next story. He stepped on a loose board, which tilted. Happily he fell on his feet and only scraped his back a little. He was not at all hurt & was walking about as usual yesterday morning when I went over."[35] Landing on his feet would prove to be an apt metaphor for the auburn-haired leader of the company's fortunes.

In the autumn of 1853, Victorine contented herself by making daily trips to the house to observe the progress of the workers. As she neared the silent manse one evening, she found no one about: "I went all over the distorted house, entirely alone, for all the workmen were gone to dinner, & I felt very sad as I wandered through it, so different from what it used to be, and I thought of bygone times!"[36] The reconstruction process had been more painful to Victorine than she had anticipated. Although she had been one of the voices advocating for renovation, she was not fully prepared for the raw pangs of nostalgia that now assailed her. To Irénée's eldest daughter, the house had become the symbol of all that had been—and was now passing.

The workmen deposited salvaged lumber and other materials beside the company office, which Alfred had built near the house in 1837. Victorine noticed the piles and returned to the spot the following day. "I took two of the ornaments of the top [of the piazza columns] in my arms and carried them to my green house," she informed Sophie, "from whence I shall have them conveyed here, keeping one for myself & reserving the other for you. It is a very natural wish for both of us to keep some memorial of that beloved place. . . . I never spoke of this to you before you left home, because I knew how painful it would be to both of us."[37]

On the day the old porch was to be removed, young Henry Algernon came by to alert her. She told Sophie, "I went over to Louisa's after breakfast to take a last look at our dear old piazza. . . . You may imagine the feelings with which I took a last, solitary walk upon it!"[38] The piazza had served in both a business capacity and a personal one. Many were the times when Eleuthère Irénée du Pont would stride out upon its wide wooden floorboards and survey the ever-expanding scene below him; his eyes would take in the rolling mills, the out-buildings, the steadily turning water wheels, the various activities of the powder men, and the slow, plodding progress of the wagons carrying materials back and forth. On other occasions, megaphone in hand, he could be heard shouting orders from his lofty vantage point to an attentive foreman or worker below.

To Victorine, however, the piazza was more closely associated with family than business. It had been one of the du Ponts' favorite spots to congregate on warm summer evenings. Situated on the east side of the building, with the setting sun behind them, the house would cast a cool shadow over their company. For fifty years, the du Ponts and their friends had laughed, told stories, sipped wine, read aloud, stitched and chatted, or simply sat together in trusting silence. Gazing down upon the quiet beauty of the softly flowing Brandywine, the river seemed like an old friend. Many a reflective hour had been spent listening to its contented gurgling where it greeted the narrow dam that Irénée had strung across its watery neck. As she heard the echo of her footsteps upon the old floorboards, other memories would have surely stirred. She might have recalled those long ago evenings when only one other person had sat beside her on the quiet veranda, his youthful face

smiling over at hers in the moonlight. One of the poems in her files perhaps sum-
marizes the power of such memories best:

> Once in my childhood there was one
> Who lov'd me more than tongue can tell—
> Departed days, *all, all* are gone—
> Yet bear to him my last farewell.
> When all things else of death are past,
> Tell him "I lov'd him to the last—"[39]

CHAPTER 17

A Time to Build

While Henry's mansion was being torn apart in the summer of 1853, a "palace" in New York City was receiving rave reviews. Over the course of the year, nearly all the Brandywine du Ponts made the one-hundred-mile trek to view the Exhibition of the Industry of All Nations. Generally accepted as America's first World's Fair, it "featured four thousand exhibitors and displayed the industrial wares, consumer goods, and artworks of the nation."[1] Twenty-four countries also hosted exhibits. Of special interest to the family was that their own Samuel Francis Du Pont had been appointed general superintendent of the exhibit, serving directly under New York City mayor Jacob Westervelt. Sophie joined her husband in New York and Victorine followed later in the summer. She viewed the trip as a dual opportunity to visit the wonders of the fair and to spend time with her favorite niece, Victorine Kemble.

The ever-curious woman visited the grounds as often as she could. Her favorite place was the centerpiece building, the Crystal Palace, and the thousands of items displayed in its galleries. "I should never tire of visiting that beautiful place!" she exclaimed to Sophie.[2] In a letter to Lina she reported, "I am going again this evening to see it lighted up. I wish I could go there every day while I am here; there are so many objects of interest that it would take an age to examine them all. . . . for instance, the machine gallery, which I walked through with Frank, in order to see the celebrated washing machine, which I promised dear Brother [Bidermann] to examine for him."[3] The Brandywine schoolteacher also spent hours strolling with her niece in Manhattan, exploring the various shops and sightseeing. They took the "omnibus" (a horse-drawn trolley) whenever they could find one. "A very pleasant mode of [transportation]," she assured Eleu.[4]

Progress was also on display at the powder mills. Alfred's twenty-two-year-old son, Lammot, following in his father's footsteps, was changing the company's industrial landscape. One such marvel raised biblical imagery for Victorine, as she strolled through the yards one evening with Alfred's daughter Emma Paulina:[5] "We visited Lammot's improvements at the refinery, just passing through it. They have been making tremendous chimneys lately; one of them is so high that I call it the tower of Babel. It looks quite well through the trees since they have painted the bricks brown."[6]

STORM CLOUDS

Following his conversion, Alexis du Pont attended the afternoon services at Christ Church but, on Sunday mornings, he accompanied Joanna to Trinity Church in Wilmington, where Rev. Van Deusen still presided. Although Trinity's rector had accepted a position at St. Peter's Church in distant Pittsburgh, his departure had not been immediate. The extra months proved sufficient to convince Alexis of Tractarian positions. Just two weeks after being baptized by Rev. Samuel Brincklé, Alexis paid the Brandywine minister a "painful" visit, informing him that he "now avows himself a high churchman."[7] Brincklé's disappointment was palpable, but he also expressed concern for those du Pont relations who did not share Alexis's high church views, among whom were now Victorine, Sophie, Samuel Francis, Mary Van Dyke du Pont and her brother Victor, the Shubricks (Julia and Irvine), and Henry's wife, Louisa.

Brincklé recalled Victorine's prediction that should Alexis ever be convinced of the Gospel message, "He would never be a half-way Christian, but when once converted he would give heart and soul to the work."[8] The youngest brother was immediately vocal about his new faith and involved himself in a variety of Christian endeavors, including a local temperance movement. At the mills, he spoke frequently to his workmen about spiritual matters, and although associated with Trinity, became a new voice advocating for the building of Christ Church.

Victorine thought it unfortunate that her brother had so quickly—and so fervently—embraced high church positions. Although Alexis did not share Van Deusen's personal animus toward Rev. Brincklé, he became increasingly outspoken against the Brandywine minister's low church, evangelical practices. This did not abate even when revelations came to light after Van Deusen's departure as to how he had tried to undermine Brincklé's missionary status. "He was trying to get another clergyman to take his place in Newcastle [sic]," confided Victorine to Sophie. "For my part, I never cease rejoicing that the Alleghenies are between us!"[9]

Despite tensions over their ecclesiastical differences, tragedy would again bind the family together in grief. In late September 1853, Alexis and Joanna's toddler fell ill. Vic told Sophie that little Thomas Mackie, only thirteen months old, had "summer complaint" (infantile cholera).[10] His parents watched helplessly as the boy succumbed on October 3. "Dear Sophie," wrote Victorine, "Poor little Tom died this morning at 3 o'clock! His disease took a sudden turn Saturday evening and he sank under it."[11] The death was a severe blow to his parents and also to Eleuthera, who was still grieving the connected loss to the child's namesake.

Five months later, Alexis sought to renew efforts to find a home for Christ Church. On Sunday afternoon, February 12, 1854, he invited two men to his home to discuss the future of the church: Rev. Samuel Brincklé and Samuel Francis Du

Pont. Although Victorine had been involved in Brincklé's plans for a church since the beginning, Alexis did not ask her to take part in the discussion. He was, in fact, a bit disturbed that his sister was allowed so much direct influence in church affairs. The zealous brother had also been appalled at some of the practices going on at the schoolhouse, such as permitting Presbyterian children to learn from their own catechisms (rather than the Episcopal one), and at his sister's stubborn insistence that the school's hours continued to occupy the Sunday morning schedule. Brincklé admitted that Alexis had "alluded to some complaints that Mrs. Bauduy, & not the vestry had authority here." And even though the minister agreed with Alexis regarding the Sunday morning monopoly, he told him that, "as she had been accustomed to sole authority [at the school] before the church was organized, she could scarcely forego it now."[12]

Although the Sunday school had been around since 1816, the year Alexis was born, he appears to have lacked an appreciation for its founding purposes. His zeal for an Episcopal church in the neighborhood made it difficult for him to understand the continuing necessity for secular education and blinded him to the rationale for its nondenominational approach to religious instruction. While Rev. Brincklé was more sympathetic to the school's history, he too chafed at the inconvenience it posed to what he considered the more important work of planting the church. Both men would have profited by reading the recent summary of the school's history written by Victorine, which read, in part:

> [Church] services are in the afternoons & do not interfere with the school which still continues in operation on Sunday mornings from half past 8 till 12. . . . Children of all denominations still receive instruction in the Sunday school, as heretofore, in those doctrines, which all protestants hold in unison. There are now within a range of 2 miles five other churches, 2 Presbyterian, 2 Methodist & 1 Roman Catholic, they all have Sunday schools. Still many of the children come to ours and are welcome, for it has always been the opinion of the superintendent, that all Christians may and should unite together in promulgating the great truths of the Gospel and that it is a great pity it is not done oftener.[13]

But the primary issue Alexis wished to discuss with the two Samuels on that February afternoon was finding suitable land upon which to build a church. The hunt for a permanent location had all but stalled since the death of Dr. Smith, who had spearheaded the initial attempts. But 1854 was a new season, and the landseekers believed that fresh opportunities had presented themselves, not the least of which was the additional clout that Alexis now brought to the effort. Both he and Samuel Francis had found themselves with time they could spare: Alexis was needed less at Trinity Church since Van Deusen's departure, and Cousin Frank had resigned his post as general superintendent of the New York exhibition two months earlier.

While Alfred and Henry consistently rejected proposals for a church on du Pont property, Alexis felt that his good relationship with Henry might persuade him to relent. Teaming up with Frank, he suggested they approach the company's president individually. They knew it was one thing for the two older brothers to ignore the wishes of religious women (be they sisters or not), and to dismiss the aspirations of a local clergyman, but to avoid discussions with a brother who was an equal partner in the mill, and a cousin so highly esteemed as the Captain, would not be as easy. Their intention was to present four sites to Henry—all of them on du Pont property.

But if the spring of 1854 seemed advantageous to the church planters, it couldn't have been worse for the company. On May 31, three large wagons loaded down with 450 kegs of Du Pont powder blew up in sequential order in downtown Wilmington on their way to the wharves. An estimated five tons of gunpowder exploded at the corners of Fourteenth and Orange Streets, killing nine people and destroying several homes, including that of Bishop Alfred Lee. The three drivers, Thomas Talley, John Keene, and Thomas Chambers were killed immediately, along with six townspeople, including one woman and an African American servant named Henry. Numerous other citizens were badly injured.

The *Delaware Republican* conjectured that leaking powder kegs may have caused the explosion. The *New York Times* estimated the damages at "not less than $75,000, including the powder and teams, valued at about $5,000. Messrs. DUPONT were on the ground actively engaged in doing all they could to relieve the sufferers. They declare their intention of paying for all the damage done to property."[14] The story made headlines all over the nation, inciting many towns and cities to pass legislation restricting the transport of gunpowder through populated areas. The du Ponts themselves immediately revised their own practices and, with difficulty, sought alternative routes to the wharves.

The emotional weight of the catastrophe took a toll on Alfred's frail health and only served to darken his mood. When he picked up a local paper three weeks after the Wilmington blasts and read that the du Ponts were planning to erect an Episcopalian Church on their property, the news struck him like lightning. The thought of a church on company property, let alone the hallowed ground containing the remains of his beloved parents, grandfather, and aunt and uncle—none of whom were Episcopalians—was insufferable. Alfred had felt so deeply about the cemetery that he had volunteered to be the sibling responsible for its upkeep.

The outraged brother immediately sat down and wrote two long and scathing letters. The first was addressed to all of his siblings. He reminded them that "Our father's intentions were that no partiality or leaning to any Sectarian Creed should be shown . . . [and he] resisted every application made for land to be used for this purpose; the case of the Sunday School is no exception. He saw with regret the purpose it was gradually being converted to."[15] He argued that their father had been no "religionist," but had he been, "his road to Heaven would never have been through the Church of England." He asserted that the whole world knew their father would never kneel to either the Pope *or* to Henry the Eighth. In a final volley, he argued that "true Du Ponts" would, on any given Sunday, empty and fill an ale house "with the same pleasure as they would sit on velvet cushions in a pew."[16]

His second letter was to Victorine, whom he perceived as the family's primary influence behind the movement to build a church on the grounds. He accused her of pursuing a reckless course and said that if the idea had "been proposed to our father to give land to a church, his answer would have been one word, 'NEVER.' . . . [As for the church being] located in close proximity to our family grave yard; the thing was truly ridiculous; how could my sisters insist in forcing our brother Bidermann & myself to . . . remove the graves of our grandfather, father, mother & aunt."[17] Alfred was convinced that placing an Episcopal church next to the family graveyard would imply that all who were buried there were adherents of that sect, thus forcing the removal of those family members who had not ascribed to it. Victorine later countered that it "would have led to the preservation of the graveyard, *not* into its conversion into any sectarian cemetery, as has been most untruly stated."[18]

Alfred concluded, "I was willing to give money but *not* land; there is space enough beyond the limits of the homestead to locate a church without desecrating the soil left us by our father. . . . I know I am too late, but how could I suspect my sisters . . . would be willing to sever the most sacred ties to smooth the road to heaven; . . . it would have been better to have paid some little respect to the memory of our father."[19] Victorine was stung by the letter. It grieved her that Alfred could feel so deeply prejudicial against their motives, but it was clear how deeply the proposal pained him. The idea to build next to the family graveyard was immediately—and permanently—withdrawn.

The second of the four possible locations was the apple orchard on the hill above the schoolhouse, but the site was thought too vulnerable to explosions. Had not Hagley House, which was adjacent to the orchard, been damaged several times already? Alexis supported a third location, next to Phillip's Mill, but the Captain thought it too distant from numerous local communities. Victorine agreed, saying that some members would find the way too circuitous by carriage and be tempted to go back to Wilmington before making the journey out to Phillip's Mill.

The fourth parcel was one that was clearly visible from Eleuthera's windows—the wooded area above Flea Park,[20] close to her own property line. The location had long been a favorite of Anna Brincklé's, which she had recently reiterated to her father. The Captain, too, had eyed the spot favorably and suggested it to Brincklé one week later. The minister noted that it was "the very place Anna remarked last Sunday (without knowing it was thought of), she would prefer to any other."[21] As the discussions continued, Henry felt conflicted, a state of mind that did not please the ordinarily decisive man. He was unaccustomed to being challenged, and he did not like it. Alexis and Captain Frank had launched their individual negotiations with him in April—six weeks prior to the explosions in downtown Wilmington—and these discussions had been fiery at times. The battle-experienced captain concluded that his visit with Henry had been a victory, "but such a one as he should not often wish to have."[22] Alexis reported that in his meeting, "poor Henry fretted like a bull in a net."[23]

Henry made several demands before he would agree to relinquish the property. The first was that his name should not appear anywhere on the deed. He wanted no record that the current president of E. I. du Pont de Nemours and Company had sold a piece of their property to an Episcopal church. He then stalled the advancing land-seekers with a series of defensive maneuvers, which Victorine countered one by one: "You had other objections. First, that a graveyard would be wanted. This was not an unreasonable objection, & we immediately gave up all thought of such a thing.[24] You then objected that a parsonage would be wanted sooner or later; this we likewise promised to forego. You then spoke of damages from explosions; we promised to bind the church or its trustees forever from making such a claim."[25] Henry had hoped that at least one of his objections would succeed, but when each defense was breached by a concession, he was reluctantly forced to yield. Although Victorine considered the area around Flea Park (with its noisy children, squawking chickens, bleating goats, and barking dogs) a "very unpleasant neighborhood for a church," she rejoiced that a location so close to the Sunday school had been procured—and on du Pont property!

Before Henry could change his mind, Captain Du Pont hired the Philadelphia architect Richard Gilpin to draw up plans for a 250- to 300-seat building. Alexis, in the meantime, set some of his men to work quarrying the beautiful native bluestone indigenous to their area. Known as Brandywine Blue Gneiss by geologists, or "Wilmington Blue Rock" by the locals, the remarkable vein stretched from the shores of the Delaware River all the way to the Brandywine banks of du Pont's mills. Alexis gave special instructions to his quarry foreman, Mr. Conley, that the largest and prettiest stones were to be reserved for the church's exterior walls.

But Henry was still unsettled by the whole affair. A dinner conversation with his siblings at Eleutherian Mills one Sunday afternoon grew heated, and his latent discontent quickly resurfaced. He excoriated family members who supported the church and reiterated some of Alfred's former arguments. The chastened evangelicals temporarily retreated. In Henry's present state of mind, everyone agreed that another confrontation would avail them nothing, and possibly put the whole project in danger. Victorine suggested that a letter to Henry might have better results, and submitted a draft to the small group a few days later. With minor edits, the church-planting members of the family signed their names to it and sent it off. It read, in part:

My dear brother, when a subject discussed among relations & friends has led to misunderstanding, irritation, & perhaps heart burnings, it is wiser to leave verbal altercations, & resort to a different mode of intercourse, one more likely to insure calmness, circumspection, & the preservation of that spirit of kindness and affection which in this instance truly exists on our part, however *apparently* forgotten by some of us during moments of warm discussion.

. . . [The school house] was incorporated by the legislature of the state, & thus a public character was given to it, notwithstanding its location in the midst of private property. The great good which it would do to the children of the work-

men, & to gratify his daughter who took a warm interest in the scheme, were the
motives which induced your father to build the school house. In addition to the
use for which it was built, it has likewise been used with scarcely any interruption
as a place of religious worship during a period of 37 years, & by different denominations. . . . We ask you for the use of that little piece of ground, . . . believing that
a calm review of the case will very much modify your objections to it, & lead you
to feel towards us the same spirit of kindness in differences of opinion that we
most cordially do towards you. We remain dear Henry yours very affectionately,
V. E Bauduy, Alexis I du Pont, E. D. Smith, S. F. Du Pont, S. M. Du Pont.[26]

The overall tone of the letter was conciliatory, referring as it did to the innocence
of the group's motives and the reaffirmation of familial relationships above personal aspirations. Victorine confessed that had they known the depths of the
"evident distress it cause[d] you, we would never have proposed or encouraged
it, however unjust & unkind we might have considered the opposition on your
part."[27] Composed by his eldest sister, the letter bore a tone that, for Henry, no
other living person could have replicated—a maternal quality whose familiar
guidance had been earned over the period of a lifetime. Were it not for the subtle
influence Victorine carried within the family structure, it is unlikely that Christ
Church would be sitting on its present location today.

Whatever the letter's impact, one thing was clear: opposition to the building
project ceased from that point on. The pragmatic businessman seemed to genu-
inely put the matter aside and move on to the innumerable other concerns demanding his attention. By late July, even Rev. Brincklé felt comfortable enough to stop
by and spend a pleasant afternoon in conversation with Henry: "He seemed dis-
posed to sit & talk with me all the time. . . . [I] could not but think of his sister's
wish that I could see him oftener, that from personal interest in me, he might, by
God's blessing, be attracted to the same blessed hope. Thought of this again & again
while conversing on apparently indifferent subjects, with an earnest desire to win
him to the Saviour."[28]

The return to normalcy in relationships proved merciful in terms of timing. In
early September, Henry and Louisa suffered the devastating loss of their baby girl,
little Mary Constance. Not quite seven months old, she died after a brief battle with
a high fever. "My dear Sophie," wept Victorine to her sister, "Our little darling will
know no more suffering on earth. She died at 4 o'clock this afternoon. The disease
went to her brain & she went suddenly. Dear Louisa is as composed as we could
expect."[29] Victorine stayed with the grieving mother until ten on the evening of
the infant's death and awoke early the next morning to send Sophie an update: "The
dear babe will be buried this afternoon at half past 5. . . . I must not omit telling
you that our brother H[enry], though deeply afflicted, is softened not hardened by
it. He was very affectionate by me, & I know he will feel & dearly appreciate all
Alexis' kindness."[30]

Brincklé too noticed this softening. The day of the funeral, "Henry D.P. walked
with me from the grave, & seemed much affected, & was very kind in his manner.

Figure 24. *Victorine du Pont Bauduy (Mme. Ferdinand Bauduy)*. Unknown artist, watercolor on ivory, c. 1850.

Saw Mrs. Bauduy, who spoke of their prayerful anxiety for him."[31] Louisa too was comforted by Henry's attitude. It appears that the grief caused by the loss of their seventh (and final) girl had the effect of refocusing his priorities, and the tender concern for his grieving wife was manifest. Henry had witnessed how much his wife's faith meant to her when, in the maelstrom of her sorrow, she had requested that Rev. Brincklé come to the house to pray for them. Alone in a room, with just their son and this tall, empathetic pastor, Henry had been grateful for the pastoral words that were comforting his quietly weeping wife. Although not particularly religious himself, he judged the white-haired minister to be a sincere man, and truly appreciated the support he was providing Louisa at that moment.

———

Work on the church progressed at a steady pace, despite the replacement of an entire wall that had sprung in April of 1855. As the building neared completion, Alexis suggested that, in light of Henry's former opposition, it might be a good idea to ask Bishop Lee to officiate the laying of the cornerstone. As presiding bishop for the State of Delaware, Lee's presence would add dignity and prominence to the project. The bishop had, in fact, just returned from laying the cornerstone of the new St. Peter's Church in Lewes, Delaware, when his stately home in Wilmington was obliterated by du Pont powder.

Christ Church, meanwhile, continued to yield the morning slot to the Brandywine Manufacturer's Sunday School. Although the school's doors remained open to anyone who wished to attend, the scholars were now predominantly Episcopalian—though not exclusively. A minority of children from other denominations continued to attend and, as long as that was the case, Victorine maintained the nonsectarian principles upon which the school had been established. When Alexis complained to Bishop Lee that the Presbyterian catechism was still being taught, Victorine defended the practice: "When I came to consider the thing as a superintendent, I see it very differently, & I cannot make it a rule that the Presbyterian catechism shall not be taught, when the girls, Mary Mitchell [and others] are willing to learn & say it. As long as those children come they must be allowed to learn it if they choose."[32]

CHAPTER 18

Bells

I always felt I must take our dear mother's place.

—Victorine to Sophie, April 17, 1857

For different reasons, the widowed sisters of Smith Lane wished to remain close to home: Eleuthera, because she had yet to resume an appetite for social gatherings, and Victorine, because she considered any trip away from the Brandywine a journey in the wrong direction. "I begin to feel as if I must be at home now," she confided to Sophie in the summer of 1857.[1]

This new season of life with Eleuthera had become one of particular contentment for the elder sister. Except for their ecclesiastical differences, which they tacitly agreed not to discuss, the two women could not have been more compatible. Remarkably alike in their tastes and interests, they shared the same bed, rose at the same time, prayed, and dined together. Their recreational hours were spent gardening, walking, sewing, playing the piano, reading, and caring for their birds. As winter approached, Victorine informed young Henry that "We fixed all our birds in two cages, and brought the large one into the green house. There are 19 inmates in it, and 11 in my own cage which we mean to keep in the office. . . . We raised 18 young birds this summer . . . [and] have given six away. I think we could spare a few more, for they eat a great deal of feed."[2]

If Eleu's fingers weren't gripping a book or a pen, they were busy with a sewing needle. "Needlework," observed Vic to Sophie, "has become one of the necessities of life to her."[3] Shopping excursions to the "trimming stores," such as Vanharlingen's on Chestnut Street in Philadelphia, or Jones & Sharpe's in Wilmington, were regular stops on their jaunts to the city. The latter town had long suffered in negative comparison with its well-supplied, cultural big sister to the north, but times were changing. Victorine told nephew Henry: "I don't intend going to Philadelphia before Christmas, so I shall depend on Wilmington for all my new year's gifts. The stores are so well filled now, however, that I dare say I shall make out very well."[4]

On most summer evenings, the sisters of Smith Lane could be seen strolling together through their flower and vegetable gardens. The connate naturalists maintained a pair of greenhouses, where they wintered the more delicate varieties and experimented with plants not native to the area. "I hesitate about [wintering] the big cactus," Vic commiserated with Eleu, "though I should think [Mr. Carpenter's] greenhouse more favorable to cactus than mine."[5] All of the du Pont women hired men who meticulously tended their grounds to nurture their personal *jardins des fleurs*. Every du Pont home, from Louviers to Winterthur, took pride in the appearance of their gardens. When Victorine read that the Bidermanns had visited the Jardin des Plantes while in Paris, she admitted to Evelina that "Of all places in the world, it is the one I should most like to see."[6] Locally, she admired the conservatory of Joseph Shipley, which the merchant had built at Rockwood, his residence in Wilmington.[7] "Nothing can be handsomer than his conservatory adjoining the parlour full of the most beautiful flowers one can imagine," she glowed to Cousin Amelia. "It was like fairy land. The place is in beautiful order. The immense lawn was an expanse of green velvet, so smooth & close shaven."[8]

Reading, however, remained their favorite pastime and their formidable library continued to expand. Victorine had commissioned a carpenter to build new bookshelves, and she anticipated "great comfort in having room for my books which are in triple rows in my present bookcase."[9] As for their vocation, the two sisters shared the same overarching commitment—the Brandywine Manufacturer's Sunday School (BMSS). It had, in fact, been the attachment to the girls of her class that prompted Eleu's first forays out of the house after Tom's death.

As construction of Christ Church neared completion in the spring of 1856, Victorine grew more conscious that her beloved school was approaching the end of an era. She knew the coming changes were inevitable but, after forty years of involvement with the BMSS, the transition to a denominational entity was going to be a difficult adjustment. She could accept that the school would come under the auspices of Christ Church, but confessed to Anna Brincklé that she wished its name didn't have to change. The pioneer school had been called the Brandywine Manufacturer's Sunday School since her father's day, and although the students were nearly all from Christ Church now, she still felt an attachment to the name. Rev. Brincklé, however, had waited a long time to bring the schoolhouse under the Episcopalian wings of Christ Church, and he made it clear to Victorine that its nondenominational days were over. In the minister's mind, the old name had to go. No longer was it to be thought of in terms of "Brandywine manufacturers," but as an Episcopal entity. "I fear the old name will commit us to old practices," he explained, "and we propose a complete revolution. This school has been in existence under one head (our friend Mrs. B[auduy]) for about 30 years—at first rather secular, and still teaching writing—using all catechisms. . . . Some of the children are teachers, much more fit to be learners."[10]

The minister meant well but, like Alexis, he appears to have had an incomplete appreciation for the rustic, uneducated status of the valley's earlier days. His arrival in 1848 made it difficult for him to envision the primitive nature of the Brandywine in 1816. By the time he arrived, two churches had already been built and a third was in process. The passage of the Delaware Free School Act in 1829 had established state-sponsored schools and, though they had yet to reach rural mill communities, would soon be available. He thus believed that secular subjects such as reading, writing, and spelling were no longer necessary. The minister's single-minded pursuit of planting a church, though admirable in terms of dedication, may have hindered his ability to appreciate peripheral realities, such as the social impact the BMSS had already made upon the community. In a setting formerly devoid of schools and churches, literacy and the Christian religion had been taught to nearly every child in the neighborhood for over four decades under Victorine's direction.

The minister could perhaps be excused for not recalling that she had led the Sunday school for *forty* years (instead of his stated thirty), but after eight years on the Brandywine, his ignorance of other details seems mystifying. For example, on concluding his first Sunday school session under the auspices of Christ Church, he commented that he "closed school with a hymn. There had never been singing at the school."[11] In reality, however, hymns had been a weekly part of the school's routine since the early 1820s.[12] Yet, while singleness of purpose may have narrowed his perspective in some areas, he was realistic enough to expect a period of adjustment for his old friend.

> Had a conversation with Mrs. Bauduy about the S. School. Relieved her mind in regard to her own position in the new organization—viz.—that she would be immediately under me, to act as my deputy in my absence. She was full of apprehensions & misgivings about the shortness of time teaching—[the need for] punctuality of teachers, &c. Told her a new leaf would be turned over . . . & that the time being so short, punctuality would be the order, and that secular instruction being abandoned (spelling & writing) for which there was no necessity now, we could apply ourselves to the great object of religious instruction. I could not but see that through so many years engaged in [Sunday school] teaching, her ideas were very confused about it. I have a great work before me. May I have grace for it.[13]

He later acknowledged that, although Sophie Du Pont agreed with him regarding the name change, "she feels for her sister, who had been identified with the school so many years, & of whom she said, so many would rise up and call her blessed."[14]

On May 4, 1856, Christ Church held its first worship service in the new stone building. "A glorious day," rejoiced the minister.[15] Across the creek, Sophie was marking the event in her diary: "Christ Church Christiana [Hundred] was opened today. The Lord was very merciful and permitted all should go well. It cleared at five o'clock in the morning, and was a perfectly lovely day. . . . We met Alexis, he was very cordial and kind, and gave his arm to show me the pew. I threw myself on my knees and prayed fervently for God's blessing upon this house of worship."[16]

Although religious instruction would continue to be held at the old schoolhouse until 1899, Brincklé pronounced of the BMSS that "Henceforth it is an Episcopal school."[17] The vestrymen agreed that the name should be changed in actual practice, but they saw no need to alter the incorporation papers. As far as the State of Delaware was concerned, the Brandywine Manufacturer's Sunday School remained its official title. But on the local level it simply became known as the "Episcopal school," or "the church school."

ALFRED

While these transitions were taking place at Christ Church, Alfred's health continued to decline. The devastating effects of the explosion in downtown Wilmington in 1854 had shaken the entire family, but it had taken its greatest toll upon the eldest son. There were those who believed that Alfred's health problems had begun with the earlier blast of 1847, which had occurred during his watch as head of the company. Historian William Dutton wrote that after that event he had become "a broken man."[18] Although Alfred had been living in a semi-invalid status for some time, by August of 1856 he was confined to his bed. His sharp decline throughout the summer presaged a more serious change. "He is averse to seeing anyone," wrote Vic to young Henry. "[He] takes very little nourishment, and unless he would take more, it is impossible he should recover strength."[19] To Sophie she confessed, "I almost dread what the news will be today—and yet it is wrong to wish to keep him in his present state, poor dear Brother! I pray for him constantly. Oh dearest Sophie how sad is such a death bed. What an inexpressible comfort would be a few words of trust in Christ, intimation that he recognizes the value of our Religion, but there is nothing of that sort though he is fully aware of his situation."[20]

Later, she quietly entered his room and found Alfred's twenty-one-year-old daughter, Mary Sophie,[21] reading to him.

> He scarcely noticed me except giving me his hand when I came in. He is very low indeed, can scarcely speak to ask what he wants & it is very difficult to understand what he says. Yet he still wishes [Mary] Sophie to read to him & she does so almost constantly, only stopping when he sleeps, which he often does. It is harrowing to see her, dear child, commanding her feelings so as to read in a slow, distinct voice, (the life of Attila!) while the whole expression of her face is so sad; and she is so pale she looks like a beautiful marble statue! I could scarcely refrain from weeping when I looked at her. Meta does not stir from Alfred's side.[22]

Eleuthera described Meta's state as "the image of rigid, fixed despair," and said that James Bidermann "thinks that unless she is most carefully nursed & tended after this she will never survive the blow!"[23] On Saturday, October 4, Victorine saw her brother alive for the last time. She left him at one o'clock, visited again at three, and then departed temporarily to spend time with Joanna, who was suffering from a severe headache and was being leeched. "On that account I stayed longer than I had intended. Alas! When I returned to Alfred's all was over—."[24]

Two days later, Alfred was buried in his beloved cemetery at Sand Hole Woods, attended by a huge crowd of family, friends, and workers. In an ironic twist, the mourners were just descending from the graveyard when the fire bell started ringing frantically from the Hagley Yards. A blaze that had ignited in the composition house had already spread to the sawmill. The company's three leaders, Henry, Alexis, and Alfred's son Lammot, rushed down the hill to join the men who were attempting to douse the flames.

The following day, Victorine defined what had been the family's greatest fears to Sophie: "The events of yesterday have left me extremely tired. I expect you were, like ourselves, in a great agony, for you must have known where the fire was and how many near & dear ones were at it! I followed Eleu to Joanna's . . . and remained there till all was over, watching that terrific fire, sometimes hoping & oftener fearing it could not be kept under [control]. I never suffered so much at any of our explosions. It was a wonderful preservation & we cannot be sufficiently grateful for it."[25] The lives of all three leaders could have been erased simultaneously had an explosion resulted from the fire.

Three weeks later, Victorine learned that her old friend, Rebecca Ralston, had also passed away. Becky had been living in Dedham, Massachusetts, with her third daughter, Hannah, and died on October 28, 1856. Victorine recalled the many happy hours of their youth, and the first influences of Christianity upon her soul by Rebecca's family. The loss of Becky and Alfred in the same month may have explained why the wistful aunt sat down to pen a nostalgic letter to Henry Algernon.

> Not a day passes without my thinking of you, and our long separation is one of my severe trials. I remember you as the lovely infant I used to nurse, as the entrusting child whose unfolding powers I watched from year to year; as the promising boy, who though a little wayward and lazy at times, bid fair to become all that we wished him to be—and now that you are on the threshold of manhood, that most important era of your life, I must remain far, far away from you, with the conviction that if we ever meet again, we will be of necessity much estranged from each other. I know you will always love me, but it cannot be the same thing as if you had remained near us. . . . We have had a very sad time lately. Not only on account of your dear Uncle Alfred's death, which I feel very deeply, but so many of the family have been sick.[26]

ALEXIS

The death of the eldest brother brought one type of pain to Victorine, but disagreements with the youngest brought another. Alexis's high church views had not abated, and he had, if anything, become more firmly entrenched in them. Rev. Brincklé was just as intransigent in his positions, and these differences eventually led to a schism between the two men. Visiting the minister on January 29, 1857, Alexis verbally withdrew his membership from Christ Church, citing several low church practices of which he disapproved. Brincklé recalled: "Finding me immovable, which [Alexis] said he expected, he announced his intention of communing in future at Trinity church."[27]

These ecclesiastical differences between family members made for occasionally awkward social moments. Eleuthera, especially, found herself caught in the middle.

Joanna was her deceased husband's sister, and Alexis was her brother, but having to listen to his accusations against Victorine's "latitudinarian practices," or that she was running a "petticoat government" at the Sunday school, were hurtful and unfair criticisms.[28] Yet Eleu herself sided with her brother's high church opinions and was not always in agreement with her sister. As gentle as she was, she could be inflexible on certain points. "It is perfectly useless to argue with Eleu;" wrote Vic to Sophie, "it does nothing but harm. She is now convinced that you & I are very unjust to Alexis [and that] I view all he does through a false, prejudiced medium."[29]

If sincerity were the only requisite for unity, then harmony may have been attainable, for surely the members on each side of the issues were earnest in their positions. Alexis, as Victorine predicted, had become no common Christian. In the five short years since his conversion, he had committed many passages of the Bible to memory and demonstrated an unflagging zeal for Christian causes. Most recently, he had thrown himself into the construction of yet another new church, St. John's Episcopal in Brandywine Village. Joanna recalled that "The very day before [Christ Church] was opened for divine services, he had secured the ground in a neighboring village for the planting of another."[30] The temperance-minded Alexis had felt an extra sense of triumph in the purchase, for he knew that the site for the new church had once been home to the Green Tree Inn, a former tavern.[31] Although he had withdrawn his Sunday presence from Christ Church, Alexis continued to attend its various meetings. Samuel Francis frequently confronted Alexis on various issues. He seemed the only one capable of standing up to Alexis, and often defended his minister against the younger man's complaints. An appreciative Brincklé recorded that Samuel Francis had "expressed his indignation at the aggression of Alexis, and . . . promised to protect me from annoyance I had suffered from time to time—invasions of my province as Rector."[32]

But the Captain's protection was about to be removed. On the evening of April 15, 1857, Frank broke the news to Sophie that his extended shore duties had come to an end. The Navy had officially promoted him to captain (the rank his admiring family and neighbors had already bestowed upon him), and he was awarded command of the newly commissioned USS *Minnesota*. The powerful, sixty-gun frigate was about to depart on a two-year mission to the other side of the world. Its assignment was to deliver U.S. ambassador William B. Reed to China, a visit that would culminate in the historic signing of the Treaty of Tientsin.[33] On Frank's final Sunday at Christ Church, he exhorted the vestrymen of Christ Church to "stand fast, & keep out high church influence."[34] But if his departure was a discouragement to his minister, it was devastating to Sophie. The following morning, she sent word of her husband's impending departure to her big sister across the creek. Victorine responded:

> Oh my dear sister, I do pray for you! May you be sustained under this great trial, and may I be able to do all in my power to lessen it. You know dearest, that you have always been my first object when your husband is away; you are my [particular] charge then. I always felt I must take our dear mother's place towards

her Sophie—depend on me always beloved sister. I know exactly how you must
feel. I know it is the most painful separation that could have been thought of,
and no one can support you under it but *Him* who has ordered it.[35]

A large contingency of the family, including Victorine, went to Philadelphia to see
Frank off and explore the *Minnesota*. Sophie was permitted to sail to Virginia with
her husband and remain with him until his ship sailed out of Norfolk Harbor on
July 1, 1857. She would not see him again for two full years.

During an unfortunate three-year period from 1855 to 1857, no less than thirty
explosions occurred at Du Pont's mills, resulting in the deaths of ten men. The dou-
ble blasts of August 22, 1857 had accounted for six of them. "Several powder mills
exploded at 5 P.M.," wrote Brincklé that evening. "Several persons hurt, & was
shocked to hear that Alexis [du Pont] was among them."[36] The youngest son of Irénée du Pont had been mortally wounded in the second explosion. Eleuthera, who
stayed with Joanna throughout the ordeal, described how her brother had "ordered
the removal of an old mixing box from the grainery near the upper Press Room,"
and with seven other men had assisted in the transfer.[37] As they were moving the
heavy box out of the building, one of the corners struck a stone wall, which created a spark that ignited some powder sweepings. The building blew, and five of
the men were seriously burned.

Alexis was thrown onto the roadway, badly seared. He immediately jumped into
the waters of the mill race to drench his burning clothes and, as he was climbing
out, noticed that flaming debris had landed on the roof of the press room. He
ordered the other men to back away but ran toward the building with the intent of
extinguishing the flames. Eleu recorded that while he was halfway up his climb to
the roof, "the entire building exploded, throwing him back on the tables used for
drying powder in the sun. He was fatally injured, but in spite of the chaos, never
lost his self-command. He ordered his son, Eugene, to tie his suspenders around
his leg to stop the bleeding, and when placed upon a shutter to be carried home,
sat upright until brought into the house."[38]

Suffering from broken bones, a punctured lung, and third-degree burns, Alexis
was carried to his room on the second floor of Hagley House and laid upon his
bed by two of his workers. Doctors Bush and Jones arrived to tend his wounds and
administer pain medication. Brincklé recorded that, in addition to his charred
and broken flesh, Alexis suffered "a compound fracture of the thigh, & two ribs
broken, which punctured his lungs."[39] The following morning, a Sunday, Alexis
lucidly dictated the terms of his will to his brother Henry, while Mr. Belin stood
by as a witness. He began, "In the name of God, Amen. Alexis I. du Pont . . . being
suddenly overtaken by a dispensation of our Heavenly Father, but of sound mind
and steadfast faith through Christ, does hereby devise and bequeath the following sums . . ."[40] The terms provided for his family and included generous gifts to
the Episcopal Diocese of Delaware, Trinity Church, and the completion of St. John's
Church. Alexis then bade each of his older children goodbye, with individual mes-
sages of love and guidance. The youngest pair, seven-year-old Francis and

three-year-old Joanna Maria, were not permitted to see him in his terrifying condition. As Aunt Sophie led the weeping little Francis downstairs, she whispered to him, "We shall meet in Christ."[41]

The ministers then entered his room for a private communion service, which Alexis shared with Joanna, his daughter Fanny, his in-laws, and his three pious sisters. Eleuthera reported, "He went through the whole service in a perfectly distinct voice, and when it was over, exclaimed, 'What a glorious termination.'"[42] Alexis then asked his sister Sophie to convey a final farewell to her husband, deeply regretting that he would not see the Captain again. At this point, Victorine threw herself beside his bed, "and bursting into tears said, 'Oh, have you not a word for me, Lex?' He turned at the sound of her voice, and seeing her, held out his hand and said 'Goodbye sister, you have been a mother to me.'"[43] From Victorine's perspective, the dying man could not have chosen kinder words.

Of the du Pont brothers, none had been more respected by the powdermen than Alexis, whose constant presence in the yards had been a reassurance to them. A large number of the hardworking veterans of the company had waited downstairs or were milling about outside the house when Alexis invited several of them upstairs for a final farewell. To each man who filed respectfully through the room, he gave an appropriate word. To those who shared his religious convictions, he urged them to "be steadfast in the faith." To others, he used this final opportunity to urge them to "turn to Christ for my sake."[44] The following day, Victorine and Sophie told Rev. Brincklé how Alexis had urged several people in his last hours to seek Christ, without making a single reference to denominational preferences. Eleuthera recorded his last words—a quote from the Bible: "Heaven and earth shall pass away, but Thy words shall never pass away."[45] He then fell into "a quiet sleep from which he never woke . . . Dr. Bush broke the silence by saying 'Alexis is with God.' His sisters knelt down in prayer, rose, kissed him and left the room."[46]

Alexis had desired that Christ Church have a bell for its new steeple. In July 1857, a bold Mr. Brincklé had approached the merchant Joseph Shipley to see if he might be interested in contributing toward the purchase of one.[47] Shipley, a lifelong Quaker, was sympathetic to the Episcopal minister's plea and pledged him one hundred dollars. Victorine and Sophie each gave fifty dollars, and when Joanna and Eleuthera had heard about the project, the sisters-in-law had conspired to surprise Alexis by secretly contributing toward the effort as well. But the bronze herald would not arrive until a year and a half later, at which time Eleu recalled her conversation with her brother's widow: "[Joanna] spoke of the bell of Christ Church, which had arrived a few days before & was in the vestibule of the church. I said to her that there was always now a pang of pain with the thought of that bell for me— because we had first projected the getting it in July, 1857 and intended it should be a surprise to our dear brother Alexis, & that my first thoughts in connection with having a bell, had been the pleasure it would give him. [Joanna] said . . . she had thought of that too."[48] Victorine shared Joanna's sorrow, having now lost two of her three brothers in less than a year.

CHAPTER 19

Feeling an Interest

Sitting at her desk in the spring of 1857 as she approached the age of sixty-five, Victorine shared her nostalgic reflections with her sister Sophie:

> I have been spending part of the afternoon looking over some old papers in my *secretaire* in the dining room. They reminded me of many things I had forgotten, so I may say I have been making acquaintance with my former self!—I remember the time when these reminiscences would have saddened me, but they have not that effect now. I am thankful I can look back on the past with calm, quiet feelings & to the future with cheerfulness. How can it be otherwise after the innumerable blessings I have received from our Heavenly Father?[1]

As an integral link between the former generation and the succeeding one, Victorine sensed that identification with the family's past was not as deeply rooted in her nieces and nephews as she would have preferred. She didn't blame them for this; they were, after all, a new generation. But her letters reveal occasional annoyance at what she perceived to be a lack of historical appreciation for the family's sojourn. Tales of France and of grandfather Pierre Samuel (and even of her father's many sacrifices) were not experiences "the youngies" had shared. Grand and marvelous stories they were, to be sure, but the next generation did not feel them with the same visceral connection as those who had actually lived through them; theirs was a totally American experience.

The aging aunt also found the youngies to be inconsistent in their displays of social etiquette, sometimes even thoughtless. Victorine had been raised to believe that some virtues, such as respect for elders, should be transgenerational. The occasional violations of this unspoken code by the younger relations annoyed (and sometimes wounded) her, but her biblical perspective usually prevailed in calming her spirits. "As we grow old," she mused to Sophie, "we are very prone to think ourselves slighted. I feel it, because now there often happen things that worry me in those I love, which I dare say they do not mean will hurt me. It is best it should

be so; it loosens our earthly ties and reminds us how well the world can get on without us!"[2]

A local woman named Mary Elliott, who attended Christ Church, replaced
Mrs. Waterman as Victorine's housekeeper and proved to be a most favorable fit.
She not only shined as an efficient cook and seamstress, but she also joined Vic
and Eleu on the teaching staff at the Sunday school. With so much time spent in
each other's company, the three women became fast friends. Mrs. Elliott stayed
with the sisters for four years. In June 1858, the proficient housekeeper moved with
her husband, Robert Elliot, to Chester, Pennsylvania, where the couple rented living quarters near the wharves. This move initiated a lengthy correspondence
between Mary and Victorine, providing many new insights into the latter's reflections and activities during the closing years of her life.

Now that the Sunday school was officially under the auspices of Christ Church,
Rev. Brincklé could finally hold his worship services on Sunday mornings. He discovered, however, that his increased administrative responsibilities at the church
forced him to reduce his level of involvement at the Sunday school. The fortuitous
result for Victorine was that she was able to continue with much the same autonomy
she had previously enjoyed. Although the time slot for the school had been drasti-
cally shortened to two hours and secular subjects eliminated, her teachers now
focused on Bible lessons, recitations, and the Episcopalian catechism. Mr. Brincklé
continued the quarterly practice of awarding premiums to students, which now
consisted primarily of the American Sunday School Union's nondenominational
publications; he was familiar with the du Pont sisters' discerning criteria for the
approval of books and trusted their selections.

Although the waning era of the Brandywine Manufacturer's Sunday School had
saddened the pioneer educator, Vic engaged her new duties with the same level
of integrity she had brought to her former administration. The du Pont sisters
established a parish library for the adults of Christ Church, stocking it with many
of their own personal volumes. Whenever the quarterly "Premium Sundays"
approached, the dutiful siblings spent their evenings readying individual awards
for nearly 150 children. Sophie continued to assist at the school whenever she could,
but she struggled with intermittent bouts of neuralgia that often exempted her from
the teaching rotations.

It is likely that Victorine would have engaged the Sunday school at some level,
regardless of her marital status. She had been fully convinced of its importance,
both educationally (as had her father) and religiously. By 1858, Mrs. Bauduy was
aware that although the Lower Brandywine was now sprinkled with common
schools and churches, there were still a number of manufacturing enclaves where
neither institution existed. "I had a visit on Saturday from Mary Hamilton," she
wrote to Mrs. Elliott. "She & Louisa work in a mill belonging to a person called
Daniel Lord. They have neither church nor Sunday school. The nearest is 3 miles

off! I always feel very sorry when I hear of a manufactory where the operatives have no religious privileges. I gave Mary a good many tracts for herself and friends."[3]

When Mrs. Elliott launched a similar Sabbath school in nearby Marcus Hook in 1859, Victorine kept her friend well supplied in materials and advice. She and her sisters had also been instrumental in helping launch a Sunday school in the Rockdale area.[4] These examples of support for efforts beyond her immediate community reaffirm Victorine's continuing belief in the Sunday school as a transformative social construct. In her own neighborhood, the high level of commitment demonstrated by the superintendent and her faithful band of teachers proved to be the primary reason Siddall's seedling had continued to thrive after his departure.

LITERARY PURSUITS

Throughout their lives, the academic siblings maintained their passion for reading. Between 1850 and 1860, Victorine and Eleuthera consumed hundreds of books and articles covering an eclectic range of topics. The widowed sisters read both secular and religious works in French and English, and were especially fond of history, biographies, and novels. "We read aloud every evening as usual till 9 o'clock when we have prayers," Victorine told Mary.[5] Together, with longtime friends Sarah Gilpin and Anna Brincklé, they kept up with the latest authors in both America and England. "Did you not enjoy [William Cullen] Bryant's discourse on Washington Irving?" inquired Vic enthusiastically of Sarah.[6]

Like many other Americans of the day, they read the popular tales of Charles Dickens, which were released through periodicals in serial installments. Although Victorine thought his subjects "caricatures," she readily forgave him for "the sake of his exquisite pathos, his knowledge of human nature and his skill in delineating some of its best traits."[7] Another favorite of hers was George Eliot, whom she was delighted to discover was actually a woman named Mary Ann Evans: "I got the other day The Mill on the Floss after discovering that the author of Clerical stories [Scenes of Clerical Life] & Adam Bede were one!"[8]

Works on the lives of famous French women were perennial favorites. She informed young Henry that "Your aunt and I spend our evenings in reading aloud to each other while she sews and I cut labels. We are enjoying [Madame] de Sevigne's letters.[9] They give us a lively account of what was passing in France at the time of Louis 14th & she writes so delightfully that everything she says is interesting."[10] They read the works of Victor Cousin, a French biographer and philosopher who had been born in Paris the same year as Victorine:[11] "We began last evening, a very interesting book, La Jeunesse de [Madame] de Longueville by Cousin. . . . [And] of two other French ladies by the same author . . . [Madames] de Chevreuse & de Hautefort. The latter was a lovely character very superior to most of the Ladies of those times."[12] (The former woman, Madame de Chevreuse, was known for her palace intrigues and escapades and, although interesting to read, Victorine could not applaud her morals.)

The sisters also tackled massive historical works, such as *Lectures on English History* by Henry Reed, and the last two volumes of T. B. Macauley's *History of England*. "It will be quite an undertaking for there are upwards of 1400 pages," Victorine wrote to Henry Algernon.[13] They had begun William H. Pickering's *History of the Reign of Phillip II*, but were "very sorry" that his untimely death precluded his finishing the work.[14] By the time the sisters were hunkering down for the winter of 1858–1859, Victorine told Mary that "We are now reading aloud in the evenings Motley's history of the Dutch Republic, a very interesting book in 3 large Volumes. We are at the second Volume."[15]

Religious works like the popular *Pilgrim's Progress* by John Bunyan and *The Saint's Everlasting Rest* by Richard Baxter were standard fare, as were sermons and works by other well-known theologians. The sisters were inspired by the biographies of famous Christians, such as *The Life of Captain Vicars*, the pious soldier of the Crimean War, and *The Life of Lord Teignmouth*, the former Governor-General of India.[16] Victorine had been so impressed by the godly example of the latter that she sent his biography to Henry Algernon at West Point.[17] Works by female writers of strong moral character were also popular with the sisters, such as Maria Edgeworth, Hannah More, and Elizabeth Gaskell. The latter had written *Cranford* and her much-lauded biography *The Life of Charlotte Bronte*, which Victorine had enjoyed "extremely."[18] Lydia Howard Huntley, better known as "Mrs. Sigourney" after her marriage, was admired by Victorine for her literary and moral inspiration to young women. "I am reading Lydia Howard's Journal and I like it very much," wrote Vic to Sophie in the closing weeks of her life. "It will be an excellent book to give to one of our nieces. It is interesting and improving."[19] Ever the teacher, one of the last books she would ever read had been chosen with the benefit of her young charges in mind.

"I Feel an Interest"

Due to the economic depression that followed the Panic of 1857, when it had appeared that the American banking system was on the verge of collapse, several cotton mills along the Brandywine failed. Although the economic disaster had reached its nadir by the close of 1858, many local families were still suffering. At Flea Park, like many other millworkers' communities, the predominant social problem was alcoholism. Long an issue in the Brandywine community, drunkenness had plagued the neighborhood since its earliest days. Although inebriation had been suspected in several mill accidents, including the Great Explosion of 1818, alcohol remained a strong temptation for many a hardworking mill hand at the end of a long day. Victorine's letters record the death of more than one man who had drowned in the Brandywine Creek after a night of carousing. On one occasion, a somewhat peeved Victorine told Sophie about a recent visit she had received from Mrs. James Bayard[20] and her two youngest daughters: "We saw very little of the young ladies, who chose to remain out of doors during nearly all the visit watching the proceedings of a very drunken man at our gate."[21] On another occasion,

Vic and Eleu were awakened by sounds emanating from the parlor below their bedroom. Their verbal outcry spooked a would-be burglar, who quickly exited through the backdoor. They suspected that the man had been intoxicated. In July of 1859, Vic told Evelina that they were still without a gardener. "The difficulty will be to find one . . . who does not drink. The temptations here are so great; it is a great deal worse than at your house."[22]

A single page from her diary for April of 1860 reveals how seriously she took the issue of drunkenness:

> April 7th—I went over the new bridge, called to see W[illiam] Allisson, the Mitchells, W[illiam] Dougherty and W[illiam] Sterling, spoke to the latter on the subject of temperance.

> [April] 21—again in Flea park, called at Nat Browns, Mrs Murphy, Mrs Gill, and M Lance, spoke to the latter on temperance, told me he had been a year without drinking, made the promise [to quit] after having been drunk one day in town.[23]

Her diary notations reveal that many of her visits (which she sometimes referred to as her "pastorals") were intended as much for the parents of her scholars as they were for the scholars themselves. She believed it was within the realm of a teacher's responsibilities to address any issue that affected a child's well-being, including alcoholism. In addition to her native boldness and frankness of speech, it didn't hurt that she was also the boss's big sister.

Victorine turned sixty-six on August 30, 1858, and, except for sporadic bouts of stomach cramps, which she referred to as her "cholics," she remained healthy and active. Her tall figure was a familiar sight on the neighborhood's trails as she made visits to students and parents, conducted medical calls, or performed various errands of mercy. Her status as a widow enabled her to be more socially proactive than most married women of means, and likelier to be available when needed. While the majority of medical requests she dealt with consisted of treatments for cuts and bruises, rashes, earaches, fevers, digestive issues, and other common complaints, parents knew that she would send for a doctor if she encountered a situation beyond her own skill level.

Eleuthera, who had been transcribing the family's papers and letters, discovered that Victorine was not the first female physician of the family. Their paternal grandmother, Marie Le Dée, had occupied the position long before her—to the apparent chagrin of her clientele. Vic noted that Eleu had been "amusing herself reading our grandmother's letters (Grand papa's first wife) and she occasionally treats me to curious extracts, which amuse us very much. She was the *doctress* at Bois de Fosses and inflicted awful doses of medicines on her patients."[24]

Encouraged by such genes, "Doctor Bauduy" was unafraid to dispense medical advice whenever she thought it might help. A recent prescription for Sophie had included taking, "a small dose of oil with 8 or 10 ten drops of laudanum," followed by quinine, "or . . . paregoric if you do not take the oil."[25] When young Henry

Algernon wrote from West Point complaining of frequent digestive issues, his aunt assured him that if he followed her directions, he would be feeling much better by the time he arrived home on furlough. "In the meantime, if you have not yet tried it, suppose you take a wine glass full of cold Chamomile tea three times a day, before your meals? . . . If your disease comes from the stomach this tea may help you very much. At any rate, it cannot hurt you."[26]

Victorine's files contain an attractive medical notebook she had made for herself. The cover shows the title "Dr. V E Bauduy" above a colorfully drawn array of her remedies (such as lemons, chamomile tea, and chicken water). Among its entries were found instructions by the old family physician, Dr. Didier, on how to purify a patient's blood, and a three-page note by Dr. Thomas Mackie Smith on how to conduct the vaccination process. Dr. Smith had inscribed: "To Dr. Bauduy, this description of the progress of vaccination is humbly dedicated by a brother of the *Noble Science*."[27]

In 1857, a local girl named Victorine Boulé had acquired a severe case of worms and her mother had called for her namesake, Mrs. Victorine Bauduy. *La femme docteur* prescribed a regimen of medicine and herbs that proved successful in ridding the poor girl of her frightening guests. Updating Sophie a few days later, Vic wrote: "Madame Boulé was here on Saturday. She told me her little girl was much better after passing 49 worms, some of which were enormous!"[28]

In her dual roles of teacher and visiting nurse, she was often in a position to observe the needs of millworkers' families firsthand and would discreetly find ways to meet them whenever she could. In the case of Victorine Boulé's mother, for example, Mrs. Bauduy mentioned that "I gave her a counter pan, pair of sheets, shirt & chemise for Victorine and a nice black silk hood of mine, made like a hat which she thinks will do to go to church in, so she was delighted. I feel an interest in the poor woman."[29]

The phrase "I feel an interest" appears several times in Victorine's letters as an expression of compassion. For example, she had tried to find a live-in position for the needy seamstress Mrs. Ryan, telling Sophie that "I feel very much interested for the poor creature."[30] On a trip to Winterthur, she had stopped to see the mother of one of her scholars. "I found the poor woman had no wood, & only flour to last till next week," she told Sophie. Feeling an interest, she arranged for a local man to send the woman half a cord of wood, and said she would send her some flour, "but I really don't know how she is to be supported through the winter."[31] On another occasion, when she learned that Daniel Simpson (who had five children attending the Sunday school) had lost his job, she told Mary Elliot that she didn't know what the family would do: "The girls have no work. I gave the mother some bags to make for the factory this fall. I will give her some more but it will not be much for them all."[32] Victorine's responses to those in need were as varied as finding a nurse for family friend Polly Simmons, or taking up a collection for a poor family with an injured son. Sometimes they were as unique as supplying a French newspaper to a woman who spoke very little English. When she learned that such a paper arrived regularly at West Point, she asked her nephew Henry to send her the used copies: "I know they will amuse that poor French woman who speaks too little English to associate much with her neighbors."[33]

Lately, however, her "interest" lay much closer to home. The health of their mother's brother, Uncle Charles, had been deteriorating for some time, and was now complicated by increased mental confusion. In former years, the sisters had questioned some of his decisions and behavior, but they loved their uncle and admired him for his creative talents. He was an accomplished artist, musician, gardener, and woodcarver. Although he remained more comfortable speaking his native French, he enjoyed life in America and the freedom it gave him to pursue the varied interests of his independent spirit. He seemed content to be a bachelor but voiced a desire to the sisters that he wished to "marry a rich woman."[34] On one occasion, Eleu complained about a social impropriety she felt Uncle Charles had committed (visiting the wife of their handyman during the lady's confinement). Victorine defended him by saying, "He goes on just as usual, poor man! He is much to be pitied, having nothing to do & no one to love."[35]

By the autumn of 1858, Uncle Charles's cough had grown worse and his dementia had advanced. Throughout the winter, Victorine made daily walks to Louisa's to visit him. For a brief time in December he seemed to rally, but the disease continued to take its toll, and on March 25, 1859, just nine days after his eighty-second birthday, Charles Dalmas expired in his bedroom at Eleutherian Mills. "His malady was long and tedious," wrote Vic to Mary Elliott, "but he did not suffer much acute pain. He had lost his mind very much, for some time past. The funeral took place on last Sunday."[36] Victorine felt his loss deeply; Uncle Charles had been a part of her life since birth.

His was already the second funeral Victorine had attended in the young year. Henry and Isabella Belin's daughter, Louisa Wales, had died giving birth to her first child at the close of another sad January. Vic had admired the twenty-two-year-old's sweet and pious character, and her cheerful presence as a teacher at the Sunday school. "One can hardly realize that she is no more," wrote Vic sadly to Mary. "She was so young, so full of life & health. It seems but a little while ago I went down to see her married. Her husband is in deep grief, but I cannot help feeling most for her parents. Mrs Belin has the little boy just two weeks old. Louisa gave him to her while she was yet conscious. Towards the last she was totally out of her mind. Her disease was one of those bad fevers that sometimes come in confinements."[37]

She visited Mrs. Belin during the ensuing weeks and thought Louisa's orphaned baby was "beginning to grow finely."[38] But little Henry, named after his grandfather, would not survive the year, leaving his grandparents brokenhearted. "Oh Lord," prayed Victorine, "I must not despond when sorrow comes to sit musing upon [my heart] but I must arouse each active power within me & strive to be always employed about my duties; by so doing I shall conquer grief & be more useful to my friends. Oh grant my Lord that amidst all the sorrow & exigencies of life I may be a comfort to those dear friends & that I may support their spirits instead of letting their sorrows prey upon my mind."[39]

In June, sorrow was turned to joy when cousin and captain, Samuel Francis, returned from China. After an absence of two years, the USS *Minnesota* pulled into the docks at Boston on June 2, 1859. The veteran seaman arrived from the Far East bearing gifts. To his beloved Sophie he presented an exquisitely carved ironwood table with Chinese patterns and a marble top.[40] Victorine and Eleu received a pair of cats, a Persian male they named "Selim" and a female Japanese Bobtail they dubbed "Derzina." Victorine took an immediate liking to the Persian, but he died six weeks later, causing her to lament: "I did not think I could have become so much attached to an animal in so short a time. . . . We buried him behind the green house near a grapevine."[41]

Health-wise, the past year and a half had been less kind to the nurse of Smith Lane. Rheumatism in Victorine's left shoulder had been giving her trouble, and her "cholics" had become more frequent. Regarding the latter, she told Sophie: "If I could only get rid of that difficulty I should do very well."[42] At first she had not been too concerned with these occasional bouts, but by early fall she had suffered another series of painful attacks in her lower abdomen.

She was still recovering on the morning of October 21, 1859, when four buildings in the lower yards were blown to pieces in rapid succession. Victorine broke the news to Sophie: "I have . . . to tell you of an explosion which occurred this morning at Hagley . . . several men lost their lives. It was the new press room at Hagley that first blew up, because a cart backed against it so as to strike fire. . . . Joanna's house is much injured. She and her children have dined here."[43] Within half an hour of the blast, Henry sent two men to check on Joanna at Hagley House and his two sisters atop Smith Lane; they informed the women that the only victims they knew for certain were William Moran and Hubert Jacquot.[44] They feared for the half-dozen men who had been in the immediate vicinity but at this early stage they were still uncertain of their identities. Victorine knew that Jacquot was the husband of Justine Jacquot, the woman for whom she had been collecting the French newspapers. Justine, not quite thirty-four years of age, was caring for five children below the age of ten. Her eight-year-old, Julie Marie, had nearly drowned in the creek earlier in the summer.

The next day she wrote to Cousin Amelia, who was now living in Scranton with her daughter Ella Breck and her husband. "The pressroom in front of our house first went off, then two rolling mills, a little composition house & last the glazing mill. It was dreadful. [Seven] men lost their lives.[45] . . . We deeply grieved for the families of the poor men. One of the women is the wife of a French man named Jaquot whose little girl nearly drowned when they lived over the creek. She does not speak English, so that her neighbors cannot converse with her. Eleu went to see her yesterday and I this morning. Her grief is most touching."[46]

The du Pont sisters were concerned that the poor woman would not understand what was being said to her by the company's representatives and, since Vic was still indisposed, Eleu went over to Justine's to assure her that she and the children would be provided for. A couple of hours later, the gentle sister returned in tears, saying that the sight of the distressed woman weeping with her children was almost too much to bear. Victorine went to the house the next day and found it the same. Nevertheless, the warm welcome the sisters always received from the distraught mother and her children encouraged them to keep returning. Victorine felt an interest in the young woman and did what she could to provide for her family in supplementary ways.

On December 28, Victorine felt compelled to squeeze in one more letter to her nephew before the year ended. "Dear Henry," she began, "I am determined not to let [the year] end without sending you a few lines. It is a time at which we think a great deal of [our] absent friends & regret they cannot be with us."[47] By "absent friends," she had meant those who, like Henry himself, were separated by physical distance. But 1859 had carved deeper wounds. Uncle Charles's departure had been the most personal, but her grief for others, like Justine Jacquot and Henry and Isabella Belin, had also pierced her heart. On the periphery of her year-end reflections may have been other 1859 obituaries, which included literary men she had read, like William H. Prescott, Horace Mann, and Washington Irving. Even as she was folding her letter to young Henry, she had no way of knowing that Thomas Babington Macaulay, whose three-volume *History of England* she had recently finished, had died that very day in London.

CHAPTER 20

Nearing Home

As talk of Southern secession and rumors of war were mounting across the nation, daily life for the two sisters atop Smith Lane was relatively calm. Thomas Flemming, their new outdoor man, was an experienced gardener and handyman who kept their greenhouses, gardens, and yards in tiptop shape. Rachel Smith (a young relation of Eleu's by marriage) moved in with the sisters when her brother left to seek work in Philadelphia, and Phoebe Sharpless, an eager girl who had won Victorine's heart with her efficiency and cheerful demeanor, started as their new cook. Mrs. Riggs, a hard-pressed woman to whom Victorine had formerly given sewing tasks, turned out to be an adept washing woman as well, so the sisters took her on permanently. Victorine assured Mary Elliott, however, that no one could ever take her place, and that she would always be considered their "jewel of a housekeeper."[1]

On January 1, 1860, du Ponts far and wide gathered at Eleutherian Mills for their traditional New Year's celebration, an annual time of gaiety, feasting, and exchanging of gifts. This year's event was rendered all the more joyful when Eleuthera came over to the house to join the family "for the first time since eight years."[2] "Auntie Tata" was met with a chorus of joyful welcomes by the youngies—and several tearful embraces by the adults.

But before January came and went, it added the name of Henry Dilworth Gilpin to its growing list of epitaphs.[3] A successful literary critic, editor, and lawyer, Henry had served briefly as President Martin Van Buren's attorney general.[4] But to Victorine and her sisters, he had simply been "Henry," their friend Sarah's older brother. "We have spent that long month of January pleasantly and quietly enough, but it is always a sad month to me on account of some very sad anniversaries it brings around," confessed Vic to Mary Elliott.[5]

Names like Gilpin, Shipley, Tatnall, and Ferris symbolized more than future street names in the city of Wilmington to Victorine; they belonged to acquaintances. Families like the Canbys and Bayards were frequent visitors to the sisters' home. Victorine herself bore the name of Bauduy, daughter-in-law to one of old Wilmington's most influential men. Ultimately, however, it would be her own

maiden name—the family's name—that would top Delaware's list of most recog-
nizable names and come to be known across the country.

Victorine's trip to the Crystal Palace in 1853 had introduced her to myriad technological advances that were being made in her generation. Photography was one
that especially delighted her. To have been born in the last generation that knew
only paintings, sculptures, and drawings, it seemed miraculous to her that a person's real-life image could be captured. Elwood Garret's studio, at 720 Market Street
in Wilmington, had become her favorite establishment for purchasing daguerreo-
types.[6] Usually not interested in having her own picture taken, she cajoled others
into posing so that she could distribute pictures of them as New Year's presents.
"I have not as yet seen my gift to you," she told Evelina on the first day of 1859. "It
is our dear Brother Henry's picture. I prevailed on him to go to Mr Garret's that
I might have his likeness for Louisa and for you."[7]

Reports of inventions and discoveries that seemed to appear almost weekly in
the newspapers enthused her. The laying of the first transatlantic telegraph cable,
completed in August of 1858, was "the most wonderful thing, and appears like
magic to me," she marveled to Mary two weeks after the event.[8] Having long been
accustomed to waiting four to six weeks to receive news from France, she could
barely comprehend that it was now possible to receive transcontinental communication within a matter of minutes. As a girl, a trip to Philadelphia by carriage
had required an overnight layover in Chester, but since the arrival of the railroads,
she could say, "We were whisked off at such a speed that we reached Wilmington
in less than an hour. . . . I never travelled so fast in my life!"[9]

Since the dawn of history, sewing by hand had been an essential component of
every young woman's domestic education but, by the 1850s, improvements to the
sewing machine had evolved to the point where it could be mass produced at afford-
able rates. Although initially awkward to learn, the contraption was embraced by
Victorine's friends and family members. Even the experienced seamstress Mary
Elliott quickly made the transition. "I am much pleased you have bought a sewing
machine," cheered Vic, . . . [Louisa] has bought one lately, but she does not yet
understand how to manage it very well."[10] The progressive granddaughter of Pierre
Samuel du Pont de Nemours subscribed to periodicals such as *Littell's Living Age* for
worldwide articles of interest and received newspapers such as the *Delaware
Gazette* and the *National Intelligencer* to stay abreast of local and national news.

By 1860, tensions between North and South were dominating the headlines.
Although Delaware was officially a slave state, sympathies were divided between
pro-abolitionist forces in the industrial north, and pro-slavery forces in the state's
southern, agricultural regions. The sisters thought it inconceivable that the South
would actually resort to the threatened "madness" of secession, as Sophie had put
it.[11] The youngest sister's avid interest in national affairs was fueled largely by her
husband's role in the U.S. Navy. When they learned that Frank had been appointed
to oversee the Philadelphia Naval Yard, the sisters had felt relieved. In a hastily
scribbled note she sent across the creek to Sophie, Vic exclaimed: "Dearest, I cannot

tell you how grateful I feel for the piece of news you tell me! Since the late troubles I had been thinking much about [Frank being assigned to] Annapolis. . . . But this appointment to Philadelphia is what we wished for."[12]

———

As much as Victorine welcomed technological change, transitions on a personal level were much more difficult for her. In a letter to Henry Algernon, she wistfully stated, "I hope I shall not find you too much changed, and that I shall still be able to recognize my darling nephew in the big West Point Cadet. . . . I really believe I would rather have had you remain as you were when you left us. But that was impossible, and at my age I ought to be reconciled to the inevitable changes of this life. You will find great alterations in your nest of sisters; they are all growing up very lovely and what is better, very good girls."[13]

To the judicious aunt, the fact that Henry's sisters were growing up to be *good* girls, was the most important facet of their development. (She had expressed the very same sentiment about him on past occasions.)[14] Louisa's six remaining daughters were, each in their turn, making open professions of Christian faith. Most recently, Ellen Eugenia had made her public commitment on May 13, 1860. Now seventeen and attending school in Philadelphia, Ellen traveled home so she could be confirmed at Christ Church by Bishop Alfred Lee. Henry supported these events with his attendance, but it is safe to say that it was Louisa's pious efforts that provided the family's spiritual guidance. Of the nine others confirmed with Ellen on that same day, six were from the Brandywine Manufacturer's Sunday School. "This is a great encouragement to one's efforts," stated Vic honestly to Sarah Gilpin.[15]

Christianity had become the primary lens through which Victorine perceived her world, and through her role as first tutor, she introduced that same biblical perspective to each of her American-born siblings. Her influence provided an atmosphere in the home that was distinctly Christian in its values. Later, when devout women like Louisa and Joanna married into the family, that receptive atmosphere made it easy for them to raise their numerous children in their faith, even if their own husbands took little interest. Prayers, Bible readings, and church attendance were interwoven into the normal patterns of their week. Among Victorine's female friends and family members, a like-minded Christian worldview sprinkled their conversations as a natural element of their discourse, as is reflected in this letter from Victorine to Mary Elliott:

What you say is most true "that every station in life has its own peculiar troubles and vexations," and our happiness depends on the manner in which we bear them. We must remember *who* it is that sends them and for *what* purpose: it is to loosen our hold on earthly things and to raise our affections to things that will not perish in the rising. If we lean on the creature we are sure to be disappointed; if we cling to the Saviour we must be happy. It is just as important to let this consideration influence us in little things as in great ones, but we are too apt to forget it.[16]

Like most religious people of her day, Victorine's theology revealed a mixture of influences, but the virtues of love and compassion remained the pre-eminent characteristics. Even when the embers of evangelical faith had first stirred in her, she had been sensitive to the religious beliefs of those closest to her. Sophie remembered that "the bonds of friendship influenced her to consider intimately the doctrines of the Roman Catholics [Aunt Gabrielle] & also of the Swedenborgians [sister-in-law Margaretta] yet the light derived from the Word through the Holy Spirit induced her to select the Episcopal church."[17] As for the deistical views she once shared with her father and grandfather, she had come to reject them out of hand. She believed they reduced the divine authority of the Bible to a plane lower than that of the humanistic opinions of Enlightenment philosophers.

At the Sunday school, she urged her scholars to keep their biblical interpretation simple, and to remember that God's purpose was to communicate with them. It was more important, she stressed, to focus on the clearer passages than to delve prematurely into controversial or difficult texts. Quoting English evangelical Rev. Edward Bickersteth, she taught: "Let us study & practice what is plain, and God will discover to us all that is needful we should know."[18] Her approach to piety, the application of faith to behavior, was marked by practicality. Victorine was keenly aware that opportunities to demonstrate the compassion of the Gospel were seldom lacking, especially in her manufacturing community where so many families struggled to make ends meet.

"SOMETHING LIKE CHOLERA MORBUS"

On August 8, 1860, Henry du Pont turned forty-eight. Victorine went over in the early afternoon to pay him a visit and to bring him a small present. Upon arriving, she found him sitting in the parlor with his eldest daughter, Evelina, and she passed a pleasant two hours with them. Better known as "Linette" to the family, young Evelina would be turning twenty in just a few weeks. As Vic listened to her niece's animated description of a social event she and her friends had attended down by the creek, it may have crossed the older woman's mind that she had taught both Linette and her father. Twenty years separated Henry from his daughter, but twenty years separated him from his older sister as well.

As she left the old familiar parlor for home, she told Henry that she would be writing his son at West Point and would convey his love. On the way home, she stopped at Nemours to see her favorite niece, Mrs. Victorine Kemble, down from New York City to visit her mother. She found Little Vic sitting on the piazza with Meta, along with "a grand meeting of all the younger children; Sophie, Vic and Willie being there too."[19] Although she had begun to feel unwell during the visit, she was content to enjoy the interaction of the youngies and to catch up with her namesakes. With Henry's eleven-year-old daughter present, three Victorine Elizabeths were together in one place.

By the time she reached home, the discomfort she had begun to feel at Meta's had worsened. Abdominal discomfort continued intermittently for the next few days, but in the early hours of Sunday, August 12, she was awakened by severe pains. Dr. Francis Gurney Smith, now a prominent physician in Philadelphia, was visiting his sister Joanna, so Eleu sent for him. The following morning, Vic felt well enough to inform Sarah Gilpin:

> I had been well for the last two weeks but I suffered yesterday with a severe attack of cholics, since 4 o'clock in the morning till noon. I was better in the afternoon and came downstairs to see several members of the family who called after church. I am wonderfully well today, indeed better than Saturday when I had premonitory symptoms & felt uncomfortable all day. Dr Smith thinks this complaint is occasioned by undigested food which passes in the lower intestines . . . [and gives] me so much pain. He wants me to take charcoal every night before I go to bed. Dr Bush had ordered it to me last fall, but I never gave it a fair trial. So I believe I will recommence it.[20]

The recurring episodes were beginning to concern the Brandywine nurse. At first, she attributed them to the time of year, having noticed that the hottest months were when the pains were more likely to appear. After suffering a severe attack in June, she described it as "something like Cholera Morbus,"[21] a nineteenth-century term defined as "a gastrointestinal disturbance characterized by abdominal pain, diarrhea, and sometimes vomiting."[22] July had followed with alternating episodes of constipation and diarrhea. The painful attack that began on August 12 continued sporadically throughout the month, forcing her to cancel her customary trip to Rockdale to visit Elizabeth Beach Smith, the mother of Sophie's friends Harriet and Clementina. As she had hoped, her condition improved when the cooler temperatures of September arrived.

———

All eyes were now on the presidential election. On November 3, 1860, Victorine mentioned to Mary Elliot that "We have heard very little about politics here, but the torch processions have been innumerable in Wilmington, & I believe the people down the creek went a great deal to those gatherings."[23] The following week, Abraham Lincoln was elected the sixteenth president of the United States. Forty-four days later, South Carolina seceded from the Union. As a silent white army of snowflakes overcame the branches of the majestic oak outside her window, Victorine lamented her country's sad condition to Sarah Gilpin:

> I feel the increased distance between us very much. It is a real pleasure to sit down quietly to converse with you this morning, when we are having the first snowstorm of the season. It tells us that winter is coming indeed, and that all our bright days are ended. Alas! I fear it is so in more ways than one. Is it not too sad that our country will be separated and that there is so little patriotism left in the land? I could not believe it. I always flattered myself that matters would be

adjusted. But Frank, who is just returned from Washington says, that South Carolina will certainly secede the 17 of this month; there is no telling what evils will follow. It is dreadful to think of it.[24]

By year's end, Victorine was feeling better physically and, in the letters she exchanged with Sarah Gilpin, she turned from current events to reminiscing about old times and sharing their literary critiques of various works. Victorine had purchased *Danesbury House* earlier in the year ("an excellent temperance tale")[25] by Mrs. Henry Wood, and "Bryant's discourse on Washington Irving."[26] She then read George Eliot's *The Mill on the Floss* and, in December, finished *Hopes and Fears* by Charlotte Mary Yonge. December also saw the release of the first installment of a work called *Great Expectations* by Charles Dickens. Already entranced with the tale, both friends expressed hopes that the time would not be so "unconscionably long"[27] between releases.

Victorine had achieved a measure of fulfillment through devotion to family and friends, the maturity of her Christian faith, and a life of selfless service to her community. Ferdinand's death had altered the course of her life, but it had not succeeded in defining her. She had resolved that the love she was unable to lavish on him would be shared with those around her.

Given the level of social standing her family had attained, she could have easily pursued a more self-indulgent lifestyle, but this was not the path she chose. Personally frugal, yet generous with others, she was happiest (as she herself had once stated) in contributing to the happiness of those around her.[28] Perhaps an excerpt she had copied from one of Wordsworth's lengthier poems described her outlook best:

> She welcomed what was given & craved no more;
> Whate'er the scene presented to her view
> That was the best, to that she was attuned
> By her benign simplicity of life.[29]

CHAPTER 21

Pathway's End

I became convinced she had death in her.
—Sophie Du Pont to Amelia du Pont, January 24, 1861

January 1861 started with a small glitch. Former student John Lowery had sent his annual gift of two handsome Bibles to be given away to the Christ Church Sunday School's most diligent boy and girl of the previous school year. When Lowery's package arrived in Wilmington on January 3, the postmaster, George Canning, sent a notice to Victorine stating that a fifty-cent surcharge for shipping was due. Since he had already paid the Philadelphia branch for the delivery, he would not release the item until he had been reimbursed. She responded by stating that Mr. Lowery had just sent a letter reminding her that he always prepaid the express rate in New York, and that she should never "at any time" be liable for shipping expenses.[1] The indifferent Mr. Canning (already out his fifty cents) refused to release the package without payment. Annoyed, but over a barrel, Victorine sent a man with the money to retrieve the volumes. She knew it was a trivial matter, but such things vexed her on principle. After all, the scholars were looking forward to Premium Sunday with joyful anticipation and, at the dawn of 1861, most Americans would have agreed that joy was an element in short supply. A sense of powerlessness and disbelief was beginning to grip wary citizens as it seemed like an irreversible slide toward the inconceivable kept unfolding day by day. Could it really be possible that this precious union of states was about to dissolve?

Earlier that morning, Captain Du Pont had received an unexpected summons to Annapolis and had already departed. The sisters, so recently relieved over his appointment as commandant of the Philadelphia Naval Yards, were now in a heightened state of alarm. Writing to Frank a week later, Sophie expressed, "I feel your absence doubly at this time, when so distressed about national affairs. Alas! The madness of the Southern people continues! The delusion which hurries them in to destroy themselves & us, I cannot comprehend."[2] The wife of the soon-to-be admiral held out hopes that cooler heads in both the North and South would prevail. "I think men are feeling that civil war would be the worst of all evils—even the South may soon recover sense enough to realize that it would be worse than submitting four years to a republican President."[3]

As one of President Buchanan's last decrees in office, he proclaimed Friday, January 4, 1861, a National Day of Fasting, Humiliation, and Prayer. It was to be a country-wide appeal. "In this the hour of our calamity and peril," pleaded Buchanan, "to whom shall we resort for relief but to the God of our fathers? His omnipotent arm only can save us from the awful effects of our own crimes and follies—our own ingratitude and guilt towards our Heavenly Father."[4] Churches across the nation opened their doors to anyone wishing to pray in solitude or to attend a public gathering. Christ Church Christiana Hundred was no exception, and the sisters made plans to attend Rev. Brinckle's special service. It was snowing heavily that Friday morning as faithful members of the Brandywine neighborhood made their way to the doors of the blue-stone church. When Sophie arrived, she glanced over at "Pew 77," which was rented quarterly by the sisters of Smith Lane. She could see Eleu sitting with Rachel Smith, but Victorine was missing.

The service began with Isaac Watt's appropriate hymn "O God, Our Help in Ages Past." In keeping with the president's desire for the *United* States to humble themselves before God, Rev. Brinckle avoided all mention of politics and spoke from the text: "Who can tell if God will turn and repent, and turn away from his fierce anger, that we perish not?"[5] After the service, Sophie learned that Victorine had experienced severe colic pain shortly after breakfast. This was disappointing news, for everyone had begun to hope that the troublesome malady might be gone for good. "For the three last months of the year," wrote Eleu to Ella Breck, "she had been in such excellent health, looked so well, & was so active, that we had been rejoicing in the hope that those attacks, which had caused this long uneasiness, had entirely passed away."[6]

With Frank gone to Annapolis, Sophie accompanied Eleu and Rachel back to the Smith house. They were met at the door by a distraught Jenny Mullen who blurted out that Victorine had experienced severe stomach pains "and thrown up!"[7] This last bit of news alarmed Eleuthera because it was the first time that vomiting had accompanied her sister's symptoms. The trio rushed upstairs and found Victorine in bed, resting quietly under her quilts. Although paler than usual, she assured them that she felt better. Eleu then asked why she thought she had thrown up, and Vic suggested that it was probably due to her earlier pains interfering with the digestion of her breakfast. She remained healthy for the remainder of the day and felt so well on Saturday that she invited a few of the older nieces to tea, as she had been wanting to see them.

The following day, she and Eleu made the short trip to the schoolhouse, accompanied by Jenny and Rachel, who assisted them in carrying the extra supplies for "Premium Sunday." Despite its transition to a denominational entity, the school had maintained a large enrollment. The last few years had recorded an average of 157 children per Sunday and attendance would, in the coming year, increase to 180.[8] As Eleuthera watched the children approach one by one that January morning, she would later recall the moment to Mary Elliott: "This was the 6th of January, the last time she was ever in our dear Sunday school or at Church, Oh! How little I then imagined we should never again be there together! There, where we have been every Sunday, excepting when I was ill or away, for 45 years!"[9]

The following Tuesday, Victorine and Sophie spent a leisurely overnight visit with Lina and James Bidermann. Due to its distance from the noisy mills, a trip to Winterthur was usually considered a respite.[10] Vic had left instructions with Eleu that if it were to snow, they would extend their visit for another day. As it turned out, it did snow—heavily—so Eleuthera did not bother to send the carriage. Thus she was "greatly surprised" when her sister strode into the parlor at half past four on Wednesday afternoon, with the wintry wind swirling at her back.[11] Bidermann had driven her home because Victorine had felt the onset of stomach pains, and she wished to be available to her "remedies" if the episodes increased.

The attack subsided, however, and the threat did not materialize. At nine o'clock on Thursday evening, a telegram arrived from Alexis's daughter, Fanny, who had been traveling back and forth to Philadelphia for the past several weeks due to her grandmother's failing health. The news was not good, and indicated that Mrs. Eliza (Mackie) Smith, Francis Gurney's wife, was sinking fast. The telegram called for the immediate presence of Smith's daughter Joanna, and her daughter-in-law Eleuthera. Due to the storm, the women waited until the following morning to take the train. Although Vic had caught a cold, her stomach pains had not returned, and they agreed that Eleu's place should be in Philadelphia with her in-laws. Paulina Fowle,[12] an old friend of the family, was due to arrive in Wilmington on a four-day visit, and Victorine assured her sister that she felt well enough to entertain.

Shortly after Joanna and Eleu departed, Vic sent a note across the creek to Sophie to say that her cold had worsened and that some stomach pain had returned. Fearing that Victorine might overexert herself, Sophie immediately packed her bags and arrived at the Smith house in the early afternoon: "So tho' it came in to snow hard I went over—& was with her from that time till she died."[13] Paulina Fowle arrived shortly after and, though sorry she had missed Eleuthera, insisted on helping Sophie with Victorine's care.

The youngest sister discovered that V's cold had worsened and that she had lost her appetite. "She took *enema's* & said she was costive—& she had some colics Sunday. I insisted Sunday night on writing to Dr Bush to come & see her. He did so Monday evening late."[14] When the doctor arrived, he "prescribed a preparation of senna & other things" to help with V's constipation, "and that was all," noted Sophie.[15] It was obvious to her that Dr. Bush did not think her sister's condition any more serious than her previous attacks had been.

Mrs. Francis Gurney Smith passed away at her Philadelphia home on Monday morning, January 14. Eleu sent a message home, saying, "[Joanna and I] sat watching our beloved Mother in the agonies of death! She was unconscious when we reached her, & never knew us!"[16] That afternoon Victorine sent a note over to Winterthur to apprise Lina of her present condition: "My dear Sister, I am a great deal better today [in] every way. I coughed much less last night. I do not cough in the daytime, and I have no colics since I went to bed last evening with a hot pillow on my stomach." [The following sentence, inserted in French, translates as:] "Besides I went naturally this morning which had not occurred since about a week. . . . [Sophie] has been wanting to write you a long note ever since she is here, but she has not had a moment of leisure between keeping company to Mrs Fowle & nursing me. She is the most admirable nurse I ever knew. She is like our dear Mother, is she not?"[17] Those remarks would have meant the world to the youngest sister.

On January 15, Victorine was feeling so much better that she entertained a visit from Meta and Mary Van Dyke du Pont. The next morning, a Wednesday, she came down to breakfast and spent an enjoyable hour feeding and talking to her birds. By noontime, however, the pains in her lower abdomen returned. Sophie said she then, "went up & laid down & applied warm flannel (& took) flax seed enemas, her usual remedies."[18] Later in the day a note arrived from Evelina, inquiring about her sister's health. Wishing her not to worry unduly, Victorine scribbled off a short reply: "Dear sister, Thank you for your kind note. My cold continues much better. I have been downstairs yesterday and today, but I am troubled with cholics [sic] which are very annoying though they are not so violent as I have had them. Ever yrs, V."[19] This short note was to be her last. It seemed somehow fitting that Evelina, her "first friend," would be the last person for whom Victorine would ever again lift her pen.

A tired Eleuthera returned home at suppertime on Wednesday evening, January 16. Recounting the day's events to Mary, she would later report:

> I found Sister dressed, but on her bed, having again suffered some in the afternoon. We sent her up her tea & afterwards we talked to her all evening, sitting by the bed. [Sophie] slept with her . . . & she slept as usual, & had no pain. Thursday she rose & dressed & wanted to come down to breakfast, but we persuaded her to let us serve it to her. She took a cup of tea with some toast & appeared quite well. At 10 o'clock she said she felt very sick, & we put her to bed; she threw up her breakfast. She continued to suffer. The Dr was here at 12 o'clock & remained with us till near five, doing everything he could think of to produce an evacuation, but in vain. She underwent the most terrible pain, & told us unless the remedies had effect, she could not live! At [4:00 p.m.] the pain passed away, & she was [more at ease]. The doctor left medicines, but they were either thrown up, or had no effect.[20]

Rev. Brincklé stopped by and was surprised to hear that Victorine was so sick. The respectful minister had a brief prayer with Sophie and then departed. Sophie telegraphed Dr. Bush that the medicine had not worked; his reply was to continue administering it. She and Polly Simmons took turns giving Victorine the dosages every two hours throughout the night, but without effect.

At 5:00 a.m. Friday morning, the worried sister sent the doctor another update. Sophie had expected the physician to come out himself, but he instead sent a woman to apply leeches. "The leeching was very tedious," Sophie acknowledged to Cousin Amelia.

The nausea at her stomach continued & she had thrown up her medicine. She craved ice—which we gave to her in little pieces. I felt very much worried & alarmed. But when the doctor came [at 1:30 p.m.] he said that she was not dangerously ill & reassured us. About 4 o'clock however I became convinced she had death in her. I went & told Henry who was there, that she would not recover, & begged him to send for Lina. Henry thought I was too frightened, but he would speak to the Doctor. [Later] he told me the doctor said he saw no cause to send for [the Bidermanns] . . . & if the Dr saw any change then they could be sent for.[21]

It was now Friday evening, January 18, and Sophie had not left Victorine's side for eight straight days. Whether it was by vague premonition or because she was so attuned to her sister's condition, Sophie was the first to sense that an unbidden guest more serious than sickness was present. Even Eleu, who'd heard Victorine's painful cry that she could not live unless she could pass her food, had yet to consider death a possible visitor.

Sophie sent word of her presentiments to Hagley House, and Joanna immediately packed a small bag and came over to spend the night. When the Bidermanns' rider from Winterthur arrived at seven, the doctor told him there was no immediate danger and that they should inquire again in the morning. Sophie, however, detained the man at the door and scribbled a quick note to Lina, stressing that she should come herself in the morning. As she recounted, "I thought then that she would not recover—but I had no idea she would be taken from us so soon. Eleuthera was not at all aware of her danger."[22] When Eleu came into the sickroom to urge that Sophie should get some sleep, the younger sister begged to stay. As Eleuthera hesitated, Victorine's voice rose weakly from the pillow, "Yes, let her stay a few hours more."[23]

At about ten in the evening, Sophie noticed a change in her sister's breathing. She descended the stairs and found the doctor standing by the front door, bidding Henry goodbye. She asked Dr. Bush if he had noticed any change in Victorine's breathing. The weary doctor said no, but dutifully followed her upstairs. After taking Victorine's pulse, he quickly rose and called down to Joanna, asking if Henry had departed yet. She replied that he had, but thought he could be no farther than the gate. The doctor rushed to the front door, opened it, and summoned Henry back. Sophie, listening from the top of the stairs, felt relieved; the doctor had at last been convinced of the impending danger. When she asked him in confidence how much time he thought her sister had left, he responded soberly that if she continued to fail as rapidly as she had in the last half hour, she could not live till morning.

Sophie then told Henry to alert Louisa and the others, and to send a swift rider to Lina and James Bidermann at Winterthur. She awoke Polly, and then went into the dining room and roused the exhausted Jenny Mullen, who had been sleeping on the sofa. Sophie appraised her of the sudden turn of events and asked Jenny to be available when family members began to arrive. She then went upstairs and joined Eleu and Joanna, who were sitting silently in the dimly lit room. Without speaking to anyone, Sophie went straight to the bed and laid quietly down beside her sister. She quietly recited Bible verses that spoke reassuringly of Christ's promise of eternal life. Although the quotes came no louder than a whisper, Victorine opened her eyes and began to repeat the familiar lines along with her sister. After a time the patient paused and, without any sign of fear or agitation, stated what should have been a question, "You think, then, that I shall not recover."[24]

Glancing around at each of their faces, Victorine seemed to put everything together. She smiled weakly and then asked for whomever else was present in the house to come to her room. Sophie remembered that "Meta & Paulina, & Irénée, & Henry & Louisa, & Joanna, Eleuthera, Polly & I with, at the last hour or two, Brother & Lina, were round her."[25] Eleu would later recall:

> We were all with her. She was perfectly herself till three or 4 minutes before she left us, without a struggle & gently breathing! She spoke to us in her own dear voice. I never have seen such perfect peace & calm. Such trust & faith! When she first took in the idea of danger, she asked [Sophie] "if the Doctor thought she would not live." Sophie could only bow her head. "Well" [Victorine] replied, "I am not afraid. I know in whom I have trusted."[26]—And not a doubt or fear ever disturbed her. She left all her directions to Sophie & myself, "her two dear daughters" as she called us. She named every absent member of our family, leaving a message for each & for her two friends Miss [Sarah] Gilpin & Mrs Richard [Elizabeth Beach] Smith.
>
> About 15 minutes before she died, she said to me, "O Eleu, is it not a blessed thing to have one's consciousness this way to the last!" And oh! It was a mercy for which I never can feel grateful enough. Since we had to lose her, our heavenly Father sent us all the consolation we could have in our suffering! The knowledge that nothing could be done to save her, so that we have not that terrible thought "O if such or such a thing had been done!" . . . Dr. [Frank] G. Smith came down on Saturday night, alas! Too late; but he assured me he could have done nothing. From all the symptoms he said . . . it is a very rare disease & no remedies can either prevent it or cure it![27] O dear Mrs Elliott, . . . I pray fervently that when [God] summons me to rejoin the loved ones gone before, I may have such a death as hers. To follow the example of her life, must now be our constant endeavor.[28]

As Victorine's breathing grew more shallow, Sophie recalled that "Joanna read the prayer for those in danger of death & the Lord's prayer—& [Victorine] answered 'Amen' in as strong a voice as anyone. Her voice changed but a few moments ere she died, when she seemed to fall asleep—& then came a few moments of heavy breathing—& all was still."[29]

It was 4:30 in the morning. Victorine lay peacefully on her back, with Sophie kneeling on one side of the bed and Eleu on the other, each holding one of their sister's hands. Humble Polly Simmons, ever in the background, wept softly as she sat in an armchair in the shadowed corner. James Bidermann and Henry, each

holding a wife who was quietly weeping into their shoulders, looked down disbe-
lievingly at the still figure upon the bed.

Brandywine Farewell

Sophie had been the first to realize that death was near, but she was still surprised
at how quickly it came. Even Victorine had thought she had more time, for when
Henry made the suggestion around 1:00 a.m. to call for Rev. Brincklé, she urged
the family not to bother him until morning. Although she would not live to see the
minister again, his diary recorded the events of the day.

> January 19th. Received a great shock this morning, in hearing of the death of
> our dear friend, Mrs. Bauduy. She was not considered in danger until last night,
> & even then did not think it so imminent as it proved. Went to the house & saw
> her sisters, who told me the particulars. Her death was most peaceful. No per-
> turbation, sudden as the message was. She quietly leaned upon the Saviour whom
> she had loved in life, & who did not forsake her in the hour of her soul's need.
> She sent messages of love & recollection to everybody. She spoke very earnestly
> to her brother Henry on the great subject, pressing him to go to church, & tell-
> ing him it was in her heart to have asked him to go with them on the National
> Fast-day, but that she had not courage. He was much affected. O that our pre-
> cious Saviour would send it home to his heart! It is note-worthy that he proposed
> to his sister to send for me; but she, not supposing her end so near, said, "Oh
> not to-night! I should like to see Mr. B. very much, but wait till morning." Just
> at the early dawn her happy spirit went to heaven. She was conscious to the last.
> Seeing the Dr. with his hand on her pulse, she asked, "How is it?" He answered,
> "Very low, I can scarcely feel it." She calmly said, "I thought so," & closed her eyes,
> never speaking again. Her brother-in-law, Mr. Bidermann, who loved her as a
> sister, said, "What a glorious death!" . . . Our departed friend was the eldest
> child of her parents . . . and was actively engaged in [the Sunday school] to the
> last. Many of those trained will rise up & call her blessed. She was a true friend,
> warm & impulsive in her feelings, & if betrayed into a hasty word, the readiest
> to crave forgiveness, often with tears. None so ready to forgive as herself. "Blessed
> are the dead who die in the Lord."[30]

The following morning, a Sunday, Mr. Brincklé oversaw the school program in her
place. "At [Sunday school] in the morning, . . . Missing an accustomed face there,
when her little old basket with the books & keys came in, but not its owner whose
kind greeting we have always met. All seemed to feel the sad event."[31] As the minister surveyed the room, he observed that many of the children were openly
crying.

News traveled quickly throughout the neighborhood. By the time of her funeral
service on Monday morning, Christ Church was filled to overflowing. So large was
the crowd that latecomers were forced to stand along the walls or squeezed into
any nook where space could be found. Henry had set about making the funeral

arrangements. He contacted the McClary brothers, Samuel and Thomas, who operated a combination cabinetmaking and undertaker business at 605 Market Street
in Wilmington. Henry selected a finely crafted, red cedar coffin lined with fine
cloth, and a cashmere pillow for his sister's head. After contracting for the use of
McClary's hearse and carriage, the grieving brother hired two of his workers to
dig the grave.[32]

Bishop Alfred Lee had been scheduled to speak at the funeral but was unable
to return from a trip in time. Rev. Brincklé took his place and gave the eulogy; many
of the participants felt that Providence had intervened for "dear Mr. B" to have the
privilege of speaking for his old friend. The good minister faithfully described
the ceremony:

> Conveyed the mortal part of dear Mrs. Bauduy to the "narrow house." The
> Assemblage was immense, more than could be seated. I did not know until I
> reached the church that [Bishop] Lee whom I had relied on to make an address,
> had not returned from the North. I spoke 25 minutes—of her Christian charac-
> ter & example, pressing it especially upon those most dear to her, who had been
> the subjects of many a prayer of hers, . . . & of her words of entreaty in her
> dying hour that they should not neglect the great Salvation. All the Du Pont
> connection from far & near were present. . . . They all seemed to feel the occasion
> much—She was buried with her family, & not with her husband at [Old Swedes]
> Church.[33]

After the service, the large crowd of mourners followed the hearse to Sand Hole
Woods, where family and friends gathered near the open grave.

Two years previously, the death of Uncle Charles had prompted a special decision. As the unmarried brother of Sophie Dalmas, the most logical place to bury
him was in the next open spot after Irénée, but that position was not to be his.
Instead, the width of one grave had been measured off, and Uncle Charles was laid
to rest on the farther side of the reserved space. On Monday, January 21, mourners
watched as the reservation was filled. Irénée's daughter was laid beside him, and
everyone in attendance knew he would have wished it no other way. The two women
from whom he had drawn the most love and loyalty in life, would finish their
earthly journeys on each side of him.

Encompassing the graves of the earliest occupants of the family cemetery are
panels of ivory white sandstone, running the length of the sepulcher and rising to
a height of two and a half feet above the ground. Because the top panels lie flat and
are exposed to the elements, the original words have worn away and are today
largely unreadable. For this reason, du Pont descendants of the twentieth century
attached a small bronze plate to the top panel of each grave, preserving the essential details of their ancestors. These plaques, however, were not large enough to
duplicate any additional phrases that may have been carved into the surface, as
was true in Victorine's case. Her plaque simply replicates the words: "Sacred to the
memory of Victorine Elizabeth Bauduy, Eldest daughter of E.I. & S.M. du Pont and

widow of Ferdinand Bauduy. Born in Paris August 30th, 1792. Died January 19th, 1861."

But three longer quotations had been carved into the surface panel—each thought to have been submitted by a surviving sister. In the order in which the faded phrases appear on the stone, they read:

Let your light so shine before men, that they may see your good works, and glorify your Father which is in heaven.[34]

Favour is deceitful, and beauty is vain: but a woman that feareth the LORD, she shall be praised.[35]

To live in hearts we leave behind is not to die.[36]

CHAPTER 22

Epilogue

In the weeks following Victorine's death, Rev. Brincklé made several visits to du Pont homes to pay his respects and to offer spiritual comfort. On Monday, January 28, 1861, he rode out to Winterthur to pay a visit to the Bidermanns. He observed that Evelina felt "crushed by her sister's death" but that "she seemed much softened."[1] After watching the minister depart, Lina returned to her desk and penned her feelings to Sophie:

> We are like you dear Sophie, and cannot realize yet our great loss, but every moment unconscious thoughts of her arise as she was to us, and it required [mighty] struggles to say, His will be done! The greatest consolation is that now her troubles are over and that as Mr. Brincklé says, she has indeed left a bright example for all to follow. She was my first friend, and she is still, for I trust she will still know me if I am permitted to be with her, which is my hope, but I know I am not good as she was. Still, there is mercy for all I trust. Dear Sophie, you know how much I wish I could do anything for you, but you cannot have the same trust in my judgment as you had in hers; and I am afraid I shall oftener have recourse to you now for I, too, will miss her oh so much![2]

Sophie and Eleu grieved at a level that was akin to that which they experienced over the loss of their mother, but while Sophie had her husband to lean on, the family was concerned for the widowed Eleuthera. "We all do try to be with her a great deal," wrote Evelina to her nephew Henry.[3]

Ultimately, the faith that Victorine had transferred to her two "daughters" proved to be their mainstay as well. Writing to Sophie, Eleuthera confessed: "I never thought I could bear to lose her! I could not even endure to think of it, & yet she has gone & I am quiet. . . . Nothing can so comfort us to the bitter parting, as to feel a full & entire comfort in their faith, to know they are certainly with God & the Saviour, & awaiting & expecting us."[4] Nevertheless, Victorine's absence left gaping holes in their lives. There were surely times when Eleu half expected to see Victorine stride into their parlor, book in hand, to read a line of prose, or to remark upon some recent discovery or invention. Eleu especially missed the evening read-ings that had begun in childhood. "It is one of my greatest enjoyments," she remi-nisced to a cousin in France, "to read books aloud with friends. We were always accustomed to it at home, when sitting at our [embroidery] with my mother & sister Victorine."[5]

Resuming her sister's correspondence with Mary Elliott, she expressed: "I hope you will always write to me as you did to [Victorine] & let me try, in some man-ner, to be in her place to you. I know I never can in any way be to her friends what she was, but it will be a great comfort to me to keep up all the interests she had, & besides you know I am much attached to you for my own account."[6]

When Mr. Brincklé appointed Eleu as the new Sunday school superintendent, she assumed the mantle that her sister had worn for the past forty-five years. And like her sister before her, it was a position she would hold until death. Eleu's over-all service at the school would prove to be the longest in its history—a span of sixty years. With the exception of her own schooling in Philadelphia, and her year abroad, she had been teaching at the schoolhouse since she was ten years old.

Sophie, for her part, continued to find solace in the role she had played in the final days of her sister's life, never forgetting the providential series of events that had led to it. Describing the happenstance to Cousin Amelia, she acknowledged:

> One thing I was truly thankful for . . . was that Frank happened to be away (except that I would have liked for his own sake he had seen her that night & received her farewell). But had he been at home I would probably not have been here at all—for there was dreadful weather & high freshet & they were so little frightened [of Victorine's danger] they would not have sent for me. . . . I would not have had the consolation of being with her these two weeks—the only com-fort as regards myself that I have. I have never suffered so much before in my life—for I have always had *her* to love & comfort me in all my trials before.[7]

Victorine du Pont Bauduy succumbed on January 19, just two days shy of the forty-seventh anniversary of her beloved Ferdinand's death but, in a romantic sense of symmetry, her body was lowered into the ground on that very anniversary. Nearly a year before, Victorine had remarked that she found the month of Janu-ary seasonally depressing "on account of some very sad anniversaries it brings around,"[8] a sentiment she expressed numerous times over the years. The ravenous month had consumed a disproportionate number of her friends and relations. It had claimed the life not only of her husband, but of Eleuthera's as well, both of whom died on January 21. One can only imagine the wistful directions their con-versations may have taken as the melancholy anniversary rolled around each year. January had also claimed little Lucille, the sister who had been born in France on January 1, 1795, and lived but two days. Uncle Victor had died in January (1827), as would his son Charles Irénée I (1869) and his grandson Charles Irénée II (1873). The gravestone of Henry's youngest son, Willie, would eventually be inscribed with January 20, 1928; and Alexis's son Eugene would have January 28, 1902, entered upon his. The month would also claim the lives of Victorine's two "daughters":

Eleuthera on January 1, 1876, and Sophie on January 9, 1888. Thus, of the five girls born to Irénée and Sophie Madeleine du Pont, only Evelina would escape January's cold grasp.

Eighty-three days after her death—to the very minute—a fusillade of artillery shells exploded off the walls of Fort Sumter in Charleston Harbor, plunging the country into civil war. Although she had speculated with dread "what evils would follow," she did not live to experience them—but many of her scholars would. Ten months after her death, a letter of condolence arrived for Eleuthera from James Perry, a former student who had anglicized his name from "Perrier" since leaving the Brandywine. His family had relocated to Iowa and, in June 1861, James enlisted in the Second Iowa Regiment. Writing from the unit's headquarters at Benton Barracks, Missouri, he expressed, "It was with deep sorrow that I received the news of the death of Mrs Bauduy. I shall ever kindly remember her."[9] James would go on to experience some of the war's bloodiest fighting at places like Fort Donelson, and the "hornet's nest" at Shiloh. He was killed in battle in 1864, serving as a lieutenant with the First Alabama Cavalry, one of that state's six anti-secessionist regiments fighting for the Union Army.

Other scholars-turned-soldiers also wrote. Among them were James Buchanan serving with the Twenty-Third Regiment of Pennsylvania Volunteers, and William Green with the First Delaware Regiment at Camp Dare, near Havre de Grace, Maryland. Thomas Brown, who entered the Sunday school in 1848, was now a part of the Marine Corps contingency stationed aboard the forty-gun USS *Colorado*, the flagship of the fleet blockading the mouth of the Mississippi River. Writing to Victorine from its deck in November 1861, Thomas was unaware that his former teacher had died: "I often look back to the time when I went to your Sunday School, and think if I had followed your advice and teachings I would have led a better life than I have."[10]

Alexander Phillips, whose family had moved to Iowa in the early 1850s, was now serving in the infantry of the 9th Iowa Regiment. His older sister, Mary Ann, was struggling to make ends meet as her husband slowly succumbed to tuberculosis. Writing to Eleuthera in February 1862, Mary lamented:

> I hope you do not think that I have forgotten you. Sickness and trouble prevented my writing. O! My dear Teacher, how I long for one look at that beautiful place [the Sunday school] where I was so happy in the days of my childhood. I did not know how to appreciate it when I had it as I do now! When I think of . . . the kind & dear teacher who is now enjoying the reward of her many labors of love in her heavenly home, then I could tell those who are able to enjoy those privileges to lay up for a future day all the faithful advice of their teachers![11]

Eliza Jane Flemming had been four years old when she entered the Brandywine Manufacturer's Sunday School (BMSS) in 1829. She had married and moved west. She wrote to Sophie two months after Victorine's death: "Your dear Sister will be greatly missed. What a record has she left of a life well spent and devoted to the service of God! And how bright an example of constant and faithful discharge of duty! It was a great pleasure to me, seeing her and Mrs. Smith & yourself, when I was on; and a constant recurring pleasure to think over. She was so kind!"[12] Mary McCartney, who had entered the school in 1839 at the age of ten, was now married and living in Philadelphia. She wrote to Eleu in December 1861:

> Seldom a day passes, but I think of you and of the dear old Sunday School, and all the pleasant associations connected with it. But perhaps you have forgotten me, forgotten the little girl, Mary McCartney, that entered your class many years ago, & there grew up under your kind & gentle care, and after awhile, passed away into the world to other scenes and cares. My life since then has been a very happy one, yet still my thoughts wander back to those days that are gone and past forever as amongst the happiest of my life, & how often in fancy do I find myself again in school, & listening to her who was wont to preside over our school with so much gentleness & dignity! . . . Our dear Superintendent is no more, her voice will no more be heard within those walls! She has been called to her blessed reward! How my heart ached and how many tears I shed when I heard of her death. Sorry to think of the loss her own family had sustained, and also the great loss to the Sunday school and the neighborhood. But our Heavenly Father saw best to call her away from a long life of usefulness, and how many there are this day to rise up and call her blessed![13]

An examination of Victorine's class books, ledgers, and files reveals that she touched the lives of nearly three thousand children during her forty-five-year ten-ure at the school, spreading an educational and spiritual influence that traveled far beyond her own neighborhood. During the school's nondenominational years, she and her team of volunteers worked faithfully to bring literacy and Christian instruction to children who would have otherwise been denied them. With com-passionate "interest," Victorine demonstrated the sincerity of her motivation by surrendering much of her life to that task. An obituary that appeared in April 1862 validated the effectiveness of her approach: "At Philadelphia, April 3rd, 1862, Mrs. Margaret Armstrong, in the 51st year of her age. . . . The subject of this brief notice, was born in Wilmington, Delaware. . . . She was a pupil in the Sabbath School at Brandywine, Del., under the care of Mrs. Bauduy, a relative of Commo-dore Dupont, and to its influence she ascribed her conversion."[14]

In a broader moral sense, Victorine's influence upon the first two generations of American du Ponts played a significant role in maintaining the legacy of benev-olence and paternalism that her father had initiated. Her conversion to Christian-ity in her late teens was the single largest rudder that turned the family's drift toward deism (under her grandfather's influence) back to the biblical heading of their Huguenot ancestors. As first tutor of her American-born siblings, her reli-gious influence was early felt and would eventually extend to the next generation as well. Henry and Louisa's daughter Ellen, writing to her older brother at West Point, commented: "Think how proud and happy dear Aunt Vic would have been to know 'her dear boy' had graduated head of his class; she was so pleased and proud of your standing last time. . . . I pray to God that the memory of her life and of her death may be ever in our hearts so that we may imitate her Christian virtues, and finally be with her in everlasting felicity. Think of all these things dear [Henry] and of us. I once heard her express it, 'her dearest wish for you was that you should be an earnest Christian man.'"[15] In 1864, Captain Henry Algernon du Pont received the Medal of Honor for his exceptional bravery at the Battle of Cedar Creek. Upon his marriage to Mary Pauline Foster in 1874, the couple received Winterthur and its four hundred-plus acres as a wedding present from Henry and Louisa.[16] The newlyweds became faithful members of Christ Church.

––––––

An unexpected trace of Victorine's lingering influence along the Brandywine has survived in local lore in the form of a ghost story. Patricia Martinelli, in her book *Haunted Delaware*, records over a hundred tales of ghostly sightings in the First State, including certain members of the du Pont family who had their own "reasons to linger on after death."

> One such familiar phantom who is occasionally glimpsed around the grounds of Hagley is Victorine Elizabeth du Pont, the oldest child of Eleuthère Irénée and Sophie Madeleine du Pont. [After her husband's death] . . . she devoted the rest of her life to teaching Sunday school for the children of the mill workers and managing the household after her mother was injured in an explosion at the mill. Victorine died in 1861, but her trim figure, dressed in the height of French fashion, is still seen from time to time crossing the grounds, carrying a Bible in one hand and a basket of food in the other. She apparently is determined to continue her good works even in the afterlife.[17]

While the real Victorine may not have chosen to appear in the height of French fashion, the folklore is significant for the truth it does retain. She is depicted as "crossing the grounds" (on one of her pastorals, perhaps) with a basket of food in one hand and a Bible in the other. For all its apparitional imagery, this account is remarkably accurate in terms of preserving those essential qualities for which she was best remembered—spreading charity and biblical instruction throughout the Brandywine community.

A more terrestrial account appeared in the *Delaware Republican* on January 13, 1876, in a letter to the editor. Written upon the occasion of Eleuthera du Pont's death on January 1 of that year, it reads:

> The funeral notice of Eleuthera D. P. Smith . . . brought back to my mind the many happy days I spent, twenty-five years ago, while Mrs. Smith was my teacher at Du Ponts' Sunday School on the Brandywine. At that time the school was under the superintendency of Madame Bauduy and Mrs. Smith, both of them working every Sunday with a large school of boys and girls. . . . I never can forget the many fervent prayers offered up by these good ladies for the scholars . . . many of whom had poor parents and were compelled to work in the cotton factories, during the week. Hence the education of many of them . . . was very

limited, but, before attending long, they were, through the perseverance, patience and instruction of these good ladies, taught to read.

... These Christian ladies did not only spend their time and means for the success of this Sunday school and the benefit of the children of parents of all denominations, but they were ever ready and constantly doing good among the people of the Brandywine going about comforting the sick, and relieving the poor. [signed] G. R. R.[18]

Evelina died two years after Victorine, on March 19, 1863. Her husband, James Antoine Bidermann, and Sophie's husband, Admiral Samuel Francis Du Pont, died within two weeks of each other in June 1865. Sophie was laid beside her husband on January 9, 1888. In a conversation former BMSS scholar Samuel Brown had with Sophie shortly before her death, he recalled that "She was longing to go and join all her dear ones who had already gone and were waiting for her to come and join them. 'All the children and grandchildren of our family,' she said, 'are lovely to me and very considerate in every way, but they do not quite fill the place of those who were my sisters, brothers and companions.'"[19] When Henry passed away on his birthday, August 8, 1889, the last of Irénée and Sophie's children was laid below the long white rows of sandstone at Sand Hole Woods. Apart from his years at Mt. Airy and West Point, and his subsequent military assignments,[20] Henry lived his entire life at Eleutherian Mills, the home into which he had been born.

At the time of her death, Victorine's estate amounted to just under $144,000, all of it derived from the two shares she had held in her father's business.[21] After leaving a portion to Henry and Cousin Frank as executors, and a sum to her beloved Sunday school, the largest share bequeathed to an individual was to her niece, Victorine (du Pont) Kemble. Ten thousand dollars would be held as principle, so that Little Vic could draw an annual income for life from the interest. The remaining 85 percent, $122,137.90, was to be returned to her father's company—a decision that had more to do with loyalty and love than corporate need.[22] Whatever her thoughts about the family motto, it can surely be said that Victorine's life and character exemplified the concept of *Rectitudine Sto*. Her inner resolve to "stand upright" and do the right thing as she saw it, in spite of potential fallout, can be seen in many of the decisions both big and small that she made throughout her life. This insistence on rectitude, both by word and example, was conveyed to those on whom she had wielded the greatest influence. "Let not false shame or a fear of giving offense," she had once instructed the school-aged Eleuthera, "ever prevent you from doing what you feel to be right."[23]

While her accomplishments have been largely overlooked by history, such was not the case in her own day. "The assemblage [of mourners] was immense, more than could be seated," noted Samuel Brincklé at Victorine's funeral service on January 21, 1861.[24] Although it was a Monday, men and women, young and old, could be seen making their ways to the stone church from every direction. Mrs. Bauduy had been in their homes and shared their sorrows, nursed them, and even vaccinated them. She gently, but firmly, had admonished fathers for drinking their family's money away. She taught their children about God and how to read and write. In 1835, Joshua Gibbons, a former schoolmaster at the BMSS, wrote to Victorine to say that he had named his first child "Victorene" [sic], whom he earnestly prayed would imitate "in every trait of character, the lady after whom she is named."[25] For many parents, Victorine had become someone they hoped their children would, as Gibbons had hoped, model themselves upon.

Ultimately, however, it was to her family that Victorine had been most devoted. Each of her siblings, in their own time and manner, had felt the guiding hand of her maternal instruction. Its reach had extended to her nephews, nieces, and cousins, and left a lingering influence upon future generations. Francis Irénée du Pont, a direct descendant of Alexis du Pont, says that Victorine was, without doubt, the educational and spiritual "force" behind the family. He further concludes that "Her life as a strong Christian and well-educated woman served as a great influence on both her own family and the greater, early American du Pont family."[26] Today, Francis attends Christ Church Christiana Hundred, the very church his great-great-grandfather helped to build over 160 years ago and that Victorine was so instrumental in establishing.

But of all her relations, none received more intimate nurture than had Eleuthera and Sophie. On the occasion of Eleu's eighteenth birthday, when Victorine was in her early thirties, she had expressed: "When I thus see you turn your attention to pursuits which will improve & mature your character & think that I have in some measure contributed in instilling those tastes in you, I feel satisfied I have not lived in vain, and that in after years my two dear daughters will acknowledge I had no other end in view but their happiness, no wish so much at heart as their improvement."[27]

As the words upon Victorine's grave were slowly erased by the weeping rains, so too were the details of this remarkable life. Today, thousands of vehicles rumble daily across the towering bridge above the old Hagley yards on nearby Route 141, most of their occupants oblivious to the tale of love and loyalty that once flourished on the riverbanks below them.

Notes

PREFACE

1. Irénée du Pont Jr., letter to the author, January 15, 2018.

2. Francis I. du Pont, letter to the author, November 3, 2018.

3. John Beverley Riggs, *A Guide to Manuscripts* (Greenville, DE: Eleutherian Mills Historical Society, 1970), 280.

CHAPTER 1 — FRANCE, 1792–1795

1. Sophie (Dalmas) du Pont to Eleuthère Irénée (hereafter E. I.) du Pont, September 26, 1792, in du Pont, *Life of Eleuthère Irénée du Pont*, vol. 2, ed. and trans. Bessie Gardner du Pont (Newark: University of Delaware Press, 1923), 18.

2. Pierre Samuel du Pont de Nemours, *The Autobiography of Du Pont de Nemours*, trans. Elizabeth Fox-Genovese (Wilmington, DE: Scholarly Resources, 1984), 87.

3. Pierre Jolly, *Du Pont de Nemours: Apostle of Liberty and the Promised Land*, trans. Elise du Pont Elrick (Wilmington, DE: Brandywine Publishing, 1977), 20.

4. Physiocracy was an economic system that included the belief that land was the primary generator of wealth and that policies favoring its implementation would benefit society. Members of the physiocrats included Pierre Samuel du Pont de Nemours (1739–1817), François Quesnay (1694–1774), Anne Robert Jacques Turgot (1727–1781), and the Marquis de Mirabeau, Victor de Riqueti (1715–1789).

5. It was during his term on the Constituent Assembly that he added "de Nemours" to his name to differentiate himself from another du Pont serving at the same time. Nemours was the district that Pierre Samuel represented.

6. Jean-Pierre Poirot, *Lavoisier: Chemist, Biologist, Economist*, trans. Rebecca Balinski (Philadelphia: University of Pennsylvania Press, 1996), 223.

7. Antoine-Laurent de Lavoisier (1743–1794). Among his many scientific contributions were the role oxygen played in combustion, the identification of sulphur as an element, and the first compilation of the list of chemical elements.

8. Charles Antoine Houdar de Lamotte (1763–1806). The son of Houdar de Lamotte and Marguerite Le Dée de Villeneuve, a cousin of Irénée's mother.

9. Victor du Pont to E. I., June 23, 1791, in du Pont, *Life of Eleuthère Irénée du Pont*, vol. 1, ed. and trans. Bessie Gardner du Pont (Newark: University of Delaware Press, 1923), 154.

10. E. I. to Pierre Samuel, August 15, 1791, in du Pont, *Life of Eleuthère Irénée du Pont*, 1:157.

11. Ibid., 164.

12. E. I. to Pierre Samuel, August 22, 1791, in du Pont, *Life of Eleuthère Irénée du Pont*, 1:165.

13. Pierre Samuel to E. I., August 26, 1791, in du Pont, *Life of Eleuthère Irénée du Pont*, 1:177, 181.

14. Pierre Samuel to E. I., December 1, 1788, in du Pont, *Life of Eleuthère Irénée du Pont*, 1:107.

15. du Pont, *Life of Eleuthère Irénée du Pont*, 2:10.

16. "A proud family tradition . . . but there is no certain contemporary evidence for it." Ambrose Saricks, *Pierre Samuel Du Pont de Nemours* (Lawrence: University of Kansas Press, 1965), 214.

17. Jolly, *Du Pont de Nemours*, 68.

18. du Pont, *Life of Eleuthère Irénée du Pont*, 2:10–11.

19. Louis XVI was guillotined on January 21, 1793, and Queen Marie Antoinette on October 16, 1793.

20. "The Jacobins were the most radical and ruthless of the political groups formed in the wake of the French Revolution, and in association with Robespierre they instituted the Terror of 1793–94." Oxford English Dictionary, www.lexico.com.

21. Sophie to E. I., March 29, 1793, in du Pont, *Life of Eleuthère Irénée du Pont*, 2:80.

22. Philippe Jean Henri Gudin was the son of Pierre Samuel's sister. A reference to Gudin and this painting can be found in du Pont, *Life of Eleuthère Irénée du Pont*, 2:42.

23. E. I. to Sophie, December 28, 1793, in du Pont, *Life of Eleuthère Irénée du Pont*, 2:42, 218.

24. The primary ingredients of black powder are saltpeter (potassium nitrate), sulphur, and charcoal. William H. A. Carr, *The du Ponts of Delaware* (New York: Dodd, Mead, 1964), 51.

25. Pierre Samuel to E. I., August 12, 1794, in du Pont, *Life of Eleuthère Irénée du Pont*, 2:350.

26. Prince Adam Czartoryski hired du Pont de Nemours in 1774 to tutor his son. The king of Poland (Stanislaw Poniatowski) appointed du Pont Secretary of the High Council of National Education for Poland. Both positions were briefly held, because in the same year King Louis XVI appointed Turgot as Controller-General of France. Turgot wanted du Pont to assist him, and Pierre was made Inspector General of Commerce. Saricks, *Pierre Samuel Du Pont de Nemours*, 59–62; Jolly, *Du Pont de Nemours*, 37–38.

27. Sophie to E. I., September 26, 1792, in du Pont, *Life of Eleuthère Irénée du Pont*, 2:18.

28. E. I. to Sophie, May 23, 1795, in du Pont, *Life of Eleuthère Irénée du Pont*, vol. 3, ed. and trans. Bessie Gardner du Pont (Newark: University of Delaware Press, 1924), 197. Their frequent use of "little" is probably the reason Victorine adopted the practice of addressing her parents as *petite Maman* or *petit Papa*. The grandparents were referred to as *Bon Papa* and *Bonne Maman*.

29. Sophie to E. I., April 19, 1793, in du Pont, *Life of Eleuthère Irénée du Pont*, 3:98.

30. Sophie to E. I., May 5, 1795, in du Pont, *Life of Eleuthère Irénée du Pont*, 3:204

31. Anne Alexandrine de Montchanin (1720–1756). Pierre's mother was the primary force that encouraged his precocious intellectual abilities. His father, Samuel du Pont, had wished for his son to follow him in the watchmaking trade.

32. Sophie to E. I., July 26, 1795, in du Pont, *Life of Eleuthère Irénée du Pont*, 3:238.

CHAPTER 2 — AMERICA'S TURN

1. Françoise (Robin) Poivre du Pont de Nemours (1748–1841). Pierre Samuel's first wife, Nicole Charlotte Marie Louise Le Dée de Rencourt (1743–1784), had died when Victor was seventeen and Irénée thirteen.

2. Sophie (Dalmas) du Pont to Eleuthère Irénée (hereafter E. I.) du Pont, October 4, 1798, in du Pont, *Life of Eleuthère Irénée du Pont*, vol. 4, ed. and trans. Bessie Gardner du Pont (Newark: University of Delaware Press, 1923), 132–133.

3. Victorine du Pont to Sophie du Pont, October 25, 1798, in du Pont, *Life of Eleuthère Irénée du Pont*, 4:165.

4. Sophie to E. I., December 14, 1798, in du Pont, *Life of Eleuthère Irénée du Pont*, 4:207.

5. Sophie to E. I., April 29, 1799, in du Pont, *Life of Eleuthère Irénée du Pont*, 4:263.

6. Sophie to E. I., May 13, 1799, in du Pont, *Life of Eleuthère Irénée du Pont*, 4:318.

7. Among the Directory's accomplishments were a return to a semblance of order, the passing of a new constitution, and renewed successes of the French military (largely influenced by a young officer named Bonaparte).

8. Pierre Samuel du Pont de Nemours, *Philosophie de l'univers*, 3rd ed. (Paris: 737 Rue Taranne, 1799), 326.

9. E. I. to Sophie, November 2, 1797, in du Pont, *Life of Eleuthère Irénée du Pont*, 4:76–77.

10. "Sara." Françoise Josephine Bureaux de Pusy (1792–1872).

11. E. I. to Sophie, September 16, 1798, in du Pont, *Life of Eleuthère Irénée du Pont*, 4:129. Also Sophie to E. I., October 11, 1798, in du Pont, *Life of Eleuthère Irénée du Pont*, 4:141.

12. Sophie to E. I., July 28, 1796, in du Pont, *Life of Eleuthère Irénée du Pont*, vol. 3, ed. and trans. Bessie Gardner du Pont (Newark: University of Delaware Press, 1924), 300.

13. E. I. to Sophie, July 20, 1799, in du Pont, *Life of Eleuthère Irénée du Pont*, vol. 5, ed. and trans. Bessie Gardner du Pont (Newark: University of Delaware Press, 1924), 81.

14. Françoise Julienne Ile-de-France Poivre (1770–1845).

15. Gabrielle du Pont, "Notre Transplantation en Amérique," Hagley Museum and Library, Wilmington, DE (hereafter HML), Winterthur Manuscripts, Acc. 1686, 3/D, in Du Pont, *Life of Eleuthère Irénée du Pont*, 5:115–116.

16. Ambrose Saricks, *Pierre Samuel Du Pont de Nemours* (Lawrence: University of Kansas Press, 1965), 281.

17. A somewhat fanciful account says that the family briefly disembarked in search of food and knocked at a door where they discovered no one at home. After trying the latch and finding it unlocked, they entered the unoccupied house, helped themselves to some food, and left a French *louie* in payment. This Goldilocks-flavored tale is quaint but has little to recommend it.

18. Pierre Jolly, *Du Pont de Nemours: Apostle of Liberty and the Promised Land*, trans. Elise du Pont Elrick (Wilmington, DE: Brandywine Publishing, 1977), 232.

19. Ibid., 233.

20. Victorine to Sophie, undated, 1801, HML, Winterthur Manuscripts 6/A, Papers of Victorine du Pont, box 6a1.

21. English was the predominant language spoken by the siblings and cousins and is confirmed by their letters. French was not, however, uncommon, especially when describing private or delicate matters.

22. Ruth C. Linton, "To the Promotion and Improvement of Youth: The Brandywine Manufacturers' Sunday School, 1816–1840" (MA thesis, University of Delaware, 1981), 29.

23. Louis de Tousard (1749–1817). Alternately rendered "Toussard."

24. Tousard served during the campaigns of 1777 and 1778 and lost his arm during the Battle of Rhode Island.

25. du Pont, "Notre Transplantation en Amérique," 196.

26. After Napoleon's coup over the Directory in 1799, his civil reforms proved enormously popular with the citizenry. He simultaneously increased France's military strength.

27. William S. Dutton, *Du Pont: One Hundred and Forty Years* (New York: Scribner's, 1942), 31.

28. Victorine to E. I., undated, 1801, HML, box 6a1.

29. E. I. to Pierre Samuel, September 9, 1801, in du Pont, *Life of Eleuthère Irénée du Pont*, 5:280.

CHAPTER 3 — WILMINGTON, DELAWARE

1. As an architect, Peter Bauduy designed several houses and public buildings, including the city's first Roman Catholic church, St. Peter's Cathedral, completed in 1818. He is also credited with designing Wilmington's old town hall, but there has been recent debate over this.

2. John Thomas Scharf, *History of Delaware, 1609–1888*, vol. 2 (Philadelphia: L. J. Richards, 1888), 664–665.

3. Jacob Broom (1752–1810). A signer of the U.S. Constitution. Quaker and pacifist, Broom served the American Revolution by drawing up local maps for General George Washington during the Brandywine campaign.

4. Peter Bauduy to Eleuthère Irénée (hereafter E. I.) du Pont, October 16, 1801, in du Pont, *Life of Eleuthère Irénée du Pont*, vol. 5, ed. and trans. Bessie Gardner du Pont (Newark: University of Delaware Press, 1924), 302.

5. E. I. to William Hamon, April 26, 1802, in du Pont, *Life of Eleuthère Irénée du Pont*, vol. 6, ed. and trans. Bessie Gardner du Pont (Newark: University of Delaware Press, 1925), 29–30.

6. E. I. to Peter Bauduy, January 2, 1802, in du Pont, *Life of Eleuthère Irénée du Pont*, 5:339.

7. E. I. to Peter Bauduy, June 25, 1802, in du Pont, *Life of Eleuthère Irénée du Pont*, 6:73.

8. Victorine du Pont to Pierre Samuel du Pont de Nemours, undated, c. 1803, Hagley Museum and Library Manuscripts and Archives, Wilmington, DE (hereafter HML), Winterthur Manuscripts, Papers of Victorine du Pont Bauduy, box 6a1.

9. William Dutton, *Du Pont: One Hundred and Forty Years* (New York: Scribner's, 1942), 35.

10. Sophie (Dalmas) du Pont to Charles Dalmas, September 1802, in Maureen O'Brien Quimby, *Eleutherian Mills* (Greenville, DE: Hagley Museum, 1973), 11.

11. Juliette Bauduy to Mimika Bauduy, January 3, 1803, in Dorothy Holland, *Garesché, De Bauduy, and Des Chapelles Families* (St. Louis: Schneider, 1963), 46–47.

12. Although officially a creek, the Brandywine is often referred to by the locals as a river.

13. Victorine to sister Sophie du Pont, undated, 1846, HML, box 6a4.

14. Victorine to her mother Sophie, December 9, 1812, HML, box 6a2.

15. Victor du Pont to E. I., May 2, 1804, in du Pont, *Life of Eleuthère Irénée du Pont*, 6:308.

16. Dutton, *Du Pont*, 41.

17. The Barbary Wars (1801–1805).

18. E. I. to Pierre Samuel, July 16, 1803, in du Pont, *Life of Eleuthère Irénée du Pont*, 6:252.

19. Peter Bauduy to E. I., December 11, 1804, in du Pont, *Life of Eleuthère Irénée du Pont*, vol. 7, ed. and trans. Bessie Gardner du Pont (Newark: University of Delaware Press, 1925), 55–56.

20. E. I. to Victor, "about December 13, 1804," in du Pont, *Life of Eleuthère Irénée du Pont*, 7:52.

CHAPTER 4 — EMERGENCE

1. For more on Madame Capron, see Edwin Hatfield, *History of Elizabeth, New Jersey* (New York: Carlton & Lanahan, 1868).

2. Mary Johnson, "Victorine du Pont: Heiress to the Educational Dream of Pierre Samuel du Pont de Nemours," *Delaware History* 19 (Fall–Winter 1980): 92.

3. Victorine du Pont to Evelina du Pont, July 18, 1811, Hagley Museum and Library Manuscripts and Archives, Wilmington, DE (hereafter HML), Winterthur Manuscripts, box 6a6, misc. family.

4. Ibid.

5. Pierre Samuel du Pont de Nemours, *The Autobiography of Du Pont de Nemours*, trans. Elizabeth Fox-Genovese (Wilmington, DE: Scholarly Resources, 1984), 204.

6. Victorine to Eleuthère Irénée (hereafter E. I.) du Pont, July 19, 1805, HML, box 6a1.

7. E. I. du Pont, *Life of Eleuthère Irénée du Pont*, vol. 7, ed. and trans. Bessie Gardner du Pont (Newark: University of Delaware Press, 1925), 205–206.

8. Victorine to E. I., May 9, 1806, HML, box 6a1.

9. E. I. to Pierre Samuel, May 2, 1807, in du Pont, *Life of Eleuthère Irénée du Pont*, 7:299.

10. Phoebe Pemberton Morris (1791–1827). Her father, Anthony Morris, was a former speaker of the house in the Pennsylvania Senate.

11. In 1812, Estelle Pageot (1795–1876) married Louis Sérurier (1775–1860), Napoleon's Consul to America (1811–1815). He was thirty-seven and she was seventeen.

12. Victorine to Evelina, December 5, 1809, HML, box 6a1.

13. Eleuthera du Pont, Transcript Books, HML, Winterthur Manuscripts, Group 10, Series E.

14. "None of the Quaker City's captains of industry conducted business upon a more extensive scale . . . or stood higher in the world of finance, than [Robert Ralston]." Frank W. Leach, "Old Philadelphia Families," *North American* (Philadelphia), July 7, 1912, http://files .usgwarchives.net/pa/philadelphia/history/family/ralston.txt. Scharf notes that his "ships traded with the West Indies, France, Ireland and China." J. Thomas Scharf, *History of Delaware*, vol. 2 (Philadelphia: L. J. Richards, 1888), 655.

15. Leach, "Old Philadelphia Families."

16. Pennsylvania Bible Society, www.pabible.org.

17. Julia (Rush) Williams (1790–1860).

18. Victorine to Evelina, undated, HML, box 6a2.

19. Pierre Samuel du Pont de Nemours, preface to *Irénée Bonfils on the Religion of His Forefathers* (Paris: Firmin Didot, 1808), English translation by Pierre S. du Pont (Wilmington, DE: Pierre S. du Pont, 1947).

20. Sophie du Pont, undated, HML, Winterthur Manuscripts, Group 9, W9-40303.

21. Victorine to Evelina, July 18, 1811, HML, box 6a6, misc. family.

22. The Brevost family had joined the French refugee colony along the Susquehanna River in North Central Pennsylvania, known as *Azilum* (Asylum). Although the ill-fated colony lasted only ten years, the Brevosts were among the first to arrive and last to leave.

23. Antoinette Brevost would become a teacher at Madame Rivardi's, and later establish two schools in conjunction with her parents, one in Pittsburgh, Pennsylvania, and the other in Natchez, Mississippi.

24. Antoinette Brevost to Victorine, June 17, 1806, HML, box 6a1; emphasis added.

25. Ednah C. Silver, *Sketches of the New Church in America* (Boston: New Church Union, 1920), 184.

26. Also spelled La Motte, or LaMotte.

27. Victorine to Evelina, undated, January 1824, HML, box 6a3.

28. Anna Potts Smith to Victorine, undated, 1813, HML, box 6a2.

29. Eugenia Victorine Lammot (August 24, 1822–September 8, 1839).

CHAPTER 5 — POST-RIVARDI YEARS

Epigraph: Eleuthère Irénée (hereafter E. I.) du Pont to Pierre Samuel du Pont de Nemours, November 22, 1809, in du Pont, *Life of Eleuthère Irénée du Pont*, vol. 8, ed. and trans. Bessie Gardner du Pont (Newark: University of Delaware Press, 1925), 228.

1. Ibid.

2. Victorine du Pont to Amelia du Pont, July 15, 1807, Hagley Museum and Library Manuscripts and Archives, Wilmington, DE (hereafter HML), Winterthur Manuscripts, Papers of Victorine du Pont Bauduy, box 6a1.

3. Gabrielle du Pont, "Notre Transplantation en Amérique," HML, Winterthur Manuscripts, Acc. 1686, 3/D, 44.

4. Mount Airy Seminary, established by Fr. Francis F. Brosius in 1807 and later overseen by P. F. Blondin Constant, taught general subjects. In 1827 it was converted to a military preparatory school by Augustus L. Roumfort. Samuel Fitch Hotchkin, *Ancient and Modern Germantown, Mount Airy and Chestnut Hill* (Philadelphia: P. W. Ziegler, 1889), 364, 350.

5. "[I have] been constantly occupied copying some papers for papa." Victorine to Evelina du Pont, undated (c. 1809), HML, box 6a6, misc. family.

6. Dorsey Wetlaufer, "Family Life at Eleutherian Mills, 1803–1834," Eleutherian Mills–Hagley Foundation research report, 1964, Acc. 1645, box 4, folder 75, MS1645_075.

7. "I will also send with this another copy of our inventory for 1809. Victorine has made 7 or 8 copies of it." E. I. to Pierre Samuel, January 25, 1811, in du Pont, *Life of Eleuthère Irénée du Pont*, 8:288.

8. Victorine to Evelina, March 3, 1811, HML, box 6a2. The friends mentioned were Antoinette Brevost and Alexandrine Carnevillier.

9. Victorine du Pont to Eleuthera, March 28, 1821, HML, box 6a2.

10. Victorine to Evelina, September 20, 1810, HML, box 6a2.

11. E. I. to Pierre Samuel, November 28, 1812, in du Pont, *Life of Eleuthère Irénée du Pont*, vol. 9, ed. and trans. Bessie Gardner du Pont (Newark: University of Delaware Press, 1925), 66.

12. Victorine to Samuel Francis Du Pont, December 6, 1818, HML, box 6a2.

13. Victorine to Evelina, February 11, 1811, HML, box 6a2.

14. Victorine to Evelina, undated letter of 1811, HML, box 6a2.

15. Jerome Keating (1792–1833) was the nephew and adopted son of John Keating (1760–1856), the Irish-born French soldier and American land developer connected to the *Asylum Project*. John Keating was also Peter Bauduy's brother-in-law.

16. Françoise (Robin) Poivre du Pont to Sophie (Dalmas) du Pont, October 29, 1809, in du Pont, *Life of Eleuthère Irénée du Pont*, 8:221.

17. Peter Bauduy to E. I., undated, 1809–1810, in du Pont, *Life of Eleuthère Irénée du Pont*, 8:213.

18. Mary Johnson, *Victorine du Pont: Heiress to the Educational Dream of Pierre Samuel du Pont de Nemours* (Philadelphia: Temple University Press, 1979), 14–15.

19. Antoinette Brevost to Victorine, August 2, 1813, HML, box 6a2.

20. Bessie Gardner du Pont, *Lives of Victor and Josephine du Pont* (Newark, DE: Kells Press, 1930), 179.

21. E. I. to Pierre Samuel, November 22, 1809, in du Pont, *Life of Eleuthère Irénée du Pont*, 8:227–229.

22. Pierre Samuel to E. I., January 26, 1810, in du Pont, *Life of Eleuthère Irénée du Pont*, 8:252–253.

23. Peter Bauduy to E. I., November 3, 1809, in du Pont, *Life of Eleuthère Irénée du Pont*, 8:222.

24. The import–export arm of Du Pont de Nemours Père et Fils et Compagnie, which had been under Victor's guidance in New York, underwent bankruptcy in 1805.

25. Peter Bauduy to E. I., May 22, 1811, in du Pont, *Life of Eleuthère Irénée du Pont*, 8:302.

26. Victor du Pont purchased the shares of Duplanty and Bauduy, and brought his son in as a partner, changing the name of the woolen company to Victor and Charles Du Pont. Frank R. Zebley, *Along the Brandywine* (Wilmington, DE: William Cann, 1940), 110.

27. Thomas Cooper (1759–1839). English educator, scientist, and chemist.

28. Mimika Bauduy married Vital Gareschè on October 24, 1809.

29. Peter Bauduy to his son, November 3, 1809, in du Pont, *Life of Eleuthère Irénée du Pont*, 8:222–224.

30. Peter Bauduy to E. I., undated, in du Pont, *Life of Eleuthère Irénée du Pont*, 8:209–210.

31. E. I. to Pierre Samuel, c. May 1810, in du Pont, *Life of Eleuthère Irénée du Pont*, 8:270.

32. Peter Bauduy to E. I., undated, in du Pont, *Life of Eleuthère Irénée du Pont*, 8:210.

33. Ibid.

34. Peter Bauduy to E. I., undated, in du Pont, *Life of Eleuthère Irénée du Pont*, 8:214.

35. Victorine to Evelina, undated but likely June 19, 1812, HML, box 6a2. "Botanizing" was the family's favorite term for this activity.

36. Probably Richard Rush (1780–1859), Madison's U.S. attorney general at the time.

37. "Madison's March" [c. 1809] by F. Meline, composed for Madison's inauguration. Accessible at the Library of Congress, https://www.loc.gov/item/2015561226/.

38. Victorine to Evelina, July 9, 1812, HML, box 6a2.

39. Both brothers were given the militia ranks of captain by the governor. Raymond F. Pisney, "The Brandywine Rangers in the War of 1812," Eleutherian Mills–Hagley Foundation research report, undated, Acc. 1645, box 3, folder 56, MS1645_056.

40. Victorine to Evelina, March 7, 1813, HML, box 6a2.

41. Johnson, *Victorine du Pont*, 101.

42. Victorine to Evelina, March 7, 1813, HML, box 6a2.

CHAPTER 6 — FERDINAND

1. Victorine du Pont to Amelia du Pont, July 15, 1807, Hagley Museum and Library Manuscripts and Archives, Wilmington, DE (hereafter HML), Winterthur Manuscripts, Papers of Victorine du Pont Bauduy, box 6a1.

2. Victorine to Evelina du Pont, May 19, 1811, HML, box 6a2. Victorine was quoting Claudian (370–404).

3. Victorine to Evelina, June 17, 1811, HML, box 6a2.

4. Victorine to Evelina, May 6, 1811, HML, box 6a2.

5. Victorine (du Pont) Bauduy to Mimika Gareschè, August 8, 1815, HML, box 6a2.

6. Victorine to Evelina, undated but likely July 18, 1810, HML, box 6a6, misc. family.

7. Peter Bauduy to Eleuthère Irénée (hereafter E. I.) du Pont, undated, in du Pont, *Life of Eleuthère Irénée du Pont*, vol. 8, ed. and trans. Bessie Gardner du Pont (Newark: University of Delaware Press, 1925), 214.

8. Peter Bauduy to Bernard de Sassenay, July 13, 1811, in Dorothy Holland, *Gareschè, De Bauduy, and Des Chapelles Families* (St. Louis: Schneider, 1963), 103.

9. Peter Bauduy to Bernard de Sassenay, March 12, 1812, in Holland, *Gareschè, De Bauduy, and Des Chapelles Families*, 55.

10. E. I. to Pierre Samuel du Pont de Nemours, November 1, 1812, in du Pont, *Life of Eleuthère Irénée du Pont*, vol. 9, ed. and trans. Bessie Gardner du Pont (Newark: University of Delaware Press, 1925), 56.

11. Marquise de Sassenay to Mimika Garesché, April 4, 1813, in Holland, *Garesché, De Bauduy, and Des Chapelles Families*, 111.

12. Ibid., 68.

13. William H. A. Carr, *The du Ponts of Delaware* (New York: Dodd, Mead, 1964), 92.

14. Victor du Pont to Pierre Samuel du Pont de Nemours, c. 1813, in Bessie Gardner du Pont, *Lives of Victor and Josephine du Pont* (Newark, DE: Kells Press, 1930), 179.

15. Rembrandt Peale (1776–1860), the son of artist Charles Wilson Peale (1741–1827).

16. Victorine to Evelina, November 26, 1813, HML, box 6a2.

17. Victorine to Evelina, December 7, 1813, HML, box 6a2.

18. Ferdinand Bauduy to Victorine, December 22, 1813, HML, box 6a14.

19. Victorine, undated, HML, box 6a13, poetry files.

20. Pierre Provenchère to Amelia Provenchère, January 30, 1814, HML, box 6a2.

21. Louise Bauduy died on September 9, 1813, of whooping cough. Holland, *Garesché, De Bauduy, and Des Chapelles Families*, 111.

22. Peter Bauduy to E. I., January 23, 1814, in du Pont, *Life of Eleuthère Irénée du Pont*, 9:168–169.

23. Clara Etienne Eugénie de Sassenay died in 1821 and was buried in a small Roman Catholic graveyard in Paris. She was twenty-two and had not married.

CHAPTER 7 — MOURNING ON THE BRANDYWINE

1. Author's conversation with Maureen Quimby, former Curator of Decorative Arts at Hagley Museum and Library. Quimby is the author of *Eleutherian Mills* (Greenville, DE: Hagley Museum, 1973).

2. Juliette and Peter Bauduy to Victorine (du Pont) Bauduy, undated, in Dorothy Holland, *Garesché, De Bauduy, and Des Chapelles Families* (St. Louis: Schneider, 1963), 114.

3. Peter Bauduy to Victorine, May 25, 1814, in Hagley Museum and Library Manuscripts and Archives, Wilmington, DE (hereafter HML), Winterthur Manuscripts, Papers of Victorine du Pont Bauduy, box 6a8.

4. Peter Bauduy to Victorine, undated, HML, box 6a8.

5. A list of itemized notes on copy paper are brief summaries of a letter by Pierre Provenchère (1740–1831), that include: "Victorine Bauduy was pregnant at the time of her husband's death but had a miscarriage." Item number 5, January 30, 1814, HML, box 6a13, misc. files.

6. Eleuthère Irénée (hereafter E. I.) du Pont to Pierre Samuel du Pont de Nemours, August 18, 1814, in du Pont, *Life of Eleuthère Irénée du Pont*, vol. 9, ed. and trans. Bessie Gardner du Pont (Newark: University of Delaware Press, 1925), 265.

7. Anna Potts Smith to Victorine, February 25, 1814, HML, box 6a8.

8. Rebecca Ralston to Victorine, February 26, 1814, HML, box 6a8.

9. Anna Potts Smith to Victorine, January 28, 1814, HML, box 6a8.

10. Anna Potts Smith to Victorine, March 27, 1814, HML, box 6a8.

11. Antoinette Brevost to Victorine, February 3, 1814, HML, box 6a8.

12. Antoinette Brevost to Victorine, March 7, 1814, HML, box 6a8.

13. Victorine to Sophie Madeleine Du Pont, May 26, 1814, HML, box 6a8.

14. John Keating (1760–1856) married Eulalie des Chapelles (1774–1803) in 1791. Eulalie was Juliette Bauduy's sister.

15. Victorine to Evelina du Pont, August 4, 1814, HML, box 6a2.

16. Victorine to Evelina, August 10, 1814, HML, box 6a2.

17. Ibid.

18. Ibid.

19. Victorine to Evelina, August 16, 1814, HML, box 6a2.

20. Victorine to Evelina, August 10, 1814, HML, box 6a2.

21. "Were I in a gayer mood I could give you some ludicrous descriptions of the personages we meet with, but instead I have neither power nor inclination at present." Victorine to Evelina, August 10, 1814, HML, box 6a2.

22. Victorine to Evelina, August 10, 1814, HML, box 6a2.

23. Victorine to Evelina, August 14, 1814, HML, box 6a2. William Cowper (1731–1800), English poet and hymn writer.

24. Victorine to Evelina, August 19, 1814, HML, box 6a2.

25. Anna Potts Smith to Victorine, January 1, 1815, HML, box 6a13, poetry files.

CHAPTER 8 — DEPARTURES AND ARRIVALS

1. By 1815, Victor's mill owed Irénée's company over $37,000. George H. Gibson, "The Delaware Woolen Industry," Eleutherian Mills–Hagley Foundation research report, 1963, Acc. 1645, box 1, folder 22, MS1645_022.

2. Pierre Samuel du Pont de Nemours to his sons, October 14, 1814, in du Pont, *Life of Eleuthère Irénée du Pont*, vol. 9, ed. and trans. Bessie Gardner du Pont (Newark: University of Delaware Press, 1925), 116–126.

3. Juliette Bauduy to Victorine (du Pont) Bauduy, January 2, 1815, Hagley Museum and Library Manuscripts and Archives, Wilmington, DE (hereafter HML), box 6a2.

4. Richard Scott and S. Fulton, "Interpretive Packet on Explosions," Eleutherian Mills–Hagley Foundation research report, 1990, Acc. 2016.201, 20090507_10.

5. Mimika B. Garesché to Victorine, June 8, 1815, HML, box 6a2.

6. Mimika Garesché to Victorine, August 1815, HML, box 6a2.

7. Victorine to Mimika Garesché, August 8, 1815, HML, box 6a2.

8. Victorine to Evelina (du Pont) Bidermann, May 3, 1817, HML, box 6a2.

9. Eleuthera du Pont, Transcript books, HML, Group 10, Series E, 13.

10. Victorine to Evelina, February 14, 1822, HML, box 6a2.

11. Ambrose Saricks, *Pierre Samuel Du Pont de Nemours* (Lawrence: University of Kansas Press, 1965), 354.

12. Saricks, *Pierre Samuel Du Pont de Nemours*, 347.

13. Anne Louise Germaine de Staël-Holstein (1766–1817), woman of letters and voice of moderation during the French Revolution.

14. Pierre Samuel to Germaine de Staël, February 26, 1805, in Anne Louise Germaine de Staël and Pierre Samuel du Pont de Nemours, *de Staël–du Pont Letters*, ed. and trans. James F. Marshall (Madison: University of Wisconsin Press, 1968), 267–268.

15. Victorine to Alfred du Pont, July 17, 1817, in du Pont, *Life of Eleuthère Irénée du Pont*, vol. 10, ed. and trans. Bessie Gardner du Pont (Newark: University of Delaware Press, 1926), 231–232.

16. Ibid.

17. Saricks, *Pierre Samuel Du Pont de Nemours*, 357.

18. Thomas Jefferson to Eleuthère Irénée du Pont, September 9, 1817, in du Pont, *Life of Eleuthère Irénée du Pont*, 10:252.

19. Marquis de Lafayette to Victor and Eleuthère du Pont, October 1, 1817, in du Pont, *Life of Eleuthère Irénée du Pont*, 10:263.

20. Pierre Samuel to Madame de Staël, April 4, 1809, in de Staël and du Pont de Nemours, *de Staël–du Pont Letters*, 350.

21. A short list of du Pont de Nemours' acquaintances would include: Louis XVI (French king); Jérôme Lalande (astronomer); Antoine Lavoisier (chemist); Voltaire (François-Marie

Arouet) (philosopher); François Quesnay, Anne Robert Jacques Turgot (economists); Anne Louise Germaine de Staël-Holstein (novelist and literary intellect); the Marquis de Lafayette (military hero); Napoleon Bonaparte (French emperor); Benjamin Franklin (American statesman); and Thomas Jefferson (American president).

CHAPTER 9 — LIFE AND SPIRIT ON THE BRANDYWINE

1. Norman B. Wilkinson, *E.I. du Pont, Botaniste: The Beginning of a Tradition* (Charlottesville: University Press of Virginia, 1972), 49–53. Irénée also sent "150 botanical items" to Empress Josephine Bonaparte, who responded kindly (34–36).

2. Two of the finest examples are Longwood Gardens of Kennett Square, Pennsylvania, founded in 1906 by Pierre Samuel du Pont (1870–1954); and the Nemours Mansion and Gardens, built in Wilmington in 1910 by Alfred I. du Pont (1864–1935).

3. Victorine du Pont to Evelina du Pont, August 20, 1810, Hagley Museum and Library Manuscripts and Archives, Wilmington, DE (hereafter HML), Winterthur Manuscripts, Papers of Victorine du Pont Bauduy, box 6a2.

4. Pierre Jolly, *Pierre Samuel du Pont de Nemours: Apostle of Liberty and the Promised Land*, trans. Elise du Pont Elrick (Wilmington, DE: Brandywine Publishing, 1977), 337. Sandrans took up residence in what later became known as the Belin House, completed in 1819. Victorine (du Pont) Bauduy to Samuel Francis Du Pont, September 14, 1819, HML, box 6a2.

5. Victorine to Samuel Francis, December 6, 1818, HML, box 6a2.

6. James M. Merrill, *Du Pont: The Making of an Admiral* (New York: Dodd, Mead, 1986), 16.

7. Victorine to Samuel Francis, August 9, 1818, HML, box 6a2.

8. Lessons for the girls included reading, spelling, writing, geography, history, French, English, sewing, piano, and dancing.

9. Victorine to Eleuthera du Pont, October 26, 1816, HML, box 6a2.

10. Mark Noll, Nathan Hatch, George Marsden, David Wells, and John Woodbridge, eds., *Eerdmans' Handbook to Christianity in America* (Grand Rapids, MI: William B. Eerdmans, 1983), 172.

11. Finney's visit to Wilmington: Charles G. Finney, *Memoirs of Rev. Charles G. Finney*, trans. Henry Reeve, 2nd ed. (New York: Fleming H. Revell, 1876), 234–238.

12. Alexis de Tocqueville, *Democracy in America*, trans. Henry Reeve, 2nd American ed. (New York: George Adlard, 1838), 285.

13. Victorine to Evelina (du Pont) Bidermann, October 21, 1816, HML, box 6a2.

14. Established in 1817. Jacob J. Janeway, "Obituary: Mrs. Sarah Ralston," in *The Presbyterian Magazine*, vol. 1 (Philadelphia: Littell & Henry, 1821), 78.

15. E. L. Carey and A. Hart, *Picture of Philadelphia: or, A Brief Account of the Various Institutions and Public Objects in this Metropolis* (Philadelphia: E. L. Carey & A. Hart, 1835), 59–60.

16. Page Putnam Miller, *A Claim to New Roles* (Metuchen, NJ: Scarecrow Press, 1985), 13–16.

17. Rebecca Ralston to Victorine, December 23, 1814, HML, box 6a2.

18. Frank W. Leach, "Old Philadelphia Families," *North American* (Philadelphia), July 7, 1912, http://files.usgwarchives.net/pa/philadelphia/history/family/ralston.txt.

19. The orphanage merged with the Elwyn School of Elwyn, PA, in 1965. *Orphan Society Records Collection 1913* (Philadelphia: Historical Society of Philadelphia, 2003), 1.

20. Among these were Bishop William White, first presiding bishop of the Episcopal Church in America, and Rev. Ashbel Green at Second Presbyterian.

21. February 3, 1817, HML, box 6a14, memoranda.

22. February 3, 1818, HML, box 6a14, memoranda. (Biblical reference is Psalm 103:2.)

23. Pierre Samuel du Pont de Nemours to Françoise Robin Poivre du Pont, January 17, 1817, in Ruth C. Linton, "To the Promotion and Improvement of Youth: The Brandywine Manufacturer's Sunday School, 1816–1840" (MA thesis, University of Delaware, 1981), 77–80.

CHAPTER 10 — THE BRANDYWINE MANUFACTURER'S SUNDAY SCHOOL

Epigraph: Pierre Samuel du Pont de Nemours to Françoise (Poivre) du Pont, September 6, 1816, in Ruth C. Linton, "To the Promotion and Improvement of Youth: The Brandywine Manufacturers' Sunday School, 1816–1840" (MA thesis, University of Delaware, 1981), 26.

1. "Hagley" is thought to be named after an estate in England. The Hagley Museum suggests it was named by the land's former owner, Rumford Dawes (1741–1814): www .hagley.org/sub/origins-our-name. Frank Zebley in *Along the Brandywine* (Wilmington, DE: William Cann, 1940), 133, speculated that it was named by John Gregg (1755–1834), the blacksmith who had originally owned the property.

2. John Gregg received the property from his father, Samuel, in 1799, and built a forge and other mill buildings. He sold it to Rumford Dawes in 1783. Zebley, *Along the Brandywine*, 133.

3. Samuel Brown, "Recollections of a Conversation I Had with the Late Mrs. Admiral Du Pont about 1885 to '87," Hagley Museum and Library Manuscripts and Archives, Wilmington, DE (hereafter HML), Winterthur Manuscripts, Group 9, Papers of Sophie Du Pont, W9-40309.

4. In 1815, it was estimated that as many as four hundred thousand students had enrolled in Sunday schools throughout England. Wes Haystead, *The 21st Century Sunday School: Strategies for Today and Tomorrow* (Cincinnati, OH: Standard Publishing, 1995), 12–13.

5. Victorine (du Pont) Bauduy, Report to the American Sunday School Union, c. 1830, HML, 6a13, box 3.

6. Siddall's Sunday school class was likely the second to be established in Northern Delaware. In 1813, women from the Second Presbyterian Church of Wilmington established the Female Harmony Society "for the purpose of prayer, mutual instruction, and Christian labor." One of their first actions was to establish a Sunday school class which began in Wilmington in 1814.

7. "Grog shops" were alehouses, pubs, or taverns that served liquor. Victorine to Sophie du Pont, undated, HML, box 6a6.

8. Victorine Bauduy, "General Observation," 1829 or 1830, HML, Acc. 389, box 6, correspondence.

9. BMSS Constitution, HML, Acc. 389, box 1.

10. The charter for the BMSS was received by the Clerk of the House of Representatives on February 20, 1817.

11. BMSS incorporation papers, HML, Acc. 389.

12. Andrew E. Sanborn, *Proceedings of Temple Lodge, No. 11* (Wilmington, DE: Temple Lodge No. 11, 1917), 218. Victor du Pont joined on February 11, 1819.

13. Karl Niederer, "The Brandywine Manufacturers' Sunday School: A History of its Construction and Recommendations for Renovations," Eleutherian Mills–Hagley Foundation research report, 1977, Acc. 1645, box 7, folder 220.

14. John Thomas Scharf, *History of Delaware*, vol. 1 (Philadelphia: L. J. Richards, 1888), 190.

15. A receipt signed by John Siddall states: "Rec'd from Mrs Bauduy a Subscription Collected at School at a sermon. 12.00," November 3, 1817, BMSS, HML, box 2, expenses, journal of 1817.

16. Rev. Thomas Love (1796–1879), pastor of both Red Clay Creek and Lower Brandywine Presbyterian churches.

17. BMSS files, HML, Acc. 389, W9-40303.

18. Brown, "Recollections of a Conversation."

19. Victorine to Henry du Pont, undated, 1854, HML, box 6a13.

20. After assisting her parents in starting the first school for young women in Pittsburgh, the family moved to Natchez, Mississippi, where they opened another such establishment in 1822. Tragically, all three died in the yellow fever epidemic of 1823.

21. In January 1829 John died unexpectedly, leaving Rebecca with six young daughters.

22. Richard Scott and S. Fulton, "Interpretive Packet on Explosions," Eleutherian Mills–Hagley Foundation research report, 1990, Acc. 2016.201, 20090507_10.

23. William Hubert du Pont, *Explosions at the Du Pont Powder Mills* (Greenville, DE: Hagley Museum and Library, n.d.), 9–10.

24. Ibid., 10.

25. Benjamin Ferris, *A History of the Original Settlements of the Delaware* (Wilmington, DE: Wilson & Heald, 1846), 21.

26. James F. Wall, *Alfred I. du Pont: The Man and His Family* (New York: Oxford University Press, 1990), 62.

27. Some discrepancy exists over the exact location of Sophie du Pont's wound. An editor's note in du Pont, *Life of Eleuthère Irénée du Pont*, vol. 10, ed. and trans. Bessie Gardner du Pont (Newark: University of Delaware Press, 1926), 278–279, states that she "received a blow on her side from the effects of which she never recovered." Eleuthera du Pont recorded that she received a "three inch wound" to the head. du Pont, *Explosions at the Du Pont Powder Mills*, 9.

28. du Pont, *Explosions at the Du Pont Powder Mills*, 2.

CHAPTER 11 — A NEW SUPERINTENDENT

Epigraph: Bernard Barton (1784–1849), excerpt from untitled poem, *The Museum of Foreign Literature, Science, and Art* (July–December 1831) (Philadelphia: E. Littell, 1831), 454, copied by Victorine (du Pont) Bauduy, Hagley Museum and Library Manuscripts and Archives, Wilmington, DE (hereafter HML), Winterthur Manuscripts, papers of Victorine du Pont Bauduy, box 6a13, poetry files.

1. Victorine to Eleuthera du Pont, March 28, 1821, HML, box 6a2.

2. Mary Johnson, *Victorine du Pont: Heiress to the Educational Dream of Pierre Samuel du Pont de Nemours* (Philadelphia: Temple University Press, 1979), 90.

3. Victorine to Eleuthera, January 27, 1824, HML, box 6a3.

4. John Thomas Scharf, *History of Delaware 1609–1888*, vol. 2 (Philadelphia: L. J. Richards, 1888), 653.

5. Victorine to Eleuthera, February 24, 1822, HML, box 6a2.

6. Roy M. Boatman, "The Brandywine Cotton Industry, 1795–1865," Eleutherian Mills–Hagley Foundation research report, 1957, Acc. 1645, box 1, folder 1, 61.

7. "It is a great pity that she is not a boy; she has such a memory and learns so easily that she can be made a charming child." Sophie (Dalmas) du Pont to Eleuthère Irénée du Pont, July 26, 1795, in du Pont, *Life of Eleuthère Irénée du Pont*, vol. 3, ed. and trans. Bessie Gardner du Pont (Newark: University of Delaware Press, 1924), 238.

8. *Directions for Forming and Conducting Sunday Schools* (Philadelphia: American Sunday School Union, 1828), 7.

9. Victorine to Evelina du Pont, undated (likely June 21, 1812), HML, box 6a2.

10. Victorine to Sophie du Pont, undated, HML, box 6a6, 1850–1860.

11. Sophie du Pont, BMSS history, c. 1870s, HML, Acc. 389, W9-40303.

12. Victorine du Pont, Report to the American Sunday School Union, March 1, 1830, HML, box 6a13, BMSS.

13. HML, box 6a13, poetry, extracts, quotations, from Richard Baxter, *The Saint's Everlasting Rest* (New York: American Tract Society, n.d. [1824?]), 442.

14. Margaret M. Mulrooney, *Black Powder, White Lace* (Hanover, NH: University Press of New England, 2002), 72.

15. Victorine to the ASSU, Report to the American Sunday School Union, March 1, 1830, HML, box 6a13, BMSS.

16. Victorine to Ziba Ferris, December 13, 1830, HML, Acc. 389, box 6.

17. Victorine to Evelina (du Pont) Bidermann, March 14, 1821, HML, box 6a2.

18. Ibid.

19. Victorine to Eleuthera, March 28, 1821, HML, box 6a2.

20. Victorine to Eleuthera, March 30, 1821, HML, box 6a2.

21. Victorine to Eleuthera, undated, 1828, HML, box 6a3.

22. Victorine to Eleuthera, March 28, 1821, HML, box 6a2.

23. Victorine to Eleuthera, May 3, 1821, HML, box 6a2.

24. Victorine to Eleuthera, April 8, 1822, HML, box 6a2.

25. Victorine to Eleuthera, April 26, 1822, HML, box 6a2.

26. Victorine to Antoinette Brevost, April 16, 1821, HML, box 6a2.

27. Victorine to Eleuthera, April 26, 1822, HML, box 6a2.

28. Sophie's diary, February 21, 1833, HML, Winterthur manuscripts, Acc. group 9, Series D, E, F, general files.

29. Sophie developed a close friendship with the Smith sisters from Rockdale, a mill community along the Chester Creek in Pennsylvania. Harriet and Clementina ("Hatty" and "Clem") Smith were the daughters of Mr. and Mrs. Richard Somers Smith. Anne-Marie and Charlotte Cazenove, the daughters of Mr. and Mrs. Antoine Cazenove, were also close friends of the du Pont sisters.

30. Sophie to Samuel Francis Du Pont, postscript added to letter of Victorine to Samuel Francis, September 15, 1821, HML, box 6a2.

31. For a fine example of these sketches, see Betty-Bright Low and Jacqueline Hinsley, *Sophie du Pont: A Young Lady in America* (New York: Harry N. Abrams, 1987).

CHAPTER 12 — SECOND MOTHER

Epigraph: Victorine (du Pont) Bauduy to Eleuthera du Pont, March 3, 1826, Hagley Museum and Library, Wilmington, DE (hereafter HML), Winterthur Manuscripts, papers of Victorine du Pont Bauduy, box 6a3.

1. *Tancopanican Chronicles* 1, no. 2 (September 27, 1823), HML, box 6A13, misc. papers.

2. *Tancopanican Chronicles* 1, no. 1 (September 20, 1823), HML, box 6A13, misc. papers.

3. Bernard Barton, *The Museum of Foreign Literature, Science, and Art* (Philadelphia: E. Littell, 1831), 454, copied by Victorine du Pont, HML, box 6a13, poetry files.

4. *Tancopanican Chronicles*, issues 1–8 (1823), HML, box 6A13, misc. papers.

5. Victorine to Evelina (du Pont) Bidermann, undated, 1824, HML, box 6a4.

6. Alfred's "Nemours" is not to be confused with the seventy-room mansion of the same name that his future grandson, Alfred Irénée du Pont (1864–1935), would build in Wilmington in 1909.

7. Victorine to Evelina, undated, 1826, HML, box 6a3.

8. Victorine to Sophie du Pont, September 23, 1824, in du Pont, *Life of Eleuthère Irénée du Pont*, vol. 11, ed. and trans. Bessie Gardner du Pont (Newark: University of Delaware Press, 1926), 120.

9. The house in which the wedding took place still stands at W. Third and Delaware streets in old New Castle, Delaware.

10. Annie Hollingsworth Wharton, *Salons Colonial and Republican* (Philadelphia: J. B. Lippincott, 1900), 227.

11. Footnote by B. G. du Pont included in du Pont, *Life of Eleuthère Irénée du Pont*, 11:138.

12. Victorine to Henry du Pont, February 3, 1827, HML, box 6a3.

13. Victorine to Eleuthera, March 4, 1822, HML, box 6a2.

14. Victorine to Eleuthera, November 1827, HML, box 6a3.

15. The precise nature of Sophie's ailment is unknown. A few historians have proffered cancer as a possibility, such as James F. Wall and William H. A. Carr, but both conceded that the diagnosis remains uncertain: James F. Wall, *Alfred I. du Pont: The Man and His Family* (New York: Oxford University Press, 1990); William H. A. Carr, *The du Ponts of Delaware* (New York: Dodd, Mead, 1964).

16. Victorine to Eleuthera, undated, 1828, HML, box 6a3.

17. Eleuthère Irénée (hereafter E. I.) du Pont to A. Girard, August 3, 1828, in du Pont, *Life of Eleuthère Irénée du Pont*, 11:210.

18. E. I. to Francis Gurney Smith, August 3, 1828, in du Pont, *Life of Eleuthère Irénée du Pont*, 11:210.

19. E. I. to Francis Gurney Smith, August 5, 1828, in du Pont, *Life of Eleuthère Irénée du Pont*, 11:211.

20. Dr. Thomas T. Hewson (1773–1849), Philadelphia surgeon and physician. Hewson also served the Walnut Street Prison and Sarah Ralston's Orphan Asylum for over twenty years.

21. E. I. to Francis Gurney Smith Smith, August 6, 1828, in du Pont, *Life of Eleuthère Irénée du Pont*, 11:212.

22. Victorine to Samuel Francis Du Pont, August 20, 1828, HML, box 6a3.

23. E. I. to J. P. McCorkle, November 22, 1828, in du Pont, *Life of Eleuthère Irénée du Pont*, 11:221.

24. Victorine to Sophie, March 17, 1825, HML, box 6a3.

25. Pierre Samuel du Pont de Nemours to E. I., July 10, 1812, in du Pont, *Life of Eleuthère Irénée du Pont*, vol. 9, ed. and trans. Bessie Gardner du Pont (Newark: University of Delaware Press, 1925), 46.

26. Ibid., 47.

27. Luke 12:48, King James Version.

28. John Beverley Riggs, *A Guide to Manuscripts* (Greenville, DE: Eleutherian Mills Historical Society, 1970), 280.

29. Victorine to Henry, February 3, 1827, HML, box 6a3.

30. Col. Augustus L. Roumfort (1796–1878), graduate of West Point, was principal of Mt. Airy from 1826 to 1834.

31. Victorine to Henry, November 9, 1827, HML, box 6a3.

32. Victorine to Henry, July 3, 1829, HML, box 6a3.

CHAPTER 13 — A GROWING FAMILY, A THRIVING COMMUNITY

1. Charles-Maurice de Talleyrand-Périgord (1754–1838). French diplomat who served under Napoleon and Louis Philippe I.

2. Eleuthère Irénée du Pont to Francis Gurney Smith, August 13, 1834, in du Pont, *Life of Eleuthère Irénée du Pont*, vol. 11, ed. and trans. Bessie Gardner du Pont (Newark: University of Delaware Press, 1926), 287.

3. Bessie Gardner du Pont stated: "Other accounts say that he died of Asiatic cholera." du Pont, *Life of Eleuthère Irénée du Pont*, 11:288.

4. *Delaware State Journal*, November 4, 1834, in du Pont, *Life of Eleuthère Irénée du Pont*, 11:288–292.

5. Felicia Hemans, *The Poetical Works of Mrs. Felicia Hemans* (Philadelphia: Grigg & Elliot, 1836), 295, Hagley Museum and Library, Wilmington, DE (hereafter HML), Winterthur Manuscripts, papers of Victorine du Pont Bauduy, box 6a13, poetry files.

6. Eleuthera du Pont and Thomas Mackie Smith were married on September 18, 1834.

7. In 1837, the siblings owned twenty-six shares between them, each worth $7,000: Alfred controlled eight, Henry and Alexis each had five, and the four daughters held two apiece. Allan J. Henry, ed., *The Life of Alexis Irénée du Pont*, vol. 2 (Philadelphia: William F. Fell, 1945), 212.

8. Peter C. Welsh, "The Old Stone Office Building 1837–1891," Eleutherian Mills–Hagley Foundation research report, 1959, Acc. 1645, box 3, folder 73, MS1645_073, 2.

9. Victorine (du Pont) Bauduy to Evelina (du Pont) Bidermann, January 15, 1838, HML, box 6a4.

10. Victorine to Evelina, October 10, 1837, HML, box 6a3.

11. Gabrielle Camille (Begue) Bidermann (1824–1905).

12. Anthony F. C. Wallace, *Rockdale: The Growth of an American Village in the Early Industrial Revolution* (New York: Alfred A. Knopf, 1972), 494n16.

13. "I cannot tell you how much I admire [Sophie's] conduct since her late disappointment. She makes a constant effort at cheerfulness and usually succeeds, but it makes me sad . . . for I often can see that it is an effort." Victorine to Eleuthera (du Pont) Smith, c. 1836, HML, box 6a3.

14. Victorine to Eleuthera, December 22, 1846, HML, box 6a4.

15. Victorine to Sophie Du Pont, July 22, 1837, HML, box 6a4.

16. Ibid.

17. Victorine to Evelina, July 30, 1838, HML, box 6a4.

18. Frances Elizabeth du Pont, born February 6, 1838. Named after her grandfather, Francis Gurney Smith (1784–1873).

19. Victorine to Evelina, May 15, 1838, HML, box 6a4. Frances ("Fanny") Elizabeth du Pont (1838–1902) married Leighton Coleman, the second Episcopal bishop of Delaware, in 1861.

20. Victorine to Evelina, January 3, 1838, HML, box 6a4.

21. Victorine to Evelina, February 1854, HML, box 6a5.

22. Mary Constance du Pont (February 10, 1854–September 3, 1854).

23. Victorine to Evelina, May 12, 1838, HML, box 6a4.

24. Victorine to Eleuthera, February 25, 1833, HML, box 6a4.

25. Victorine to Eleuthera, February 26, 1833, HML, box 6a4.

26. Victorine to Evelina, April 3, 1846, HML, box 6a4.

27. Victorine to Eleuthera, undated, c. 1835, HML, box 6a3.

28. Victorine to Sophie, August 1, 1853, HML, box 6a4.

29. BMSS records, HML, Acc. 389, expenses.

30. Victorine to Sophie, July 18, 1845, HML, box 6a4.

31. Sophie du Pont, n.d., HML, Winterthur Manuscripts, papers of Sophie Madeleine Du Pont, Group 9, W9-40303.

32. Joel Swayne to Victorine Bauduy, March 7, 1832, HML, box 6a13, medical notes.

33. Victorine to Eleuthera, October 1830, HML, box 6a4.

34. Daniel Bernoulli (1700–1782); Edward Jenner (1749–1823).

35. Victorine to Eleuthera, April 1831, HML, box 6a3.

36. Victorine to Eleuthera, 1831, HML, box 6a3, scrap.

CHAPTER 14 — NATIONAL RECOGNITION

1. At the BMSS, a male "schoolmaster" was occasionally hired to oversee the education of the boys. Male educators in this position were the only ones who received remuneration for teaching.

2. Rev. Patrick Reilly succeeded Rev. Kenny as rector of St. Peter's Cathedral in Wilmington (1840–1850).

3. Victorine (du Pont) Bauduy to Sophie (du Pont) Du Pont, c. 1840, Hagley Museum and Library, Wilmington, DE (hereafter HML), Winterthur Manuscripts, papers of Victorine du Pont Bauduy, box 6a6.

4. Alexis du Pont to Rev. Henry C. Lay, from a tribute the latter wrote in 1857 entitled "A Few Hours with a Christian Man," in Allan J. Henry, ed., *The Life of Alexis Irénée du Pont*, vol. 1 (Philadelphia: William F. Fell, 1945), 222.

5. Victorine (du Pont) Bauduy, BMSS Report, c. 1832, HML, box 6a13, BMSS practices.

6. Victorine du Pont, June 15, 1827, HML, Acc. 389, box 1, notes on establishment of BMSS.

7. "Our library, consisting of more than one hundred volumes is composed, with few exceptions, of the books published by the American Sunday School Union." Victorine du Pont, Report to the ASSU, March 1, 1830, HML, box 6a13, BMSS. She wrote almost the exact same information in a "BMSS history as written by Victorine du Pont Bauduy (c. 1830)." HML, box 6a16.

8. Victorine du Pont, letter to the ASSU, c. 1852, HML, Acc. 389.

9. Sophie du Pont, BMSS history, c. 1870s, HML, Acc. 389 (W9-40303).

10. "I find every day at school excellent subjects for caricatures—the master, in particular." Sophie du Pont, postscript included in Victorine's letter to Evelina (du Pont) Bidermann, February 21, 1825, HML, box 6a3.

11. "They have published the report of our school we gave last summer to Mr Haven." Victorine to Eleuthera du Pont, December 2, 1830, HML, box 6a3.

12. The six groupings of ASSU schools were neighborhood schools, schools in manufacturing villages, prisons and alms houses, private houses, infants' schools, and classes for adults. Frederick A. Packard, *The Teacher Taught* (Philadelphia: American Sunday School Union, 1839), 50–68.

13. Ibid., 60–61.

14. "An Article on the American Sunday School Union," extracted from *The Biblical Repertory and Theological Review* for April 1830 (Philadelphia: James Kay Jr., 1830), 10.

15. Records for the Levy Court of Delaware, 1823–1862, HML, Acc. 389, BMSS.

16. Victorine du Pont, Report to the ASSU, 1835, HML, Acc. 389, BMSS.

17. Victorine du Pont, Report to the ASSU, March 1, 1830, HML, box 6a13.

18. Victorine du Pont, Report to the ASSU, c. 1832, HML, box 6a13.

19. Thomas Gaw, June 30, 1849, ASSU papers 1817–1915, Presbyterian Historical Society, Philadelphia, Microfilm/POS 52.

20. "Ciphering" was defined in Webster's dictionary of 1828 as "using figures, or practicing arithmetic." *American Dictionary of the English Language* (New York: S. Converse, 1828).

21. Victorine du Pont, Summary of BMSS history, c. 1830, HML, box 6a16.

22. Victorine du Pont, History of the BMSS, undated, c. 1853, HML, Acc. 389, BMSS establishment notes.

23. Rev. Patrick Kenny (1763–1840), an early missionary priest in Delaware and Pennsylvania, was the first priest to serve St. Peter's Church in Wilmington, Delaware.

24. Allan J. Henry, ed., *The Life of Alexis Irénée du Pont*, vol. 1 (Philadelphia: William F. Fell, 1945), 23.

25. Victorine du Pont, Report to the American Sunday School Union, 1829, HML, Acc. 389.

26. Anne Boylan, *Sunday School: The Formation of an American Institution* (New Haven, CT: Yale University Press, 1988), 9.

27. Alexis de Tocqueville, *Democracy in America*, trans. Henry Reeve, 2nd American ed. (New York: George Adlard, 1838), 285.

28. School charts, HML, Acc. 389, box 2, mark books.

29. Victorine du Pont, Report to the ASSU, c. 1832, HML, box 6a13, BMSS practices.

30. Edwin Wilbur Rice, *The Sunday School Movement, 1780–1917* (Philadelphia: American Sunday School Union, 1917), 109.

31. Victorine du Pont, Report to the ASSU, January 29, 1831, HML, 6a13, BMSS 1816–1852.

32. Victorine du Pont, History of the BMSS, undated, c. 1853, HML, Acc. 389, establishment notes.

33. Undated letter from Victorine to Eleuthera (du Pont) Smith, c. 1842, HML, box 6a4.

34. Victorine to Eleuthera, March 7, 1838, HML, box 6a4.

35. Victorine to Eleuthera, undated, c. 1832, HML, box 6a3.

CHAPTER 15 — LEGACIES AND CONFLICTS

1. Sophie (du Pont) Du Pont, postscript included in Victorine (du Pont) Bauduy's letter to Eleuthera (du Pont) Smith, May 8, 1846, Hagley Museum and Library, Wilmington, DE (hereafter HML), Winterthur Manuscripts, papers of Victorine du Pont Bauduy, box 6a4.

2. Victorine to Samuel Francis Du Pont, May 8, 1847, HML, box 6a4.

3. Thomas Bradford Shubrick (1825–1847). Serving as a midshipman aboard the USS *Mississippi*, he was sent ashore on March 25, 1847, to take charge of a naval battery and was killed while redirecting one of the artillery guns.

4. Victorine to Sophie, undated, c. April 1846, HML, box 6a6.

5. Victorine to Eleuthera, May 8, 1846, HML, box 6a4.

6. Victorine to Eleuthera, July 6, 1846, HML, box 6a4.

7. The Lindsay clan was prominent in Scotland from the eleventh to nineteenth centuries. www.scotweb.co.uk/info/lindsay.

8. Victorine to Eleuthera, July 6, 1846, HML, box 6a4.

9. Eleuthera du Pont, Transcript books, HML, Winterthur manuscripts, Group 10, Series E, no. 126 (32), 40.

10. Pierre Samuel du Pont de Nemours, *The Autobiography of du Pont de Nemours*, trans. Elizabeth Fox-Genovese (Wilmington, DE: Scholarly Resources, 1984), 29.

11. Victorine to Eleuthera, September 25, 1846, HML, box 6a4.

12. Alfred Lee (1807–1887) was elected bishop in 1841. Edgar L. Pennington, "The Diocese of Delaware: From Its Organization to the Election of Its First Bishop," *Historical Magazine of the Protestant Episcopal Church* 5, no. 1 (1936): 23–24.

13. Victorine to an official at St. Andrew's, undated, c. April 1847, HML, box 6a6.

14. Red Clay Presbyterian in Wilmington and the "Old Log Church," known today as the Lower Brandywine Presbyterian Church.

15. Victorine Bauduy, as quoted in Samuel Crawford Brincklé Diary, April 6, 1853, Diary Extracts, 1848–1863, HML, Acc. 2437, box 2.

16. Victorine to Eleuthera, March 24, 1847, HML, box 6a4.

17. Victorine to Eleuthera, November 21, 1846, HML, box 6a4.

18. Brincklé Diary, May 8, 1848, HML, Acc. 2437.

19. Bishop William White (1748–1836). First presiding bishop of the Episcopal Church in the United States.

20. Adam Clarke (1760 or 1762–1832) was a Methodist preacher and friend of John Wesley.

21. Victorine to Sophie, February 13, 1849, HML, box 6a4.

22. "Good Mr. B" and "dear Mr. B" were common terms of endearment the sisters applied to Rev. Brincklé. "We had good Mr Brincklé to dinner yesterday." Victorine to Sophie, undated, HML, box 6a6. For "dear Mr. B" see Brincklé Diary, January 25, 1861, HML, Acc. 2437.

23. Victorine to Sophie, undated, HML, box 6a6, 1850–1860.

24. Brincklé Diary, July 18, 1849, HML, Acc. 2437.

25. Brincklé Diary, August 1849, HML, Acc. 2437.

26. St. Joseph's Catholic Church (1841), Mt. Salem Methodist Church (1847), Green Hill Presbyterian Church (1851), and Christ Church Christiana Hundred (1851). The websites of these churches all credit the BMSS as the origin of their ministries.

27. Brincklé Diary, October 6, 1848, HML, Acc. 2437.

28. Brincklé Diary, September 2, 1849, HML, Acc. 2437, box 2.

29. Brincklé Diary, November 16, 1849, HML, Acc. 2437, box 2.

30. Brincklé Diary, May 1850, HML, Acc. 2437, box 2.

31. Brincklé Diary, May 1850, HML, Acc. 2437, box 2.

32. Brincklé Diary, April 18, 1851, HML, Acc. 2437, box 2.

33. Brincklé Diary, April 13, 1851, HML, Acc. 2437, box 2.

34. Sophie Du Pont, June 22, 1851, HML, Acc. 2437, Christ Church papers, box 2, Diary Entries—Sophie & Eleuthera Du Pont 1854–1859.

35. Brincklé Diary, May 14, 1851, HML, Acc. 2437, box 2.

36. Sophie Du Pont, June 22, 1851, HML, Acc. 2437, Christ Church papers, box 2, Diary Entries—Sophie & Eleuthera Du Pont 1854–1859.

37. The topographical term "hundred" was a lingering British colonial influence used to describe the approximate boundaries of districts within a state, usually for taxation or voting purposes.

CHAPTER 16 — LOSS AND RESTORATION

1. Peter Kemble (1825–1887), son of William Kemble, New York business associate of Eleuthère Irénée du Pont.

2. Victorine (du Pont) Bauduy to Sophie (du Pont) Du Pont, March 8, 1849, Hagley Museum and Library, Wilmington, DE (hereafter HML), Winterthur Manuscripts, papers of Victorine du Pont Bauduy, box 6a4.

3. Victorine to Sophie, undated, February 1849, HML, box 6a4.

4. Karl J. Niederer, "The Brandywine Manufacturers' Sunday School: A History of Its Construction and Recommendations for Renovations," Eleutherian Mills–Hagley Foundation research report, 1977, Acc. 1645, box 7, folder 220.

5. Other improvements at the BMSS included wooden blinds for the windows, a movable pulpit, new desks, and a pair of iron boot scrapers.

6. Samuel Crawford Brincklé Diary, August 17, 1851, Extracts, 1848–1863, Christ Church Christiana Hundred records, HML, Acc. 2437, box 2.

7. Brincklé Diary, April 1, 1851, HML, Acc. 2437.

8. Sophie Du Pont to "My dear young friend," May 5, 1851, HML, Acc. 389. She cited 1 Thessalonians 2:12, King James Version.

9. Victorine tutored Alexis throughout his first ten years. "Alexis remains under my care a little longer but, I fancy, he will soon require 'the hand of a master.'" Victorine to Samuel Francis Du Pont, May 29, 1826, HML, box 6a3.

10. Victorine to Alexis du Pont, February 14, 1834, HML, box 6a3.

11. Brincklé Diary, April 1, 1851, HML, Acc. 2437.

12. In the heading above, Victorine's description of "January" in an undated letter to her mother Sophie (Dalmas) du Pont, HML, box 6a6, 1850–1860.

13. Victorine to Sophie, March 9, 1852, HML, box 6a4.

14. Ibid.

15. This rocking horse may still be seen at Eleutherian Mills today.

16. Victorine to Sophie, March 9, 1852. HML, box 6a4.

17. Brincklé Diary, January 20, 1852, HML, Acc. 2437.

18. Brincklé Diary, January 22, 1852, HML, Acc. 2437.

19. Brincklé Diary, January 25, 1852, HML, Acc. 2437.

20. Brincklé Diary, June 13, 1852, HML, Acc. 2437.

21. Brincklé Diary, June 20, 1852, HML, Acc. 2437.

22. Brincklé Diary, January 26, 1852, HML, Acc. 2437.

23. Victorine to Sophie, undated, c. March 1852, HML, box 6a4.

24. Ibid.

25. Victorine to Eleuthera (du Pont) Smith, April 4, 1822, HML, box 6a2.

26. Victorine to Eleuthera, undated, 1828, HML, box 6a3.

27. Victorine to Evelina (du Pont) Bidermann, January 1, 1853, HML, box 6a4.

28. Victorine to Sophie, undated, c. March 1852, HML, 6a4.

29. Victorine to Sophie, undated, c. 1853, HML, 6a6.

30. Sarah Garesché Holland reported that during the restoration of Ferdinand's grave, a human skull was discovered in a handsome walnut box inside the monument. "No one in the family had ever heard of the skull, so it will always remain a mystery." Holland, *Garesché, De Bauduy, and Des Chapelles Families* (St. Louis: Schneider, 1963), 119.

31. Victorine to Henry Algernon du Pont, January 30, 1858, HML, box 6a5.

32. Victorine to Henry Algernon, June 15, 1854, HML, box 6a5.

33. Victorine to Sophie, July 2, 1853, HML, box 6a4.

34. Victorine to Sophie, July 8, 1853, HML, box 6a4.

35. Victorine to Sophie, August 3, 1853, HML, box 6a4.

36. Victorine to Sophie, undated, 1853, HML, box 6a6.

37. Victorine to Sophie, May 21, 1853, HML, box 6a4.

38. Victorine to Sophie, undated, 1853, HML, box 6a6.

39. Victorine du Pont, HML, box 6a13, poetry.

CHAPTER 17 — A TIME TO BUILD

1. Anne Kumer, Bryant Park archivist, www.bryantpark.org. Used by permission.

2. Victorine (du Pont) Bauduy to Sophie Du Pont, October 1853, Hagley Museum and Library Manuscripts and Archives, Wilmington, DE (hereafter HML), Winterthur manuscripts, papers of Victorine du Pont Bauduy, box 6a4.

3. Victorine to Evelina (du Pont) Bidermann, undated, October 1853, HML, box 6a4.

4. Victorine to Eleuthera (du Pont) Smith, undated, 1853, HML, box 6a4.

5. Emma Paulina du Pont (1827–1914). The sisters referred to her as either "Pene" or "Polly."

6. Victorine to Sophie, May 21, 1853, HML, box 6a4.

7. Samuel Crawford Brincklé, Diary, July 19, 1852, Extracts, 1848–1863, Christ Church Christiana Hundred records, HML, Acc. 2437, box 2.

8. Victorine as quoted in Brincklé Diary, April 4, 1852, HML, Acc. 2437.

9. Victorine to Sophie, August 5, 1853, HML, box 6a4.

10. Victorine to Sophie, undated, September 1853, HML, box 6a4. Cholera Infantum, an extreme case of diarrhea contracted by young children during the hottest months.

11. Victorine to Sophie, October 3, 1853, HML, box 6a4.

12. Victorine to Sophie, January 16, 1854, HML, box 6a5.

13. Victorine du Pont, Report to the ASSU, undated, c.1853, HML, Acc. 389, establishment notes.

14. "Wilmington Calamity," *New York Times*, June 1, 1854, http://www.gendisasters.com/delaware/10773/wilmington-de-dupont-powder-mill-explosion-may-1854.

15. Alfred Victor du Pont to family members, June 27, 1854, in *The Life of Alexis Irénée du Pont*, vol. 2, ed. Allan J. Henry (Philadelphia: William F. Fell, 1945), 185.

16. Ibid., 189.

17. Alfred Victor to Victorine, June 27, 1854, in Henry, *The Life of Alexis Irénée du Pont*, 2:190.

18. Victorine to Henry du Pont, undated, 1854, HML, box 6a13.

19. Alfred to Victorine, June 27, 1854, in Henry, *The Life of Alexis Irénée du Pont*, 2:193.

20. Flea Park, a row of Du Pont company houses originally called "Free Park." Due to the abundance of barnyard animals, it soon became known as "Flea Park."

21. Brincklé Diary, April 3, 1854, HML, Acc. 2437.

22. Brincklé Diary, April 25, 1854, HML, Acc. 2437.

23. Ibid.

24. To this day, Christ Church has not had its own graveyard.

25. Victorine to Henry, undated, 1854, HML, box 6a13.

26. Victorine to Henry, undated, c. 1854, HML, box 6a13, Brandywine Manufacturer's Sunday School 1816-1852.

27. Ibid.

28. Brincklé Diary, July 28, 1854, HML, Acc. 2437.

29. Victorine to Sophie, September 3, 1854, HML, box 6a5.

30. Victorine to Sophie, September 4, 1854, HML, box 6a5.

31. Brincklé Diary, September 4, 1854, HML, Acc. 2437.

32. Victorine to Sophie, undated fragment, c. 1853, HML, box 6a6.

CHAPTER 18 — BELLS

Epigraph: Victorine (du Pont) Bauduy to Sophie Du Pont, April 17, 1857, Hagley Museum and Library Manuscripts and Archives, Wilmington, DE (hereafter HML), Winterthur Manuscripts, papers of Victorine du Pont Bauduy, box 6a5.

1. Victorine to Sophie, June 27, 1857, HML, box 6a5.

2. Victorine to Henry Algernon du Pont, October 28, 1856, HML, box 6a5.

3. Victorine to Sophie, December 1, 1857, HML, box 6a5.

4. Victorine to Henry Algernon, November 25, 1856, HML, box 6a5.

5. Victorine to Eleuthera (du Pont) Smith, September 25, 1846, HML, box 6a4.

6. Victorine to Evelina (du Pont) Bidermann, March 13, 1838, HML, box 6a4.

7. Joseph Shipley (1795-1867). The Rockwood Museum and Park, which includes the Shipley house, is still open to visitors.

8. Victorine to Amelia du Pont, April 20, 1860, HML, box 6a5.

9. Victorine to Sophie, August 9, 1853, HML, box 6a4.

10. Samuel Crawford Brincklé Diary, April 11, 1856, Extracts, 1848-1863, Christ Church Christiana Hundred records, HML, Acc. 2437, box 2.

11. Brincklé Diary, May 11, 1856, HML, Acc. 2437.

12. "Rules for the Internal Regulation of the B. M. Sunday School," 1821, HML, Acc. 389, aisle 9C.

13. Brincklé Diary, April 19, 1856, HML, Acc. 2437, box 2.

14. Brincklé Diary, April 14, 1856, HML, Acc. 2437, box 2.

15. Brincklé Diary, May 4, 1856, HML, Acc. 2437, box 2.

16. Sophie Du Pont, May 4, 1856, HML, Acc. 2437, Christ Church papers, box 2, Diary Entries—Sophie & Eleuthera du Pont, 1854–1859.

17. Brincklé Diary, May 10, 1856, HML, Acc. 2437, box 2.

18. William S. Dutton, *Du Pont: One Hundred and Forty Years* (New York: Scribner's, 1942), 72. William H. A. Carr adds that Alfred "never recovered from this assault on his emotions." Carr, *The du Ponts of Delaware* (New York: Dodd, Mead, 1964), 150.

19. Victorine to Henry Algernon, August 5, 1856, HML, box 6a5.

20. Victorine to Sophie, undated, 1856, HML, box 6a5.

21. Mary Sophie du Pont (1834–1869) would marry her cousin, Charles Irénée II, on February 25, 1862, but would die seven years later at the age of thirty-five.

22. Victorine to Sophie, undated, 1856, HML, box 6a5.

23. Eleuthera to Sophie (postscript in Victorine's letter to Sophie), undated, 1856, HML, box 6a5.

24. Victorine to Sophie, undated, 1856, HML, box 6a5.

25. Victorine to Sophie, October 7, 1856, HML, box 6a5.

26. Victorine to Henry Algernon, October 28, 1856, HML, box 6a5.

27. Brincklé Diary, January 29, 1857, HML, Acc. 2437.

28. Ibid.; Brincklé Diary, May 10, 1856, HML, Acc. 2437.

29. Victorine to Sophie, undated, HML, box 6a6.

30. Joanna (Smith) du Pont, "Joanna's Sermon," in *The Life of Alexis Irénée du Pont*, vol. 1, ed. Allan J. Henry (Philadelphia: William F. Fell, 1945), 39.

31. Harold Hancock, "The Industrial Worker along the Brandywine, 1840–1870," Eleutherian Mills–Hagley Foundation research report, 1957, Acc. 1645, box 2, folder 35c, MS1645_035c.

32. Brincklé Diary, February 25, 1857, HML, Acc. 2437, box 2.

33. The Treaty of Tientsin, June 25, 1858, signed by France, Britain, Russia, the United States, and China, ended the Second Opium War.

34. Brincklé Diary, May 24, 1857, HML, Acc. 2437, box 2.

35. Victorine to Sophie, April 17, 1857, HML, box 6a5.

36. Brincklé Diary, August 22, 1857, HML, Acc. 2437, box 2.

37. Eleuthera du Pont Smith, "Le Brave des Braves," in Henry, *The Life of Alexis Irénée du Pont*, 1:2.

38. Ibid.

39. Brincklé Diary, August 22, 1857, HML, Acc. 2437, box 2.

40. Smith, "Le Brave des Braves," 1:6.

41. Ibid., 1:7.

42. Ibid.

43. Ibid., 1:8.

44. Ibid.

45. Matthew 24:35, King James Version.

46. Smith, "Le Brave des Braves," 1:11.

47. Joseph Shipley (1795–1867), prominent Wilmington mill owner and shipping merchant.

48. Eleuthera du Pont, March 9, 1859, HML, Acc. 2437, Christ Church Records, box 2, Diary Entries—Sophie & Eleuthera du Pont, 1854–1859.

CHAPTER 19 — FEELING AN INTEREST

1. Victorine (du Pont) Bauduy to Sophie Du Pont, April 7, 1857, Hagley Museum and Library Manuscripts and Archives, Wilmington, DE (hereafter HML), Winterthur Manuscripts, papers of Victorine du Pont Bauduy, box 6a5.

2. Victorine to Sophie, undated, c. 1860, HML, box 6a6.

3. Victorine to Mary Elliott, July 5, 1859, HML, box 6a5.

4. Anthony F. C. Wallace, *Rockdale: The Growth of an American Village in the Early Industrial Revolution* (New York: Alfred A. Knopf, 1972), 104.

5. Victorine to Mary Elliott, January 15, 1859, HML, box 6a5.

6. Victorine to Sarah Gilpin, May 1, 1860, HML, box 6a5.

7. Victorine to Evelina (du Pont) Bidermann, Spring 1848, HML, box 6a4. Victorine's reference was to Dickens's *Dombey and Son* (1846–1848).

8. Victorine to Sarah Gilpin, May 1, 1860, HML, box 6a5.

9. Marie de Rabutin-Chantal, Marquise de Sévigné (1626–1696).

10. Victorine to Henry Algernon du Pont, February 2, 1857, HML, box 6a5.

11. Victor Cousin (1792–1867), author of *The Youth of Madame de Longueville*.

12. Victorine to Henry Algernon, October 28, 1856, HML, box 6a5.

13. Victorine to Henry Algernon, February 20, 1856, HML, box 6a5.

14. Victorine to Mary Elliott, February 3, 1859, HML, box 6a5.

15. Victorine to Mary Elliott, November 15, 1858, HML, box 6a5. She is referencing *The Rise of the Dutch Republic* by John Lothrop Motley (1856).

16. Lord Teignmouth was John Shore (1751–1834), who served as Governor-General of India from 1793 to 1797. In 1804 he became the first president of the British and Foreign Bible Society. Rev. Samuel Wilkes, *The Life of Lord Teignmouth* (London: John Parker, 1845), 3.

17. Victorine to Henry Algernon, December 28, 1859, HML, box 6a5.

18. Victorine to Sophie, December 1, 1857, HML, box 6a5.

19. Victorine to Sophie, undated, December 1860, HML, box 6a5. Reference is to Lydia Howard (Huntley) Sigourney (1791–1865), *Lucy Howard's Journal* (New York: Harper Bros., 1858).

20. Anne Francis Bayard (1802–1864), wife of James A. Bayard Jr. (1799–1880), who was twice U.S. senator for Delaware.

21. Victorine to Sophie, October 19, 1860, HML, box 6a5.

22. Victorine to Evelina, July 7, 1859, HML, box 6a5.

23. Victorine du Pont, Diary notes, 1860, HML, box 6a14.

24. Victorine to Sophie, undated, 1853, HML, box 6a4.

25. Victorine to Sophie, undated, HML, box 6a6, 1857–1860.

26. Victorine to Henry Algernon, May 24, 1858, HML, box 6a5.

27. Dr. Thomas Mackie Smith notation, HML, Misc., box 6a13, Medical Notes.

28. Victorine to Sophie, Tuesday, December 1, 1857, HML, box 6a5.

29. Ibid.

30. Victorine to Sophie, April 17, 1857, HML, box 6a5.

31. Victorine to Sophie, October 27, 1855, HML, box 6a5.

32. Victorine to Mary Elliott, December 14, 1858, HML, box 6a5.

33. Victorine to Henry Algernon, October 26, 1858, HML, box 6a5.

34. Victorine to Evelina, November 24, 1837, HML, box 6a3.

35. Victorine to Eleuthera (du Pont) Smith, undated, likely Thursday, August 13, 1846, HML, box 6a6, misc. family.

36. Victorine to Mary Elliott, April 5, 1859, HML, box 6a5.

37. Victorine to Mary Elliott, February 3, 1859, HML, box 6a5.

38. Victorine to Mary Elliott, March 5, 1859, HML, box 6a5.

39. Victorine du Pont, Prayers, HML, box 6a13, religion files.

40. This impressive table can still be viewed at the family home, Eleutherian Mills, at the Hagley Museum in Greenville, Delaware.

41. Victorine to Sophie, August 2, 1859, HML, box 6a5.

42. Victorine to Sophie, undated, HML, box 6a6.

43. Victorine to Sophie, October 21, 1859, HML, box 6a5.

44. Jacques Hubert Jacquot (1820–1859). His name appeared on the explosion list as "Ubert Jacob." Richard Scott and S. Fulton, "Interpretive Packet on Explosions," Eleutherian Mills–Hagley Foundation research report, 1990, Acc. 2016.201, 20090507_10.

45. An eighth man died later of his wounds. Scott and Fulton, "Interpretive Packet on Explosions," 18.

46. Victorine to Amelia (Clifford) du Pont, October 22, 1859, HML, box 6a5.

47. Victorine to Henry Algernon, December 28, 1859, HML, box 6a5.

CHAPTER 20 — NEARING HOME

1. Victorine (du Pont) Bauduy to Mary Elliott, March 5, 1859, Hagley Museum and Library Manuscripts and Archives, Wilmington, DE (hereafter HML), Winterthur Manuscripts, papers of Victorine du Pont Bauduy, box 6a5.

2. Victorine to Mary Elliott, January 3, 1860, HML, box 6a5.

3. Henry Gilpin (1801–1860). Best remembered as the man who represented the government in the 1841 case of the *Amistad*.

4. Fred Kaplan, *John Quincy Adams: American Visionary* (New York: HarperCollins, 2014), 521.

5. Victorine to Mary Elliott, February 6, 1860, HML, box 6a5.

6. Elwood Garret (1815–1910) was one of the first in the United States to use the daguerreotype process. The machine sent to him by L. M. Daguerre was labeled "No. 6." H. Clay Reed, *Delaware: History of the First State*, vol. 2 (New York: Lewis Historical Publishing Co., 1947).

7. Victorine to Evelina (du Pont) Bidermann, January 1, 1859: "A happy new Year [*sic*] to you my dearest sister." HML, box 6a5.

8. Victorine to Mary Elliott, August 28, 1858, HML, box 6a5.

9. Victorine to Sophie Du Pont, October 19, 1860, HML, box 6a5.

10. Victorine to Mary Elliott, November 3, 1859, HML, box 6a5.

11. Sophie to Samuel Francis Du Pont, January 10, 1861, HML, Winterthur Manuscripts, Group 9, W9-22868.

12. Victorine to Sophie, undated, "Dec. 1860–Jan. 1861," HML, box 6a5.

13. Victorine to Henry Algernon du Pont, January 30, 1858, HML, box 6a5.

14. "What a pity he is so lazy; he is such a bright boy! . . . but I say with you if he is only a *good, pious* man we need not regret the rest." Victorine to Sophie, July 28, 1853, HML, box 6a4.

15. Victorine to Sarah Gilpin, May 23, 1860, HML, box 6a4.

16. Victorine to Mary Elliott, February 6, 1860, HML, box 6a5.

17. Sophie Du Pont ("Mrs. S. F. du Pont"), Col. H. A. du Pont collection, HML, Winterthur Manuscripts; Samuel Brown, "Recollections of a Conversation I Had with the Late

Mrs. Admiral Du Pont about 1885 to '87," HML, Winterthur Manuscripts, Group 9, Papers of Sophie Du Pont, W9-40309.

18. From Rev. E. Bickersteth (1786–1850), *A Scripture Help* (London: Seeleys, 1850), 137, quote copied by Victorine on scrap in HML, box 6a13, religious meditations.

19. Victorine to Henry Algernon, August 9, 1860, HML, box 6a5.

20. Victorine to Sarah Gilpin, August 13, 1860, HML, box 6a5.

21. Victorine to Mary Elliott, June 24, 1860, HML, box 6a5.

22. *Merriam-Webster Dictionary Online*, s.v. "cholera morbus," accessed August 22, 2020, https://www.merriam-webster.com/dictionary/cholera%20morbus.

23. Victorine to Mary Elliott, September 19, 1860, HML, box 6a5.

24. Victorine to Sarah Gilpin, December 4, 1860, HML, box 6a5.

25. Victorine to Sarah Gilpin, August 13, 1860, HML, box 6a5.

26. William Cullen Bryant, *A Discourse on the Life, Character, and Genius of Washington Irving* (New York: G. Putnam, 1860); Victorine to Sarah Gilpin, May 1, 1860, HML, box 6a5.

27. Victorine to Sarah Gilpin, December 4, 1860, HML, box 6a5.

28. "We are never so happy as when we can contribute to the happiness of those around us." Victorine to Eleuthera (du Pont) Smith, October 26, 1816, HML, box 6a2.

29. William Wordsworth, *The Complete Poetical Works of William Wordsworth: Imagination and Taste*, ed. Henry Reed (Philadelphia: Troutman & Hayes, 1854), 349.

CHAPTER 21 — PATHWAY'S END

Epigraph: Sophie Du Pont to Amelia du Pont, January 24, 1861, Hagley Museum and Library Manuscripts and Archives, Wilmington, DE (hereafter HML), Winterthur Manuscripts, Samuel Francis Du Pont papers, Group 9, W9-22876.

1. Victorine (du Pont) Bauduy to George Canning, January 3, 1861, HML, box 6a5.

2. Sophie to Samuel Francis Du Pont, January 10, 1861, HML, WMSS, Group 9, W9-22868.

3. Sophie to Samuel Francis, January 16, 1861, HML, WMSS, Group 9, W9-22872.

4. Edward Everett, *The Rebellion Record*, vol. 1 (New York: G. P. Putnam, 1861), 17.

5. Jonah 3:9, King James Version.

6. Eleuthera (du Pont) Smith to Gabrielle Josephine (du Pont) Breck, January 31, 1861, HML, Winterthur Manuscripts, papers of Eleuthera du Pont Smith, Group 6, Series C, box 6c16.

7. Eleuthera to Mary Elliott, February 1, 1861, HML, WMSS, box 6c21.

8. Brandywine Manufacturer's Sunday School class books, 1823–1860, Acc. 389, box 2.

9. Eleuthera to Mary Elliott, February 1, 1861, HML, WMSS, box 6c21.

10. "The change and the quiet [of Winterthur] . . . would do her good." Victorine to Sophie, undated, 1853, HML, box 6a6.

11. Eleuthera to Mary Elliott, February 1, 1861, HML, WMSS, box 6c21.

12. Paulina (Fowle) Cazenove (1806–1891). Daughter of Eleuthère Irénée's associate Antoine Cazenove and longtime friend of the du Pont sisters.

13. Sophie to Amelia du Pont, January 24, 1861, HML, Group 9, Series D, W9-22876.

14. Ibid.

15. Ibid.

16. Eleuthera to Mary Elliott, February 1, 1861, HML, Acc. 6c21.

17. Victorine to Evelina, January 14, 1861, HML, box 6a5.

18. Sophie to Amelia du Pont, January 24, 1861, HML, Group 9, Series D.

19. Victorine to Evelina, January 16, 1861, HML, box 6a5.

20. Eleuthera to Mary Elliott, February 1, 1861, HML, box 6c21.

21. Sophie to Amelia du Pont, January 24, 1861, HML, Group 9, Series D.

22. Ibid.

23. Ibid.

24. Ibid.

25. Ibid.

26. Reference to 2 Timothy 1:12, King James Version.

27. Although never confirmed, colorectal cancer remains a probability for diagnosis.

28. Eleuthera to Mary Elliott, February 1, 1861, HML, Acc. 6c21.

29. Sophie to Amelia du Pont, January 24, 1861, HML, Group 9, Series D.

30. Samuel Crawford Brincklé Diary, January 19, 1861, Extracts, 1848–1863, Christ Church Christiana Hundred records, HML, Acc. 2437, box 2. Bible quotation: Revelation 14:13.

31. Brincklé Diary, January 20, 1861, HML, Acc. 2437.

32. McClary and Holden itemizations: HML, box 6a14, estate papers.

33. Brincklé Diary, January 21, 1861, HML, Acc. 2437.

34. Matthew 5:16, King James Version.

35. Proverbs 31:30, King James Version.

36. Thomas Campbell (1777–1844), *The Poetical Works of Thomas Campbell* (London: Edward Moxon, 1837), 196.

CHAPTER 22 — EPILOGUE

1. Samuel Crawford Brincklé Diary, January 28, 1861, Extracts, 1848–1863, Christ Church Christiana Hundred Records, Hagley Museum and Library Manuscripts and Archives, Wilmington, DE (hereafter HML), Acc. 2437, box 2.

2. Evelina (du Pont) Bidermann to Sophie (du Pont) Du Pont, January 1861, HML, Winterthur Manuscripts (WMSS), Papers of Evelina du Pont Bidermann, Group 6, Series B, box 6b16.

3. Evelina to Henry Algernon du Pont, February 1, 1861, HML, box 6b16, W8-3515.

4. Eleuthera (du Pont) Smith to Sophie, undated, 1861, HML, WMSS, Papers of Eleuthera du Pont Smith, Group 6, Series C.

5. Eleuthera to Lilia Bienaymé, February 1, 1861, HML, box 6c21.

6. Eleuthera to Mary Elliott, February 1, 1861, HML, box 6c21.

7. Sophie to Amelia du Pont, January 24, 1861, HML, WMSS, Papers of Sophie Madeleine Du Pont, Group 9, Series D.

8. Victorine (du Pont) Bauduy to Mary Elliott, February 6, 1860, HML, WMSS, Papers of Victorine du Pont Bauduy, box 6a5.

9. James Perry to Eleuthera, November 20, 1861, HML, Acc. 389, box 6, scholar letters 1861–1872.

10. Thomas Brown to Victorine, November 25, 1861, HML, Acc. 389, box 6, scholar letters 1861–1872.

11. Mary Ann (Phillips) Shaw to Eleuthera, February 15, 1862, HML, Acc. 389, box 6, scholar letters 1861–1872.

12. Eliza Jane (Flemming) Collins to Sophie, March 1861, HML, Acc. 389, box 6, scholar letters 1861–1872.

13. Mary McCartney to Eleuthera, December 16, 1861, HML, Acc. 389, box 6, scholar letters 1861–1872.

14. Newspaper (unnamed) clipping, April 3, 1862, HML, Acc. 389, box 6, misc.

15. Ellen Eugenia du Pont to Henry Algernon du Pont, January 27, 1861, HML, WMSS, box 8a2, W8-3513.

16. After the death of the Bidermanns, their son James sold Winterthur to Henry (Sr.) in 1867.

17. Patricia Martinelli, *Haunted Delaware* (Mechanicsburg, PA: Stackpole Books, 2006), 44. Used by permission.

18. *Delaware Republican*, January 13, 1876. "GRR" might possibly be George R. Roberts, who appears on BMSS scholar lists for May 1848. HML, Acc. 389, box 2, scholar lists.

19. Samuel Brown, "Recollections of a Conversation I Had with the Late Mrs. Admiral Du Pont about 1885 to '87," HML, Winterthur Manuscripts, Group 9, Papers of Sophie Du Pont, W9-40309.

20. Henry served with the Fourth U.S. Artillery at Fort Munroe, Virginia, and the Indian reservation at Fort Mitchell, Alabama.

21. Estate figures for (Victorine du Pont) Bauduy, January 19, 1862, HML, Estate, box 6a13. After the reorganization of the company in 1857, the du Pont daughters no longer received shares of capital stock in the company. James F. Wall, *Alfred I. du Pont: The Man and His Family* (New York: Oxford University Press, 1990), 102.

22. Estate figures for Victorine (du Pont) Bauduy, April 11, 1862, HML, Estate, box 6a13. In 1861 the company was on firm financial footing, and the demands of the ensuing Civil War would further insure it.

23. Victorine to Eleuthera, March 28, 1821, HML, box 6a3.

24. Brincklé Diary, January 21, 1861, HML, Acc. 2437, box 2.

25. Joshua Gibbons to Victorine, June 20, 1835, HML, Acc. 389, box 6.

26. Francis I. du Pont, letter to author, November 3, 2018.

27. Victorine to Eleuthera, March 1, 1825, HML, box 6a3.

Bibliography

PRIMARY SOURCES

Archives

Hagley Museum and Library Manuscripts and Archives Department, Wilmington, DE (HML)

Bauduy, Victorine (du Pont). Correspondence. Winterthur Manuscripts, Group 6, Series A, boxes 1–6.

Bidermann, Evelina (du Pont). Winterthur Manuscripts, Group 6, Series B.

Boatman, Roy M. "The Brandywine Cotton Industry, 1795–1865." Eleutherian Mills–Hagley Foundation research report, 1957, Accession 1645, box 1, folder 1.

Brandywine Manufacturer's Sunday School (BMSS) and Christ Church Christiana Hundred Sunday School Records, Accession 389, boxes 1–6, 11.

Brincklé, Samuel Crawford. Diary Extracts, 1848–1863. Christ Church Christiana Hundred Sunday School Records, Accession 2437, box 2.

Brown, Samuel. "Recollections of a Conversation I Had with the Late Mrs. Admiral Du Pont about 1885 to '87." Winterthur Manuscripts, Group 9, Papers of Sophie Du Pont, W9-40309.

du Pont, Gabrielle. "Notre Transplantation en Amérique." Winterthur Manuscripts, Accession 1686, 3/D.

Du Pont, Sophie (du Pont) (sister). Winterthur Manuscripts, Group 9, Series D, E, F.

du Pont, Victorine, and du Pont, Eleuthera. "Tancopanican Chronicles," Accession 6A13, miscellaneous papers.

Gaw, Thomas. ASSU papers 1817–1915, Presbyterian Historical Society, Philadelphia, Microfilm/POS 52.

Gibson, George H. "The Delaware Woolen Industry." Eleutherian Mills–Hagley Foundation research report, 1963, Accession 1645, box 1, folder 22, MS1645_022.

Hancock, Harold. "The Industrial Worker along the Brandywine, 1840–1870." Eleutherian Mills–Hagley Foundation research report, 1957, Accession 1645, box 2, folder 35c, MS1645_035c.

Niederer, Karl J. "The Brandywine Manufacturers' Sunday School: A History of Its Construction and Recommendations for Renovations." Eleutherian Mills–Hagley Foundation research report, 1977, Accession 1645, box 7, folder 220.

Pisney, Raymond F. "The Brandywine Rangers in the War of 1812." Eleutherian Mills–Hagley Foundation research report, undated, Accession 1645, box 3, folder 56, MS1645_056.

Scott, Richard, and S. Fulton. "Interpretive Packet on Explosions." Eleutherian Mills–Hagley Foundation research report, 1990, Accession 2016.201, 20090507_10.

Smith, Eleuthera (du Pont). Transcript books. Winterthur Manuscripts, Group 10, Series E.

Welsh, Peter C. "The Old Stone Office Building 1837–1891." Eleutherian Mills–Hagley Foundation research report, 1959. Accession 1645, box 3, folder 73, MS1645_073.

Wetlaufer, Dorsey. "Family Life at Eleutherian Mills, 1803–1834." Eleutherian Mills–Hagley Foundation research report, 1964, Accession 1645, box 4, folder 75, MS1645_075.

SECONDARY SOURCES

American Dictionary of the English Language. New York: S. Converse, 1828.

"An Article on the American Sunday School Union." Extracted from *The Biblical Repertory and Theological Review* for April 1830. Philadelphia: James Kay Jr., 1830, 3–35.

Barton, Bernard. *The Museum of Foreign Literature, Science, and Art.* Philadelphia: E. Littell, 1831.

Baxter, Richard. *The Saint's Everlasting Rest.* New York: American Tract Society, n.d. [1824?].

Boyd, William H., ed. *Delaware State Directory 1874–1875.* Wilmington, DE: Commercial Press, 1874.

Boylan, Anne. *Sunday School: The Formation of an American Institution 1790–1880.* New Haven, CT: Yale University Press, 1988.

Campbell, Thomas. *The Poetical Works of Thomas Campbell.* London: Edward Moxon, 1837.

Canby, Henry Seidel. *The Brandywine.* Atglen, PA: Schiffer, 1941.

Carey, E. L., and A. Hart. *Picture of Philadelphia: or, A Brief Account of the Various Institutions and Public Objects in this Metropolis.* Philadelphia: E. L. Carey & A. Hart, 1835.

Carr, William H. A. *The du Ponts of Delaware.* New York: Dodd, Mead & Co., 1964.

Catanese, Lynn Ann. *Women's History: A Guide to Sources at Hagley Museum and Library.* Westport, CT: Greenwood Press, 1997.

Directions for Forming and Conducting Sunday Schools. Philadelphia: American Sunday School Union, 1828.

Duke, Marc. *The Du Ponts: Portrait of a Dynasty.* New York: Saturday Review Press, 1976.

du Pont, Bessie Gardner. *E.I. du Pont de Nemours and Company: A History 1802–1902.* New York: Houghton Mifflin, 1920.

———. *Lives of Victor and Josephine du Pont.* Newark, DE: Kells Press, 1930.

du Pont, Eleuthère Irénée. *Life of Eleuthère Irénée du Pont.* 11 vols. Edited and translated by Bessie Gardner du Pont. Newark: University of Delaware Press, 1923–1926.

du Pont, Victor Marie. *Journey to France and Spain 1801.* Edited by Charles W. David. Ithaca, NY: Cornell University Press, 1961.

du Pont, William Hubert. *Explosions at the Du Pont Powder Mills.* Greenville, DE: Hagley Museum and Library, n.d.

du Pont de Nemours, Pierre Samuel. *The Autobiography of Du Pont de Nemours.* Translated by Elizabeth Fox-Genovese. Wilmington, DE: Scholarly Resources, 1984.

———. *Irénée Bonfils on the Religion of His Forefathers.* Paris: Firmin Didot, 1808. Translated by Pierre S. du Pont. Wilmington, DE: Pierre S. du Pont, 1947.

———. *Philosophie de l'univers.* 3rd ed. Paris: 737 Rue Taranne, 1799.

Dutton, William S. *Du Pont: One Hundred and Forty Years.* New York: Scribner's, 1942.

Everett, Edward. *The Rebellion Record.* Vol. 1. New York: G. P. Putnam, 1861.

Ferris, Benjamin. *A History of the Original Settlements on the Delaware.* Wilmington, DE: Wilson & Heald, 1846.

Finney, Charles G. *Memoirs of Rev. Charles G. Finney.* Translated by Henry Reeve. 2nd ed. New York: Fleming H. Revell, 1876.

Gates, John D. *The du Pont Family.* New York: Doubleday, 1979.

Hatfield, Edwin. *History of Elizabeth, New Jersey.* New York: Carlton & Lanahan, 1868.

Haystead, Wes. *The 21st Century Sunday School: Strategies for Today and Tomorrow.* Cincinnati, OH: Standard Publishing, 1995.

Hemans, Felicia. *The Poetical Works of Mrs. Felicia Hemans.* Philadelphia: Grigg & Elliot, 1836.

Henry, Allan J., ed. *The Life of Alexis Irénée du Pont.* 2 vols. Philadelphia: William F. Fell, 1945.

Hoffecker, Carol E. *Brandywine Village: The Story of a Milling Community.* Forge Village, MA: Murray, 1974.

———. *Delaware: A Bicentennial History.* New York: W. W. Norton, 1977.

———. *Wilmington, Delaware: Portrait of an Industrial City, 1830–1910.* Charlottesville: University Press of Virginia, for Eleutherian Mills–Hagley Foundation, 1974.

Holland, Dorothy. *Garesché, De Bauduy, and Des Chapelles Families.* St. Louis: Schneider, 1963.

Hotchkin, Samuel Fitch. *Ancient and Modern Germantown, Mount Airy and Chestnut Hill.* Philadelphia: P. W. Ziegler, 1889.

Howe, Daniel Walker. *What Hath God Wrought: The Transformation of America, 1815–1848.* New York: Oxford University Press, 2007.

Janeway, Jacob J. "Obituary: Mrs. Sarah Ralston." In *The Presbyterian Magazine*, vol. 1. Philadelphia: Little & Henry, 1821.

Johnson, Mary. "Madame Rivardi's Seminary in the Gothic Mansion." *Pennsylvania Magazine of History and Biography* 104 (January 1980): 3–38.

———. "Victorine du Pont: Heiress to the Educational Dream of Pierre Samuel du Pont de Nemours." *Delaware History* 19 (Fall–Winter 1980): 88–105.

Jolly, Pierre. *Du Pont de Nemours: Apostle of Liberty and the Promised Land.* Translated by Elise du Pont Elrick. Wilmington, DE: Brandywine Publishing, 1977.

Jordan, John., ed. *Colonial Families of Philadelphia.* Vol. 1. New York: Lewis Publishing, 1911.

Kaplan, Fred. *John Quincy Adams: American Visionary.* New York: HarperCollins, 2014.

Kerr, George H. *Du Pont Romance.* Wilmington, DE: E. I. du Pont de Nemours & Co., 1938.

Lappen, James H. *Presbyterians on Delmarva.* Smyrna, DE: J. H. Lappen, 1972.

Leach, Frank W. "Old Philadelphia Families." *North American* (Philadelphia), July 7, 1912. http://files.usgwarchives.net/pa/philadelphia/history/family/ralston.txt.

Linton, Ruth C. "Brandywine Manufacturers' Sunday School." *Delaware History* 20 (Spring/Summer 1983): 168–184.

———. "To the Promotion and Improvement of Youth: The Brandywine Manufacturers' Sunday School, 1816–1840." MA thesis, University of Delaware, 1981.

Lloyd, William Freeman. *The Teacher's Manual.* Philadelphia: American Sunday School Union, 1824.

Low, Betty-Bright. "The Youth of 1812: More Excerpts from the Letters of Josephine Du Pont and Margaret Manigault." *Winterthur Portfolio* 11 (1976): 173–212. http://www.jstor.org/stable/1180595.

Low, Betty-Bright, and Jacqueline Hinsley. *Sophie du Pont: A Young Lady in America*. New York: Harry N. Abrams, 1987.

Martin, Albert. *1812: The War Nobody Won*. New York: Macmillan, 1985.

Martinelli, Patricia. *Haunted Delaware*. Mechanicsburg, PA: Stackpole Books, 2006.

McNinch, Marjorie, ed. "Elizabeth Gilpin's Journal of 1830." *Delaware History* 20 (Fall/Winter 1983): 223–255.

Merrill, James M. *Du Pont: The Making of an Admiral*. New York: Dodd, Mead, 1986.

———. "The First Cruise of a Delaware Midshipman: Samuel Francis Du Pont and the Franklin." *Delaware History* 20 (Fall/Winter 1983): 256–268.

Miller, Page Putnam. *A Claim to New Roles*. Metuchen, NJ: Scarecrow Press, 1985.

Montgomery, Elizabeth. *Reminisces of Wilmington*. Philadelphia: T. K. Collins Jr., 1851.

Morrison, Samuel Eliot. *The Oxford History of the American People*. New York: Oxford University Press, 1965.

Mulrooney, Margaret M. *Black Powder, White Lace*. Hanover, NH: University Press of New England, 2002.

Murray, Elsie. *Azilum: French Refugee Colony of 1793*. Athens, PA: Tioga Point Museum, 1950.

Noll, Mark, Nathan Hatch, George Marsden, David Wells, and John Woodbridge., eds. *Eerdmans' Handbook to Christianity in America*. Grand Rapids, MI: William B. Eerdmans, 1983.

Orphan Society of Philadelphia. *Orphan Society Records Collection 1913*. Philadelphia: Historical Society of Philadelphia, 2003.

Packard, Frederick A. *The Teacher Taught*. Philadelphia: American Sunday School Union, 1839.

Pennington, Edgar L. "The Diocese of Delaware: From Its Organization to the Election of Its First Bishop." *Historical Magazine of the Protestant Episcopal Church* 5, no. 1 (1936): 1–26.

Percival, James Gates. *Poems: Ode to Religion*. New Haven, CT: A. H. Maltby, 1821.

Pestalozzi, Johann Heinrich. *How Gertrude Teaches Her Children*. Syracuse, NY: C. W. Bardeen, 1894.

Poirot, Jean-Pierre. *Lavoisier: Chemist, Biologist, Economist*. Translated by Rebecca Balinski. Philadelphia: University of Pennsylvania Press. 1996.

Pursell, Carroll, Jr. "Peter Bauduy & His Shepherd Dog, 1814: A Note." *Delaware History Magazine* 10 (October 1962): 181–184.

Quimby, Maureen O'Brien. *Eleutherian Mills*. Greenville, DE: Hagley Museum, 1973. Revised ed., edited by D. Hughes and C. Hagglund. Wilmington, DE: Hagley Museum and Library, 1999.

Reed, H. Clay. *Delaware: History of the First State*. 3 vols. New York: Lewis Historical Publishing Co., 1947.

Rice, Edwin Wilbur. *The Sunday School Movement, 1780–1917*. Philadelphia: American Sunday School Union, 1917.

Riggs, John Beverley. *A Guide to Manuscripts*. Greenville, DE: Eleutherian Mills Historical Society, 1970.

Sanborn, Andrew E. *Proceedings of Temple Lodge, No. 11*. Wilmington, DE: Temple Lodge No. 11, 1917.

Saricks, Ambrose. *Pierre Samuel Du Pont de Nemours*. Lawrence: University of Kansas Press, 1965.

Scafidi, Polly Jose. "Doctor Pierre Didier and Early Industrial Medicine." *Delaware History* 15 (April 1972): 41–54.

Scharf, John Thomas. *History of Delaware, 1609–1888*. 2 vols. Philadelphia: L. J. Richards, 1888.

Schlesinger, Arthur M., Jr. *The Almanac of American History*. New York: Barnes & Noble, 1993.

Sigourney, Lydia Howard (Huntley). *Lucy Howard's Journal*. New York: Harper Bros., 1858.

———. *The Man of Uz and Other Poems*. Hartford, CT: Williams, Wiley & Waterman, 1862.

Silliman, Charles A. *The Episcopal Church in Delaware, 1785–1954*. Wilmington, DE: Episcopal Diocese of Delaware, 1982.

———. *The Story of Christ Church Christiana Hundred and Its People*. Wilmington, DE: Hambleton Company, 1960.

Silver, Ednah C. *Sketches of the New Church in America*. Boston: New Church Union, 1920.

Smith, Elias D. *The School Interests of Elizabeth: A City of New Jersey, U.S.A. 1664–1910*. Elizabeth, NJ, 1911.

Staël, Anne Louise Germaine de, and Pierre Samuel du Pont de Nemours. *de Staël–du Pont Letters*. Edited and translated by James F. Marshall. Madison: University of Wisconsin Press, 1968.

Tocqueville, Alexis de. *Democracy in America*. Translated by Henry Reeve. 2nd American ed. New York: George Adlard, 1838.

Wall, James F. *Alfred I. du Pont: The Man and His Family*. New York: Oxford University Press, 1990.

Wallace, Anthony F. C. *Rockdale: The Growth of an American Village in the Early Industrial Revolution*. New York: Alfred A. Knopf, 1972.

Weddle, Kevin John. *Lincoln's Tragic Admiral*. Charlottesville: University of Virginia Press, 2005.

Weslager, C. A. *A Man and His Ship: Peter Minuit and the Kalmar Nyckel*. Wilmington, DE: Kalmar Nyckel Foundation, 1989.

Wharton, Annie Hollingsworth. *Salons Colonial and Republican*. Philadelphia: J. B. Lippincott, 1900.

Wilkes, Rev. Samuel. *The Life of Lord Teignmouth*. London: John Parker, 1845.

Wilkinson, Norman B. *E.I. du Pont, Botaniste: The Beginning of a Tradition*. Charlottesville: University Press of Virginia, 1972.

Williams, John M. "Daguerreotypists, Ambrotypists, and Photographers of Wilmington, Delaware, 1842–1859." *Delaware History* 18 (Spring/Summer 1979): 180–193.

Williams, Walter S., ed. *First and Central Presbyterian Church 1737–1937*. Wilmington, DE: William N. Cann, 1937.

Zebley, Frank R. *Along the Brandywine*. Wilmington, DE: William Cann, 1940.

Index

Note: Page numbers in *italics* indicate figures.

American Sunday School Union (ASSU), 72–74, 93–97

Barton, Bernard, 69

Bauduy, Cora, 20, 24, 26, 41, 48, 54

Bauduy, Ferdinand, 20, 24; with Du Pont, Bauduy & Company, 41–42; early friendship with Victorine, 20; illness and death of, 42–43; marriage proposal of, 34–35; marriage to Victorine, 41–42; on missing Victorine, 42; Paris apprenticeship of, 39–40; restoration of monument, 115; romance with Victorine reignited, 32–36; travel to Europe, 35–36, 38; Victorine grieving for, 45–49

Bauduy, Juliette, 20, 43, 45, 52

Bauduy, Mimika, 20, 24, 26, 34, 40; billiards playing, 48–49; split with Victorine, 53–54

Bauduy, Peter, 17, *18*, 20, 22, 32; on death of son, 43–44; differences with Irénée du Pont, 22; grievance to investors, 51–52, 102; marriage pressure and, 34–35; textile mill and, 33

Bauduy, Victorine Elizabeth (du Pont), *v*, *xiv*, *7*, *126*
— academic achievement, 15, 25–26, 29
— *amour oblige*, 83
— anxiety: in childhood, 12–13; over Eleuthera, 75–76; explosions as cause of, 67–68, 131–132
— birth, xxiii; baptism administered to, 1–2; amid French Revolution, 1, 6
— botany: with father, 36; lifelong interest in, 69; study of begins, xxiv; success in, 29; walks at Madame Rivardi's Seminary, 24

— childhood, xxiii–xxiv, 7; anxiety in, 12–13; on Brandywine River, 20–21; generosity in, 10; with grandfather, 8–9, 10
— Civil War, fear of, 149–150
— compassion, 141, 148
— conversion to Christianity, and Ralston family influence, 26–27
— correspondence, xxvi–xxvii
— death of, xxiv: condolences to family, 162; distribution of estate, 165; Eleuthera on, 156, 160; Evelina on, 160; funeral, 157–158, 165–166; grave site, 158–159; obituaries, 163; sister Sophie attending, 153, 155, 157, 161; surrounded by family, 156–157
— education: academic achievement, 15; in du Pont family, 69; with grandfather, 9, 10–11; with Madame Capron, 23–24; at Madame Rivardi's Seminary for Young Ladies, xxiv, 24–29; in New York, 14; of siblings and family, xx, xxiv, 30–31, 34; study of botany, languages, literature, and medicine, xxiv. *See also* Brandywine Manufacturer's Sunday School
— first tutor, role as: Christian values in, 147; to nieces and nephews, 60; religious influence of, 163; to siblings, xx, 30, 59
— generosity of, 10, 150
— household management, 89–90, 112
— illness, 148–149, 152
— languages: lifelong interest in, 69; mastery of English, French, and Latin, 14; studied German, Italian, and Spanish, 29; summary of, xxiv

About the Author

Lennie Spitale lives in Garnet Valley, Pennsylvania, with his wife Gwen. They have two sons and five grandchildren. Lennie's primary work has been to the incarcerated, with whom he has served as a prison minister since 1977, in approximately 150 correctional facilities in several states and Canada. As an educator, he has provided professional training for numerous chaplains and volunteers, and he is the author of six publications in that field. Since 2009, he has been a volunteer at the Hagley Museum and Library in Greenville, Delaware, the site of the original Du Pont powder works established in 1802. Immediately intrigued by the life of Victorine du Pont, and that so little had been written about her, he spent the next twelve years researching and writing her biography. *Victorine Elizabeth du Pont: The Force behind the Family* is the fruit of that effort.